Educational Restructuring

International Perspectives on Traveling Policies

D1275677

A volume in
International Perspectives on Educational Policy, Research, and Practice
Series Editor: Kathryn M. Borman, *University of South Florida*

Educational Restructuring

International Perspectives on Traveling Policies

Edited by

Sverker Lindblad
Uppsala University

and

Thomas S. Popkewitz
University of Wisconsin–Madison

INFORMATION AGE
PUBLISHING

80 Mason Street • Greenwich, Connecticut 06830 • www.infoagepub.com

Library of Congress Cataloging-in-Publication Data

Educational restructuring : international perspectives on traveling
policies / edited by Sverker Lindblad and Tom Popkewitz.
    p. cm. – (International perspectives on educational policy,
research, and practice)
 Includes bibliographical references.
 ISBN 1-59311-180-0 (pbk.) – ISBN 1-59311-181-9 (hardcover)
 1. Education and state–Cross-cultural studies. 2. Educational
change–Cross-cultural studies. 3. Globalization–Cross-cultural
studies. I. Lindblad, Sverker. II. Popkewitz, Tom. III. Series.
 LC71.E349 2004
 379–dc22

                                        2004011535

Printed in the United States of America

CONTENTS

INTRODUCTION

Educational Restructuring: (Re)Thinking The Problematic of Reform

Sverker Lindblad and Tom Popkewitz

Restructuring is a major issue in education studies during the last decades. Educational systems are restructured in terms of the system aspects of education through decentralisation, deregulation, professional accountability, marketization and so forth. This is done with the goal to change the relation of the state to civil society through, for example, flattening hierarchies, increasing managerial, professional or "client" control and obtaining a more efficient and innovative organisation. The restructuring is also directed to changes in the pedagogical and teacher educational programs that focus on the relations of the child and teacher in learning communities. The changes in the curriculum are promoted in policy and research as bringing the school in relation to changes in cultural, social and economic patterns embodied in phrases such as "knowledge society" and life-long learner.

Education restructuring is a concept with changing meaning. Here we are dealing with transformations in the governing of education—from government to governance, which implies a changing role of the state. We find a shift from bureaucratic control to the introduction of other agencies, public as well as private, in the governing of education (Dale, 1998; Hirst &

Educational Restructuring: International Perspectives on Traveling Policies, pages vii–xxxi
Copyright © 2004 by Information Age Publishing

Thompson, 1999). This in turn implies changes in the management of schooling and education, often illuminated by terms such as "new managerialism," "accountability," and "teacher professionalism." Restructuring is also a term that relates to changing notions of the individual who the school is assumed to have the responsibility for producing in new relations between communities, nation and global processes in which new collective memories are being forged.

In this book we seek to trouble the concept of restructuring through empirical and historical examinations of current reforms in Africa, the Americas, Asia, and Europe. We deal with controversies on and in education restructuring in different contexts as well as research traditions. The chapters speak to the following questions: What are the discursive practices that order and differentiate the practices of restructuring in different contexts and the controversies that they produce in the production of education systems and the everyday practises of schooling?

FOCUS AND LIMITS

A number of recent studies have tried to understand the meaning of education restructuring in different ways. For instance, Papagiannis, Easton, and Owens (1992) tried to understand the objectives of restructuring and the American experiences of school restructuring. Darling-Hammond and Bullmaster (1997) identify restructuring as related to increased school autonomy and new ways of managing schools in the American context. Weiler (1989) relates decentralisation measures to aspects of legitimisation. Gewirtz, Ball, and Bowe (1995) critically examine British policy that makes education as markets that respond to parental strategies and cultural capital. Halsey, Brown, Lauder, & Wells (1998) relate restructuring to the New Right ideology and consider the implications of restructuring for the teaching profession, the curriculum, and to the neglect of relations between education and democracy (Daun, 1993). Walford (1994) studies implications of parental choice on quality issues. Whitty, Power, and Halpin (1998) comparatively concentrate on the devolution of educational systems. These literatures present different aspects of education restructuring in different settings—the preconditions for and working of restructuring in relation to school management, teacher professionalism, school outcomes and so forth. Education restructuring has also been in focus for policy studies, for example, in debates about school marketization and parents as "consumers" of education.

This book has a different focus. The chapters are based on three distinct ambitions:

First, we use the notion that similar changes are occurring around the world, even if the timing and content varies between regions. For instance, the construction of markets in the U.K. was regarded as a vital ingredient in the renewal of education in the 1980s. Similar changes are introduced in Sweden a decade later.[1] The content differs as well, for instance when considering the introduction of vouchers in education, where Sweden in turn is rather an early example. But there are a lot of familiarities in current changes labelled as restructuring throughout the world. In sum, we can talk about education restructuring as "a world movement" of cultural, social and political changes in our time (Meyer, 1999).

Second, we are interested in controversies in the restructuring of educational systems. Our use of the controversies, however, goes against the grain. Our concern is not with debates and ideological argument about what is the most appropriate restructuring of the educational system. Rather, we seek to place the arguments, procedures and programs of restructuring within historical, social and political patterns that frame and shape those restructuring arguments. That is, we are after an understanding of the rules and standards of reason that order, differentiate and distinguish the processes of restructuring across different national contexts. One of the central ambitions of this book is to ask the questions, "How is it historically and politically possible for policy makers and researchers across geographical contexts to "speak," think, and act in the ways that they do?" "What are the rules and standards that order the objects reflected on and underlie programmatic changes?"

With this interest, our attention is directed at "thought" and reason as produced through a field of cultural practices that order and differentiate the objects of reflection and action. This entails paying attention to the ordering and differentiating principles embodied in restructuring efforts as constructing/construing ways of living, "seeing," thinking, and feeling. But further, it is to think of the knowledge of educational reform as producing intent and purpose that is not merely of "the mind" or as normative properties that guide and judge the success or failure of a program. To place "thought" into a field of cultural practices is to focus on knowledge as produced within an amalgamation of an immense world of institutions, authority relations, stories, resemblances, memories, and fantasies. While we rarely focus on the system of reason or "thought" of reform as a material and governing practice, our concern is to recognize that the cultural practices of educational reforms are political practices that generate principles (systems of reason) that order action and participation.

To these two ambitions is added a third. Most literature on restructuring is produced in the Anglo-Saxon part of the world (e.g., The UK, Northern America and Australia) as indicated by the references above. Since we regard education restructuring as a world movement we want to present cases of restructuring outside this Anglo-Saxon part of the world such as in Argentina, France, South Africa, South-East Asia, and Taiwan. In this literature we are able to identify some of the conceptual difficulties of applying the analytical tools of Anglo-Saxon studies to contexts outside that sphere.

We deal with the arguments and reasoning concerning different aspects of restructuring as presentations of productive aspects of power and knowledge. What are the ideas that constrain and construct intentions and norms for action in the making and preservation of education restructuring? Thus, we understand structuring as not a "concept" applied to education, but as a word that relates to a number of different cultural and social discourses that overlap to form rules and standards that order and classify the objects of practice and the possibilities of action. We think of these rules and standards of thought as "a system of reason" (Popkewitz, 1998) that governs, normalizes, and naturalizes action. In other words, the focus of this study is not on the working of restructured education system or for example, the implications for educational outcomes over different social categories. Instead, we are concerned with the cultural practices that produce, order and make plausible education restructuring.

What are these different practices that produce meaning? What are the ordering principles that underlie how the notion of educational restructuring is used in different contexts? We can think of educational restructuring as dependent on the external circumstances through which educational systems are organized, such as local, national contexts as well as the working of international organizations and communications of educational ideas. However, restructuring also depends on the activities inside educational institutions; that is, the ways they organize themselves, their knowledge of achievement, failure and childhood that constitute their work. External as well as internal influences are both, in turn, dependent on resources, organization and how, and in what ways, they organize and position their arguments and ideas.

Here, however, our primary focus is on arguments and ideas in the making of restructuring of education. From a reflexive (we are here referring to the work of Bourdieu & Wacquant, 1992) point of view, controversies are something you would expect given the structure of positions in discourses as well as conflicting relations between the logic of theory and the logic of practise. Controversies, in this sense, are very useful for reflection and analysis of political debates as well as for the historical understanding of research and its results.

A NOTE ON CONTROVERSIES

In this book are different cases of educational restructuring in different national and international contexts. The contributors have researched educational restructuring from different theoretical perspectives and with different research approaches. Our interest in these different cases is to communicate about the assumptions and presuppositions of restructuring as controversies from different positions, perspectives and contexts, since this will, we hope, generate greater sets of distinctions and more nuanced arguments. We are not interested in stating rules for how to communicate in research or policy controversies. Nor are we interested in summarising educational thoughts and research in overarching ways. Here, we are using the work of Ian Hacking who has analyzed controversies, e.g., concerning diagnoses in psychiatry. He is interested in how different lines of reasoning are constructed and in what ways controversies are outlined as new objects of analysis for which treatments are invented.

Hacking (1999) presents an analysis of a social constructionism that undoes the dualism of nominalism and realism in social research. He argues that a precondition to stating that a phenomenon (X) is socially constructed is that X is commonly taken for granted or appears to be inevitable, in spite of the argument that it is not inevitable, but socially constructed—a result of a matrix of institutions, social demands, and so forth. Hacking is not arguing that there are not things of the world (a realism) but that these things that demand our attention are "actions under description" in which the discursive practices not only describe and construe but also function to "make" the worlds in which that action is directed.

Restructuring of education is, for obvious reasons, a social construction—a result of human action operating within certain institutional, social and historical circumstances. For instance political decisions on decentralisation and deregulation are based on, e.g., power relations in parliaments, ideas about options and limitations for decentralisation, communication patterns between different levels in educational systems and so forth. The implementation of markets in a school system is based on arguments concerning what markets can and cannot do, what potentials and risks there are with markets. But what is called restructuring in this context of different social, institutional and ideational relations not only creates a way of thinking about what is troubling about schooling, but also imposes sets of descriptions and categories from which to "see," think, and act on schooling. Restructuring is a word in which programs are produced, governmental legislation enacted, and theories of school change used to order and organize action and participation. In this sense, restructuring is embodied in a range of practices that not only construe what is the problem and solutions of education, but also "make" a world through which people are to act on the possibilities of education.

An important part of controversies is what Hacking calls "elevator words." Hacking makes a distinction between objects, ideas and elevator words. Hacking differentiates elevator words from those that exist as an object: An education system or a school exists in the world around us and in that sense it can be named an object. An idea is a conception, an attitude or a theory that someone has about an object, e.g., about education restructuring. In addition to objects and ideas we have elevator words that say something about the world but are not in the world as are things that are objects or ideas. Elevator words are things that are thought of as "fact," "truth," and "reality" and thus produce words that are circularly defined and continually undergo substantial mutations. Hacking states:

> Facts, truths, reality, and even knowledge, are not objects in the world, like periods of time, little children, fidgety behaviour, or loving-kindness. The words are used to say something about the world, or what we say or think about the world. They are at a higher level. (a. a., p 21 f)

He notes two aspects of such elevator words—they tend to be circularly defined and they tend to be free floating. A construction of a fact is something different from the construction of an object or an idea. In controversies in policy and/or research we need to be careful—or to consider carefully—the uses of elevator words.

Based on Hacking's work on controversies we try to find out about arguments in controversies on education restructuring—what are the objects, ideas, and especially, what are the elevator words? Since we are dealing with policy discourses we are expecting other formats of elevator words than in research discourses. Such formats could be what makes a certain option the "natural" one or turns a change into "progress." What the elevator words are is an empirical question, which we will contend with below.

Cases and Focuses

We asked research colleagues, who are working with issues in education restructuring in different national contexts, to write about their research and present aspects of relevance for understanding controversies in their field.

The different national and comparative studies enable us to make the case of education restructuring as central to the investigation of this book. These studies deal with different levels of educational systems: with higher education in South Africa and with teacher education in England, with secondary education in European contexts, educational reforms in Argentina, and so forth. Different aspects are focussed; discourses on globalisation, individual responsibility, parental choice, mass-media spin, and the impacts of policy-making, and so forth.

The variety in studies and their different layers of educational systems have important advantages. It makes it possible for us to cover the complexities of educational restructuring as a world movement in different settings. But the variety has its drawbacks from a traditional comparative methodological point of view. We cannot compare the different cases or relate the impact of various education measures in relation to specific operational variables. But we can compare and have argued elsewhere that there is the possibility to locate the changes through deploying theoretical entities that enable us to think about the processes of change and their implications (Popkewitz & Pereyra, 1993). That is our approach in this later part of this chapter.

In "Changing Patterns of Power: Rethinking Decentralization the Educational Reform in Taiwan," Yang-tien Chen is presenting overarching changes in Taiwanese education. These changes are related to major cultural and political changes in the current history of Taiwan. Politics of deregulation and decentralisation are presented and reframed as new regulation patterns. Of special interest are the salvation stories in reform discourses and the alchemy of knowledge in the restructuring of Taiwanese education. Inés Dussel is questioning the welfare state nostalgia among restructuring critics in "Education Restructuring in Argentina: Hybridity, Diversity and Governance after Welfare." She focuses on new patterns of governance—on demands of personal responsibility and self-government among students and restrictions in self-government in hybrid discourses on schooling. Dussel also shows how diversity is constructed as the opposite to responsibility in current discourses on education in Argentina.

In "Governance by Spin: The Case of New Labour and Education Action Zones in England" Sharon Gewirtz, Marny Dickson and Sally Power present and analyze how potential controversies in education policy are managed by spin. By spin is meant impression management in news and political communications. The authors argue that spin is a growing phenomenon due to the growing importance of media in policymaking and an increased politicalisation of media in combination with ongoing professionalisation of news management in political parties. Based on Education Action Zones as an example of spin in educational policy, the authors argue that spin is not only part of the presenting of news, but also part of the constitution of policy. Meg Maguire is presenting a case in an English context as well, but with quite a different focus. The text, "The Modern Teacher: A Textual Analysis of Educational Restructuring" is based on analyses of significant New Labour government documents focussing on the need to modernise the teaching profession. In these documents are demands of modernisation related to demands of raising standards of schooling and to reward the good teacher. The good in traditional teaching is to be preserved and integrated into modern teaching according to the documents analysed.

Agnès van Zanten is dealing with other education actors in "Education Restructuring in France: Middle-class Parents and Educational Policy in Metropolitan Contexts." Her focus here is education restructuring in relation to middle class parents' educational strategies in a restructuring educational system with public as well as private alternatives of schooling. These strategies are related to different expectations of education as well as to parents' positions in the public or the private sector. Of special concern are exclusive strategies on one side to preserve and improve the social position of the family, and on the other side the concern of social integration and solidarity. Policy is regarded not only as official decisions, but also as practice. Parent expectations influence policy in three different ways; first as aggregated implications of individual choice, second, due to interaction with school affairs, and third through parental associations. In sum, parental educational strategies are a constitutive part of educational policy-making.

Barry Franklin presents a study on restructuring in a longer time perspective and with a focus on Detroit High School and race conflicts in "Creating a Discourse for Restructuring in Detroit: Achievement, Race, and the Northern High School Walkout." He shows how a discourse on race and segregation is replaced by a discourse on social mobility and the implication of this for policy-making.

Joe Muller's text, "Responsiveness and Innovation in Higher Education Restructuring: The South African Case" provides a particular case study to examine the problematic of restructuring as that word travels through various iterations of policy borrowing and translations, recontextualization and transformations in reforms of South African universities. He examines the contradictory ensemble of logics of equalization and differentiation as universities embody a contradictory ensemble of "markets" of which state policy is placed into a network and flow of scientific disciplines and its systems of knowledge production. The results do not change cognitive or epistemic structures, but shore up basic research programs, but clothe their usual research practices in the lineaments of the new relevance. Sverker Lindblad and Thomas S. Popkewitz in "Education Structuring: Governance in the Narratives of Progress and Denials" draw from research on education governance and social inclusion/exclusion in eight countries of the European Union study. They consider how policy and education system knowledge ("the systems of reason") circulate among various institutional settings to create patterns of social cohesion and collectively, and that simultaneously produce divisions related to social exclusion. Restructuring is viewed as a salvation narrative of progress, rescue and redemption that ties the well-being of the individual to that of collective commitment and belonging. But the salvation narratives involve particular management procedures, population reasoning, and narratives that govern who the citizen is, should be, and who is outside of the pall of progress and thus to be rescued and redeemed. Fazel Rizvi in "Theorizing the Global Convergence of Educational Restructuring" explores the processes of global convergence that is occurring within educational restructuring. This involves the circulation of ideas and ideologies, international conventions and consensus that guide educational reforms; its international practices of cooperation and competition; and formal bilateral and multilateral contracts that include international agencies. The concept of neoliberalism is given a nuanced character that relates the global and the local in consider differential conditions in which convergence occurs.

To end this short review: In "Education Structuring: Governance in the Narratives of Progress and Denials" we present a discussion of an international study on education governance and social inclusion/exclusion that we carried out with the support of the European Commission. In focus are the systems of reason that order current discourses in different location. We captured narratives about change in education governance in policy texts and in interviews with actors operating at different levels of European education systems.

In Table 1 we present an overview over the different cases. These cases give a rich picture of education restructuring. Earlier we noted that there is a convergence in reform practices in the language of reform in different contexts. However, we want to make two notions in relation to that convergence. First, the notion of convergence exists in relation to distinctions and differentiations of restructuring that give meaning within the different cases with their specific historical backgrounds. Second, scholarship requires that we rethink the notion of structure and restructuring so as not to shortcut the analysis; that is, not to accept the overt practices as the focus of investigation and allow the political discourses of reform to form the conceptual apparatus for investigation.

Our comments will be presented in four sections. We start with a note on elevator words in policy discourses. Then we present some notions on ways of thinking about restructuring. This is followed by a few methodological reflections. The construction of the others in educational restructuring is in turn followed by some thoughts on the uses of standards in restructured educational systems. Based on these comments, we have a few final words on the systems of reason in education restructuring.

Elevator Words, Topoi and Planet Speaks

What elevator words do we find in the discourses presented in the different cases? These words are presented as words that suggest that they repre-

Table 1: An Overview of Chapters

Author	Title	Aspects in focus
Sverker Lindblad & Tom Popkewitz	Introduction	Cases and controversies in education restructuring
Part One: Internationalization and Globalization of Education		
Yang-tien Chen	Changing Patterns of Power: Rethinking Decentralization in the Educational Reform in Taiwan	Transformation of education governing in relation to political and cultural changes. Decentralization and the changing patterns of governing are placed in an historical context that includes internal shifts in the foci of education to international, cultural, and social relations to China, Japan, and the U.S.
Inés Dussel	Educational Restructuring and the Reshaping of School Governance in Argentina	Explores how global discourses of neoliberalism are brought into and relate to national discourses and political contexts in which Institutional and individual responsibility and diversity are constructed.
Sverker Lindblad & Tom Popkewitz	Education Restructuring: Governance in the Narratives of Progress and Denials	Using a 10 country study of educational governance, inclusion and exclusion, the restructuring of education are explored as stories of progress that relate to changing notions of teaching and the child
Fazal Rizvi	Theorizing the Global Convergence of Educational Restructuring	Globalization of the policy discourses of globalization
Part Two: Education Restructuring in Different Contexts		
Sharon Gewirtz, Marny Dickson & Sally Power	Governance by Spin: The Case of New Labour and Education Action Zones in England	Focuses on ways in which the labour government uses the mass media in policy-making related to the Education Action Zones. A central concept is "spin," the turning of negative or controversial issues into positive stories that is to manage how reforms are to be perceived and government programs understood.
Meg Maguire	The Modern Teacher: A Textual Analysis of Educational Restructuration	Teacher Education reform in England. An analysis of how the notion of Modernisation of Teachers as presented in New Labour texts, with its different sets of meaning and implications for schooling.

Table 1: An Overview of Chapters (Cont.)

Author	Title	Aspects in focus
Johan Muller	Responsiveness and Innovation in Higher Education Restructuring: The South African Case	Higher education policies and marketisation in relation to institutional organisation and intellectual capacities. Points to the ways in which institutional changes are resistant to academic traditions that have priorities other than those called forth through the restructuring efforts.
Agnes van Zanten	Education Restructuring in France: Middle-Class Parents and Educational Policy in Metropolitan Contexts	Policy-in-practice in relation to middle-class parental choice, interaction with schools and parental organisation
Barry Franklin	Creating a Discourse for Restructuring in Detroit: Achievement, Race, and the Northern High School Walkout	Decentralisation, race, social mobility, giving attention to how discourse of social mobility replaces race in a Detroit high school 1970s, and the implications of those changes to current thinking about reform and restructuring.

sent reality, are facts, and serve as truthful statements that need no further exploration or any reference to an author as they stand as unquestioned objects in need of action. The elevator words differ somewhat in the different cases, but there are striking similarities as well. The English case on spin and the Education Action Zones, for example, can be read as identifying terms such as "social justice" and "business" as elevator words. The words seem to move the particular policy into a realm of a higher "truth" about reality and fact in which there is no controversy or ambiguity. There is similar talk in the text on education restructuring in France, where notions of social integration, social mix, and new solidarity between social classes are presented and to some extent contrasted to consumerist attitudes. In the Argentine case "democratisation" and "deregulation" are combined with notions on "personal responsibility" in ways that are quite similar to the Taiwanese case. In sum we get a mixture of elevator words presented in different restructuring cases.

What role do these words play? Of course, they are written in order to convince and legitimate. They are what Antonio Nóvoa (2002) calls "planet speaks," as magical concepts that are the roots of all evil or the solutions to all problems. Planetspeak involves a new expert who creates and circulates international discourses that seem to exist without structural roots or social locations. Nóvoa calls such discourses as a "worldwide bible" whose vocabulary has no known origin and serve as a magic concept as they seem to cover the solution for all problems: globalisation, flexibility, new economy, exclusion, zero tolerance and multicultural.

One type of elevator word can be considered as topoi. In Portugal, the topoi embodied in works such as life-long education and training, the knowledge society, and globalization. These words are accepted as singular and universal terms that refer to some fact or reality and do not need to be explained. In Britain, the topoi are expressed in policy statements such as "Social exclusion is about income but it is about more. It is about prospects and networks and life changes." Or "You can't choose between a successful and stable economy on the one hand, and confronting poverty and its causes on the other" and the use of the term "zero tolerance." These words and phrases serve as banalities universally accepted as truths that do not need to be questioned. Such topoi support reasoning with no author of the words and a seeming consensus about what is to be done.

But the topoi of restructuring are words embedded in and overlapping with social and cultural discourses that give an order to the world and self. The topoi acquire a specification as they relate to different categories of children and families, for example who are to be rectified so as to gain access to employability and for social and cultural participation. The topoi of reforms embody discourses of individualization, categories of social disintegration, new monitoring strategies of the child, and changing roles of the teacher and school leaders.

It is the intersection of these different discourses that we can better understand restructuring as a system of reason that governs through its principles of ordering and differentiating. If we take one of the elevator words, individualization, there is an irony of the new reform practices of schooling. There is a "renaissance of individuality" that intersects with those of managing the practices of centralization/decentralization. The topoi emphasizes the value of the individual as opposed to that of collective equality, related to global competition and increased investment of education for the gifted child as in Finland. But this "renaissance" is not a rebirth but articulates particular historical formations that relate the state, schooling and the individual. The discourses no longer place the school in a socio-historical and cultural context in discussing issues of equity and justice. These have disappeared from state educational discourse and in their place are de-contextualized discourses about individualization that ties psychology to pedagogical innovation. Few teachers or system actors in Finland, for example, mentioned structural characteristics of social exclusion. Teachers used a common vernacular to describe those who are excluded. They were called troublemakers, truants, and children with learning difficulties. Which is a way to individualize and to personalize exclusion by means of categorizations.

Ways of Thinking About Restructuring

We are thinking about restructuring as not a project explained solely by its consequences and outcomes, but as an elevator word that interrelates with particular discursive practices to construct sets of relations and principles for ordering how the objects of schooling are seen, talked about, acted on, and felt. Our example of individualization above, for example was not about the individual per se, but of practices that disciplines who the individual is and should be. In this sense of constructivism, restructuring is the event to be understood and problematized rather than studied to see its effects.

Neoliberalism as an Elevator Word

One common elevator word of contemporary policy analysis is neoliberalism. Neoliberalism is planet-speak, a magical concept that is seen as the solution to all problems or as the evil that creates those problems. The word serves as a central "marker" about the promises of progress from conservatives and as the roots of the evil that the left sees as taking away all of the won benefits of the security nets of welfare state in care for its populations. The use of neoliberalism as a conceptual framework to understanding the social and historical transformations is clearly problematic when one considers the alliances between minority groups and conservative politicians in supporting school choice in the U.S. or the election of social democratic and Labour governments that maintained related policies but with different rhetorical configurations.

Neoliberalism is a symptom and not a cause. That is, the word never stands by itself as it is itself embedded in a number of historical patterns that exist prior to its formal label of neoliberalism and which need scrutiny. For example, neoliberalism is used in different places and with different political and cultural agendas that seem, as first glance, as strange bedfellows. If we move to Russia, although not a focus of this book, the strategies of marketization are embodied in a field of social and political practices that include a skillful Communist apparatus that moves within a shadow of strong state with little concern form democratic society agenda. As Dussel argues in this book in relation to Argentinian reforms, neoliberalism is not a "cause" but is theoretically part of the event to analyse. That is, current practices of restructuring embody a double technology that empowers and disables—includes and excludes. To understand the double technology is to investigate, as Dussel argues, a "combinatory repertoire" that relates to new patterns of governance based on personal responsibility and self-government. Fizvi, as well, argues in his chapter that neoliberalism stands as seemingly ubiquitous idea of a global context as education responds to the functional prerequisites of capitalism. This functional notion, he continues, is inadequate for considering the relation of global and educational change, as they are located in different patterns of political activity and power play, and within varied consequences.

In this volume, we view neoliberalism as a concept brought into being through policy discourses and thus a concept to be explored by placing its uses within historical configurations that make such a concept possible. Neoliberalism embodies a calculus of intervention and salvation that involves a field of cultural practices that overlap with but are not determined by the State policies associated with Reagan and Thatcher nor the Hayekian and Freedman economics. Thus, while some of the chapters in this book use the phrase Neoliberal, those policies of marketization are historicized in a manner that enables an inquiry into more complex and more profound changes occurring in the restructuring of education.

The chapters enable us to think about the notions of marketization and privatisation as words that are, in some respects, empty signifiers whose content and substance are "filled in" through a range of practices at multiple levels of educational systems across different historical contexts. For example, the notions of marketization and choice appear in the British chapters as related to rhetorical devices tied to a labour government and arguments about democratisation. Van Zanten's chapter tells about the choice of the French middle class, for example, but that notion of choice is less of a theory about marketization and more about how a fractionated middle class seeks to consecrate their social position through strategies that differentially construct school cultures. Managerial and professional groups, for example, have different priorities about what knowledge is most worthwhile for their children in schooling and in effect produce practices that make for the policy of the French State educational system.

SALVATION STORIES, NORMALIZING PRACTICES AND SOCIAL INCLUSION/EXCLUSION

We can think of schooling as embodying salvation themes. Policies and research about school reforms speak about saving or delivering the nation through the education of the child. These themes are today about democracy, equality and economic progress. There are global discourses about change in curriculum and teaching as insuring the future of the nation in the new world that is called "global" and "a knowledge-based" society. The reforms to restructure "tell" of individual and collective progress and the social obligation to rescue those who have fallen outside the narratives of progress. Neoliberal policies of privatization and marketization, for example, call for a better world through challenging the bureaucracies of the institutions of the Welfare State and prompting individual involvement in the local agencies that directly affect their lives. The modern secular salvation themes, are meant to bring progress to society and to redeem the individual who is empowered and self-actualized in the process. Traveling through the different ideological scenarios is the professional teacher who revives democracy by working more directly with parents and communities.

The salvation themes of rescue and redemption are not recent but are part of the worldwide institutionalization of schooling since the 19th century (Meyer et al., 1997). Our discussion is not to quarrel with the salvation stories but rather to interrogate historically the contemporary field of cultural practices in which they are deployed.

The salvation stories are today of an active sense of "self" whose emotional bonds and self-responsibility are circumscribed through networks of other individuals—the family, the locality, and the community. Freedom is talked about as the empowered individual who continually constructs and reconstructs one's own practice, and the ways of life through a perpetual intervention in one's life through working actively in "communities" of learning. Life becomes a continuous course of personal responsibility and self-management of one's risks and destiny as a problem-solving lifelong learner. Problem solving is not a natural process found in the child but a fabrication that responds to a humanitarian impulse of schooling that is translated and transported into particular psychologies of the mind and social interaction of the child in pedagogy. But the problem solving is a fabrication just the same, as the categories function as both "fictions" and "making" of kinds of people.

The location of responsibility is no longer traversed through the range of social practices directed toward a single public sphere—the social, but in diverse and plural communities that constitute the common good. The struggle for the soul is now in the "autonomous" learners who are continuously involved in self-improvement and ready for the uncertainties through working actively in "communities of learning." Change, contingencies and uncertainties of daily life are tamed through the rules and standards of reason of a re-visioned neo-pragmatism in which diverse communities negotiate the common good.

The school remains a site of school-family connections that re-calibrate political aspiration within the individual. Children work in "learning communities or "communities of discourses." Teachers are now asked to go into the "community," to become part of communities to "better know" their pupils and their families, to become trusted, or to "know" what they should include from "community knowledge."

The unfinished lifelong learner is also that of the teacher who is also classified as a lifelong learner. The teacher is self-actualized by remaking one's biography. That biography is continually calculated through researching one's self as the teacher. The "reflective teacher," for example, assesses the child through life histories or portfolios, and makes and remakes his or her own biography through personal assessment of self-development and self management (see Fendler, 2001).

The problem of restructuring is to consider the characteristics of this individuality that circulate as the future individual that will secure the progress of the nation. The site of change is still a soul and its rules of conduct the conduct of conduct. It is in this construction of human kinds that we can consider the rhetorical meaning of the welfare state as also embodying governing practices and thus seek rhetoric as not merely language to convince but also embodied in discourses that not only construe but also make human kinds. The materiality of discourse that is language thus construes and constructs, or fabricates in its dual sense.

Our study of education governance and social inclusion/exclusion, for example, continually "saw" policy as speaking about education as employability and preparing students for the labour market. But that planet-speak was placed in a discursive field that gave priority to cultural disorganization, social location and a need to correct and normalize deviant populations—groups defined as minorities, new immigrants, ethnic groups and so on—that were inscribed in the policy as threats to national cohesion, social harmony and stabilities.

The notions of deviance and normality existed in relation to particular human kinds. First there is the narrative of the child and teacher who can participate in the global world and produce the progress of the nation. Today's world of progress is embodied in a decentralized individual. The decentralized individual, an unfinished cosmopolitan, is categorized as a "lifelong learner." The lifelong learner is flexible, continuously active, and works collaboratively. These inner characteristics are cosmopolitan in the sense of an individuality that can chase desire and work in a global world in which there is no finishing line. The child is someone who can choose to refuse allegiance to any one of the infinite options on display, except the option of choosing. A child is, to use the planet-speak, one who is flexible, ambitious, part of a learning society. A child and teacher who relishes change for change sake. In the Meg Maguire chapter from the UK, for example, the policy of the British Secretary of Labour, wants the child to relate to business ambitions with a "competitive individualism," and as "a team member" in the learning society. The teacher who is to produce this new child is a "modern teacher who needs to be creative and imaginative."

But as this model of the child and teacher is read, its use of business language is not of business but of cultural norms relate to images and narratives that deploy the elevator of "the modern." In these instances, as Wagner (1994) suggests, it would be historically incorrect to understand the economic language without considering how that language works as cultural practices.

But embodied in the discourses of the lifelong learner and the new cosmopolitanism are links between the local and the global. The characteristics of the lifelong learner are considered global and narrated as representative of the new humanity of progress. But those distinctions are locally produced and related to its opposite - the needy as those who do not embody the characteristics inscribed for participation. That is, embedded in the distinctions and differentiations of the lifelong learner and the decentralized individual are normalizing practices that order and divide people. Dussel"s chapter, for example, focuses on how the term "needy child" produces differences and divisions. The discourses of reform and restructuring are expressed through salvation themes of justice and equity. But the concrete reform practices produce differences in which the needy (who are poor) stand in opposition to the norm individual who has self-responsibility. However, the needy is not only a single category but are present in overlapping discourses which inscribe not only economic categories related to poverty but also cultural and social discourses about rectifying moral disintegration. One can also read van Zanten"s chapter as a nuanced discussion of how different segments of the middle class inscribe their social positions in the cultural distinctions and differentiations that orders school programs.

In the overlapping of categories and distinctions of the different segments of the middle class, as they relate to categories of the "needy," or the "at-risk" or "disadvantaged youth," we are provided a way to consider the relation of inclusion and exclusion. Finer and finer distinctions are produced about the inner characteristics and capabilities of the child who lies outside of normalcy: the youth who can never be of the average because that youth is addicted, has early pregnancies, is a child of a single parent (mother), and is incapable of personal discipline. It is in the relation of these different categories and distinctions that divisions are produced and principles are presented that order the "reasonable individual" from those who do not possess reason. And it is in the rules and standards of reason that we can also begin to consider how individuals are qualified and disqualified for action and participation. That is, embodied in systems of inclusion are their opposites, the distinctions about those not qualified to be of the average. Again, inclusion cannot be considered outside of the problem of exclusion as they reside in the same mapping of the child.

The restructuring of schooling, then, is not only in the overt policies and practices that are to organize institution. Our purpose in this book is to see reforms in this double sense of restructuring. To understand how institutions are changing but also to understand the conditions of governing and thus the materiality of discourse; that is language construes and constructs, or fabricates in its dual sense. Thus, we can think about the notion of spin in relation to the discussion of the ways in which modernization is rhetorically deployed in the policies of the British government in this book. Spin, again, is a political strategy in which politicians in Britain and also the U.S. seek to provide a language in which their policies are placed in their best light, turning negative words into positive (protecting social retirement schemes by privatizing rather than fostering more business, non-public involvement in state actions) or countering negative publicity by stressing a particular aspect of the problem that would leave other parts as not part of the public debate.) But when reading these spin strategies and the topoi of policy, one quickly becomes aware of the different discourses mobilizing particular human kinds, to borrow from Hacking. For example, the use of modernization in Maguire's chapter, is not only a word that travels along with particular notions of an individual who is flexible, and a lifelong learner, but also a word that represents the "others"—the not so flexible, the non-learners.

RE-THINKING THE PROBLEM OF RESTRUCTURING

Restructuring, in the sense of this book, involves thinking of changes in education as it relates the state, society and culture. This entails two notions of the state. One is that of the changes in institutional and organisational practices, such as shifts to new relationships of the centre to the local that have occurred in the past few decades through changes, for example, to goal steering. These changes have been considered often, particularly in European contexts, as changes in the welfare state and its pact with its citizens to protect against risk. Esping-Anderson (1996), for example, has presented a topology of states that focus on its welfare policies and degrees of involvement in social security and employment among its populations. Thus, one can classify the Nordic Countries as a strong welfare state and places as the U.S. as a liberal or non-welfare state. In using such topologies, restructuring is modelled in light of the movement of government involvement as they relate to the classifications embodied in the topologies. Thus, research that compares Britain and Nordic Countries can talk about the end of the welfare state as new individualistic tendencies emerge in and as social policy.

But in the restructuring of education is also another notion of the welfare state. One can think of all modern states as welfare states in that it is, to borrow from DeSwann (1988), the placing of populations in care of the state through governing the conduct of conduct. The modern state is a welfare state not only through providing for health and social security, but also through ensuring progress through the production of the self-responsible and self-motivated citizen. This notion of all states as welfare states directs attention to restructuring as related to changing patterns of governing through the systems of reason that orders the conduct of the citizen. The complexity of restructuring to a myriad of global/ a local, state/civil society that cannot be accounted for by institutional models of the state is clearly illustrated throughout this book. If we take Muller's argument about the relation of the university and its structuring of disciplines to notions of markets, or Rizvi's discussion of the ways in which global convergence in restructuring are ordered through the consideration of differential conditions and networks. This latter sense of governing focuses on restructuring as an ensemble of institutions, procedures, analyses and reflections, calculations and tactics that connect personal conduct with specific governmental apparatuses.

The question of research is to locate the "restructuring" of the knowledge that orders and classifies in policy to construct the object of intervention and action. Thus, we can return to a previous characterization of the reforms as producing a greater individualization. The concern is not with the abdication of governance by the state, but of the new conditions of the state in governing who we are and should be. That is, the new senses of governance in which individualization occurs, embodied new relations between the state and individuals that some theorists have called "governing-at-a-distance." That is, if we think of the possibility of the welfare state as the conditions of the care of individuals, the children and teachers in the school are sites of governing that embody the multiple and heterogeneous discourses that revise the state as a condition of governing. What is significant in understanding restructuring, then, it not the seemingly economic reductionism of policy nor to place the role of the state as an institutional "body" whose rules and policies are governing, but to consider how principles are produced to order and govern the actions and participation of the subjects.

Nostalgia

The notion of nostalgia is one way to think about the discourses of restructuring. Nostalgia (from nostos- return home, and algia- longing) is a longing for a home that no longer exists or has never existed. But as a discourse of the social, nostalgia embodies a double, a looking to the past and to the future (Boym, 2001). It is a sentiment of loss and displacement, but it is also a romance with one's own fantasy that is to make for the progress of the future. Nostalgia expresses a gap between the past and the future that present action can close. Nostalgia is continually placed in relation to progress in modernity (see, e.g., Wagner, 2001; particularly chapter 4).

Wagner (2001) talks about the inescapability of the double evocation of the past in which there is a continuous claiming of origins, and the economic and cultural "globalism" that is allegedly to clear a way the disruptions produced by the traditions of the past.

One can think of this as an occurrence of modernity, which assumes a rupture in time that produces a relation between the past as tradition or in origins, as a central part of social theory and also social policy. Thus it is possible to talk about school reforms as a "back-to-basics" that entails a search for origins that are to be identified and specified in order to affirm or deny progress itself. Nostalgia stands as a double and it is both seductive and manipulative in policy documents. In current restructuring efforts, to borrow from a Russian saying, "the past has become much more unpredictability than the future" (Boym, 2001, p. xvi).

Nostalgia in the context of this book provides a way to think about restructuring as articulating a sentiment of loss and displacement, but also the construction of national fantasies that relate to inclusion and exclusion. The discussion of the modern and modernization in the policy statements that McGuire discusses is one such example. The British policies position state reforms as looking forward to the future in the present, and identifying the past and new "barbarians" coming through the gates of the nation. There is a longing for the past to invent new futures in the rhetoric of the Third Way in Britain, for example. Anthony Giddens and other major intellectuals speak for the future of nostalgia as they talk about the need to "move beyond tradition" into the formation of new sets of civil relations. Giddens argues, for example, that tradition is part of renewing the present to make possible a better future. The middle class parents that van Zanten discusses, as well, mobilize notions of nostalgia as a way of thinking about the remodeling and transforming of the public school. The nostalgia involves fantasies about what the school was, that are now devalued in the public schools that foster social disintegration, anonymity of relations, and a return to some origin of the notion of childhood in private schools that can produce the socialization necessary for maintaining their class position.

Nostalgia provides a relationship between the space of experience and the horizon of expectations. Boym suggests that one can think of nostalgia as having two different forms. One is that of restorative nostalgia that establishes a new memory of the origin for continuity and social cohesion in the transformation occurring. Restorative nostalgia is the promise of rebuilding the ideal home by a return to origins that lies at the core of many powerful ideologies today. Its danger is to relinquish critical thinking for emotional bonding. Restorative nostalgia is at the core of recent national and religious revivals and has two main plots: return to origins and the conspiracy. But the second form of nostalgia can be described as reflective, as Boym suggests. It is a nostalgia in which one can inhabit many places at once and imagine different heterogeneous zones that promote an ethical and creative challenge through the calling for doubt, and the imperfect process of remembrance (Boym, 2002, p. 41). The reflective nostalgia can open up possibilities and the movement of multiple or heterogeneous times.

One of the central aspects of the different chapters is the examination of "things" that appear as crevices or look sideways at policy and restructuring. For example, Dussel enables us to consider the statutes written by the government as systems that order the conduct of conduct, just as in the wearing of clothes is ordering of the body, (proper attire, no smoking). This poses an interesting paradox: the statutes represent children as incapable of self-government, and needing to move from traditional obeying of rules to self responsibilities, and in needing to respect for patriotic symbols: two go hand in hand but in new "hybridity." that is different from say Britain. In other chapters, there are attempts to examine the ways texts intersect with visual presentations in order to place images and narratives that seem truthful and unproblematic, as in the British examination of "spin."

A second methodological element is to think about restructuring as the fabrications of human kinds. That is, the various categories and distinctions that order policy and progress are narratives that fabricate who the teacher (and child) is and should be. These human kinds, as argued in a number of chapters, relate to populations that are categorized as outside of the normal and in need of programs to rectify their characteristics and modes of acting. The human kinds of policy, then, are ways to understand how efforts to rescue populations who are outside or excluded are also practices that normalize and divide those populations. This normalization and dividing involve the fabrication of human kinds (minorities, needy children, ethnic groups) whose characteristics involve a scaffolding of multiple categories of deviance in that they are different from what is unspoken as the normal.

Rethinking Standards In Restructuring

In multiple contexts of this study, there are continual references to standards that stand in a direct relation to strategies of decentralization and pedagogical foci concerned with an individualization. To consider the problematic of restructuring, we believe, requires understanding how these oppositions of centralization/decentralization and standards and individualization are mutually constructed.

If we focus on standards, for example, they are important to Enlightenment notions of the state and the citizen. For example, the Encyclopaedists prior to the French Revolution saw the cacophony among measurements, institutions, inheritance laws, taxation, and market regulations as the greatest obstacles to making a single people. They viewed the metric system as an intellectually important instrument to make France "revenue-rich, militarily potent, and easily administered" (Scott, 1998, p. 32). The introduction of standardized measures was to create an equal citizen.

Standards are not far from this notion of the easily administered citizen to the modern school subjects. School reforms and theories of the child/ teachers are practices of modern statecraft that make up the kinds of people who are to be productive actors. To understand how words are used and their meaning, it is not sufficient to look at a dictionary. The substantive qualities given to words are determined through their deployment in a text. But to understand the usage of words, there is also a responsibility to look at what is assumed in the text to make the writing appear as comprehensible and reasonable in the first place. There is a need to recognize that the reforms are not merely technical, but involve an amalgamation of cultural practices that relate to, for example, class timetables, notions of achievement and pedagogical organization, theories of childhood, and "standards that school performances with notions of redemption and salvation. In a word: to understand the history of schooling we need to recognize the inscription of standards that order the moral conduct of the child.

Resistance Less Difficult

Our discussion has signalled a particular type of "fatalism" in the restructuring. This fatalism is related to the discourses embedded in reform policies and the system actors' perception of the changes occurring. Why should we give attention to this in talking about restructuring?

In one part, there is a redesigning of the site of criticism. We talked about two different elements of the reforms that are related. One was the topoi, words that make change but seem to be without an author. The "spin" of public policy, for example, provides a way to turn and make it appear as though criticism is not necessary and that the certainty of the future is guaranteed. There are also ways in which the processes of change are necessary and inevitable. The discussion of modernization as a rhetorical strategy for mobilizing particular actions provides another topoi that seems to exist as authorless. The second part was the individualization of change itself. The individual is responsible in the new reforms through the continually remaking of the self as an active, lifelong learner.

When we place the rhetorical and conceptual marks together, it makes criticism more difficult. Both the ways in which problem of restructuring is stated (globalization and individual responsibility), there is little available to consider the relation of historical patterns and the formation of the type of subject and subjectivities constructed. The world is to exist as a certainty, as a systematically and clean slate in the social and political realms that is juxtaposed to the uncertainty (flexibility, relish for change), systematically/unregulated (collegial, collaboration), and unclean slate of the cleaning agents. Further, alternative notions are muted and silenced. The discourses construct a way of thinking and acting that undermines and delegimatizes competing policies and competing subjectivities. To be critical is to be "an old style teacher," to be against modernization and to subvert the position of the nation in the processes of globalization.

We focus on this issue of fatalism and the erasures of the discourses of restructuring as a way, ironically, to challenge and reinsert a historical and critical memory in the practices of education. Our concern in this book, to go back to the opening paragraphs of the chapter, is to problematize the practices of restructuring. Our strategy is to focus on the habitual ways of working and thinking in educational reform as that thinking is played out in the restructuring efforts. It is to take the "thought" of education to show how thought has played a part in holding those arrangements together and to contest the strategies that govern human possibilities.

NOTE

1.   Consider here the introduction of markets in England and Wales in the early 1980s and a little later in the 1988 education reform act (e.g., Gewirtz et al., 1995) on one side, and on the other side the presentation of a restructured educational system in The Swedish Way Towards a Learning Society in 1992.

REFERENCES

Bourdieu, P., & Wacquant, L. (1992). *An invitation to reflexive sociology.* Chicago: The University of Chicago press.

Boym, S. (2001). *The future of nostalgia.* New York: Basic Books.

Chubb, J. E., & Moe, T.M. (1988). Politics, markets and the organisation of schools. *American Political Science Review, 82,* 1065B,1087.

Dale, R. (1998). *The state and governance of education: An analysis of the restructuring of the state-education relationship.* In A.H.HALSEY et al. (Eds).

Darling-Hammond, L., & Bullmaster, M. (1997). The changing social context of teaching in the United States. In Biddle et al. (Eds), *International Handbook of Teachers and Teaching.* Dordrecht, Boston, and London: Kluwer Academic Press.

Daun, H. (1993). *Omstrukturering av skolsystemen. Decentralisering, valfrihet och privatisering.* En internationell översikt (Restructuring Education. Decentalisation, freedom of choice and privatisation. An international overview). Stockholm: Skolverket.

De Swaan, A. (1988). *In care of the state: Health care, education and welfare in Europe and the U.S.A. in the modern era.* Cambridge, U.K: Policy Press.

Esping-Andersen, G. (Ed.). (1996). *Welfare states in transition: National adaptations in global economies.* London: Sage.

Fendler, L. (2003). Teacher reflection in a hall of mirrors: Historical influences and political reverberations. *Educational Researcher, 32*(3), 3–15.

Gewirtz, S., Ball, S., & Bowe, R. (1995). *Markets, choice, and equity in education.* Buckingham: Open University Press.

Giddens, A. (1998). *The third way: The renewal of social democracy.* Malden, MA: Polity Press.

Hacking, I. (1999). *The social construction of what?* Cambridge, MA: Harvard University Press.

Halsey, A. H., Lauder, H., Brown, P., & Stuart Wells, A. (Eds.). (1998). *Education, culture, economy, society.* Oxford: Oxford University Press.

Hirst, P., & Thompson, G. (1999). *Globalization in question.* Cambridge: Polity Press. (2nd edition. 1st edition published 1996).

Latour, B. (1986). Visualization and cognition: Thinking with eyes and hands. *Knowledge and Society, 6,* 1–40.

Lindblad, S., & Popkewitz, T.S. (Eds). (2001b). Listening to education actors on governance and social integration and exclusion. *Uppsala Reports on Education 38.*

Lindblad, S., & Popkewitz, T.S. (Eds). (2001a). Statistics on education and social inclusion and exclusion in international and national contexts. *Uppsala Reports on Education, 37.*

Lindblad, S., & Popkewitz, T.S. (Eds). (1999). Education governance and social integration and exclusion: National cases of educational systems and recent reforms. *Uppsala reports on education, 34.*

Lindblad, S., & Popkewitz, T.S. (Eds). (2000). Public discourses on education governance and social integration and exclusion. Analyses of policy texts in European contexts. *Uppsala Reports on Education, 36.*

Lindblad, S., & Popkewitz, T.S. (Eds). (2001c): Education governance and social integration and exclusion: Studies in the powers of reason and the reasons of power. *Uppsala Reports on Education, 39.*

Meyer, J. (1999). *Globalization and the curriculum: Problems for theory in the sociology of education.* Paper presented at the International Symposium, Univerity of Lisbon, November.

Meyer, J., Boli, J., Thomas, G., & Ramirez, F. (1997). World society and the nation-state. *American Journal of Sociology, 103*(1), 144–181.

Novóa, A. (2002). Ways of thinking about education in Europe. In A. Novóa & M. Lawn (Eds.), *Fabricating Europe; The formation of an education space (pp. 131–156).* Dordrecht: Kluwer Academic Publishers.

Papagiannis, G. J., Easton, P.A., & Owens, J.T. (1992). *The school restructuring movement in the USA: An analysis of major issues and policy implications.* Paris: UNESCO.

Popkewitz, T., & Pereyra, M. (1993). An eight country study of reform practices in teacher education: An outline of the problematic. In T. Popkewitz (Ed.), *Changing patterns of power; Social regulation and teacher education reform* (pp. 1–53). Albany, NY: The State University of New York Press.

Popkewitz, T. (1991). *A political sociology of educational reform: Power/Knowledge in teaching, teacher education, and research.* New York, Teachers College Press.

Popkewitz, T. (1998). *Struggling for the soul: The politics of education and the construction of the teacher.* New York: Teachers College Press.

Popkewitz, T.S., & Lindblad, S. (2000). Educational governance and social inclusion and exclusion: A conceptual review of equity and post-modern traditions. *Discourse, 21*(1), 1B44.

Scott, J. (1998). *Seeing like a state: How certain schemes to improve the human condition have failed.* New Haven, CT: Yale University.

The Swedish Way Towards a Learning Society. (1992). A Report to the OECD. Stockholm: Ministry of Education and Science.

Wagner, P. (1994). *The sociology of modernity.* New York: Routledge.

Wagner, P. (2001). *Theorizing modernity.* London: Sage.

Walford, G. (1994). *Choice and quality in education.* London: Cassell.

Weiler, H (1989). Education and power: The politics of Educational decentralisation in comparative perspective. *Education Policy, 3,* 31B43.

Whitty, G., Power, S., & Halpin, D. (1998). *Devolution and choice in education: The school, the state and the market.* Buckingham: Open University Press.

part I

INTERNATIONALIZATION AND GLOBALIZATION OF EDUCATION

CHAPTER 1

EDUCATIONAL RESTRUCTURING AND THE RESHAPING OF SCHOOL GOVERNANCE IN ARGENTINA

Inés Dussel
FLACSO/Argentina

INTRODUCTION

In the last two or three years, Argentina's crisis has been widely covered by the world's principal newspapers and journals. What most of them shared was the conviction that, after having been considered the IMF's best pupil in the 1990s, Argentina's crisis was a case in point of the failure of its policies. The news spoke about unemployment, recession, political instability, corruption, and they included more or less dramatic stories about people rioting supermarkets or queuing up for a piece of bread; other journalists, in a more romantic and optimistic vein, saw a new kind of citizenship emerging from neighborhood's meetings and the unemployed picketing (*piqueteros*) movements.

In this chapter, however, instead of referring to failures, ruptures, and sinking, I am interested in pointing out the continuities and the persistent

Educational Restructuring: International Perspectives on Traveling Policies, pages 3–20
Copyright © 2004 by Information Age Publishing

3

legacies of the 1990s reform in the present. Without ignoring the dramatic and brutal effects that the crisis has had on schooling, evident, among other things, in the rise of the drop-out rates and the levels of malnutrition and other poverty-related health problems, I prefer to analyze other subtle yet pervasive dynamics that are still structuring the school system and that have powerful consequences on the way in which people think, act, and relate to each other. Erving Goffman once said that, "in a complex society, social disorganization is no more than the dismantling of one component of a totality; but the totality is never so firmly integrated that it falls totally apart" (quoted in: Grüner, 2003, p. 27). In other words, as widespread and deep as this crisis is, it has not provoked a complete disarticulation of the system. Moreover, as other colleagues and myself have argued elsewhere (Dussel & Finocchio, 2003), Argentina's school system has remarkably kept functioning, and this "keeping up appearances" in turbulent times is not a minor fact.

My concern in this chapter is to analyze the reshaping of the patterns of governance in schools during the 1990s and that are still in effect these days, which may help to explain why the school has survived in better shape the general social disorganization that took place in recent years. First, a cautionary note should be taken here. It is particularly challenging to analyze patterns of governance in a society that has become known as one of the most un-governable places in the world. To counter this view, I will argue that this lack of "social discipline," or law-abiding people, should not be read as a complete absence of law or governance. As O'Donnell (2002) has stated, the efficacy of law has been weak in Latin America for most of the 20th century, and this has not meant that societies did not organize or that no rule or hierarchy was in place. What we need are more complex ways to understand this kind of organization and governance; and this is where I believe other theoretical tools have to be put to work. These tools should combine a different take on the workings of power, such as the one provided by Michel Foucault and Nikolas Rose among others, with "microphysical knowledges" (as the ones provided by some histories and anthropologies) that inform us about the "localization" of these political practices.

A second cautionary note is referred to in my use of the concept of "educational reform," which has been thought of as a one-dimensional, single movement that exogenously or endogenously seeks to impose change in one direction. Here, again, my analysis is based on the works of Michel Foucault, Nikolas Rose, and other studies about governmentality, but especially on Tom Popkewitz's readings of this school of thought from the educational field (Foucault, 1980; Rose, 1989,1999a; Popkewitz, 1993,1998). Grounding on these works, I will propose that recent reforms have to be understood as part of government technologies that intend to shape the way people are to act, think, and feel about the world, that combine the old and the new in unique ways. These technologies of government are not the expression of a single "will to power" (Rose, 1999a) but rather have to be considered as a "combinatory repertoire" (Hunt, 1999) that adapts and relocates different discourses and strategies in the process of governing teachers.

Finally, another concern that runs throughout this chapter is to investigate how the global and the local have been played out in recent reforms. I have already mentioned that the 1990s reforms in Argentina were "inspired" by more global movements of change, which recommended school-based management, standardized testing, common curricular contents, and financial decentralization as the direction of change. But, as important as unraveling these universalistic rationale for change is, it is also necessary to analyze the "creolization" of these reforms (cf. Anderson-Levitt, 2003). In a way, my project is similar to Arjun Appadurai's when he says that: "If the genealogy of cultural forms is about their circulation across regions, the history of these forms is about their ongoing domestication into local practices." (Appadurai, 1996, p. 17) While I would speak more in terms of translation than of domestication, his pointing simultaneously to the global and the local in the construction of cultures and knowledge seems fundamental to produce a better understanding of these recontextualizations.

The chapter has two main sections. In the first one, I will take a historical turn in order to analyze the decentralization policies that were effected in the 1990s, and will describe the changes in the broader patterns of governance that were put in place by these reforms, that gave a renewed role to provincial governments and what was called the "federal government of education."[1] At the same time, the discourses of reform developed a new language for teachers and principals that set new constraints and regulations on their work in the name of reflexivity, autonomy, and responsibility. In the second section, I discuss current efforts of reform related to the construction of new patterns of governance based on personal responsibility and self-government, and will consider especially the new rules for school discipline. I will argue that these discourses, as they are read in present Argentina, are hybrid discourses that combine heterogeneous discourses, and cannot be enclosed in "neoliberal" or "neoconservative" labels. Also, I will argue against those who see the current situation as the sole product of globalization and import of foreign policies, and emphasize instead the translation and recontextualization processes that are taking place in the educational field. I hope that the unfolding of these combinations will illuminate the complex works of power, thus providing new grounds for the development of an "inventive politics" (Rose, 1999b).

RESHAPING GOVERNANCE AT THE SYSTEM'S LEVEL:
THE CENTRALIZED CONSTRUCTION OF DE-CENTRALIZATION

Argentina's decentralization policies in the 1990s were presented as the conclusion of a century-old struggle of the provincial governments against the primacy of the national state in educational matters. The notion of "federalism," which condensed the claims of the provinces to rule their own educational systems, gained currency in a context of structural reforms and financial cuts to social expenditure (cf. Rhoten, 1998). In this section, I am interested in tracing the history of decentralization policies in order to illuminate the multiple and even contradictory dynamics that they encompass today.

It can be said that, even if it is always difficult to date precisely any event without falling in the trap of declaring "origins" and "foundations," (against which Foucault (1980) persuasively argues), the emergence of this problematic can be traced back to the organization of the modern educational system in the second half of the 19th century in Argentina, while projects for a unified nation were being discussed. For the generation of liberals that led the process of unification, education was to civilize the plebe that had been mobilized during the independence and civil wars, forming a citizenship that would stop supporting the provincial leaders (caudillos) and embrace the liberal ideals. The republican order and the national union imagined by the liberal elite would rest on this "literate citizenship" (Sábato, 1992) educated by the schools.

The liberal program, and the first organization of the system, thought differently of primary and secondary schooling. The provinces that would be in charge of designing the curriculum and administration would run elementary schools. Secondary schools and normal schools that would train teachers would be run directly by the national state, which sought to keep a hold of the formation of the ruling classes. In 1905, a law was passed that authorized the creation of national elementary schools in those places where the provinces were not fulfilling the educational needs of the population. From that moment on, the national schools increased their enrollment gradually at the expense of the provinces', reaching its peak in the 1940s, when the national primary schools received almost 50% of the total population of that level (Braslavsky & Krawczyk, 1987), and the nationalization of educational services was the dominant drive until the late 1950s.

After Perón's debunkment of office in 1955 by a military coup, a reverse movement towards provincial administrations grew. At that time, some laws were passed that allowed private owners to run universities, and gave them increased power in the primary and secondary level. This shift of balance between the private and the public sector was thought of as the best means to prevent an authoritarian state from monopolizing public education.

This move implied a break with the deeply rooted republican belief that "state-owned" was the equivalent to "public" and "democratic." At this time, decentralization was led by the private sector.

During the last military dictatorship (1976–1983), the government transferred all elementary schools and preschools, depending on the national state, to the provincial governments. The government, coherent with its traditionalist, "back to the roots," ideological motto, claimed that this act was a sort of restoration of the federal origins of the educational system. In this second wave, then, decentralization was a result of authoritarian policies that intended to dramatically restructure the political field. The center of the scene was no longer occupied by the private sector, but by the provincial states, tightly controlled by the militaries.

In the 1980s, with the restoration of democratically elected governments, the strong movement towards communitarian participation and democratization also reached the educational arena. Several experiences of school boards, students' centers and parents' associations were developed, in some cases—as in the parents' and students' cases—recreating old traditions in the Argentinean educational system. Decentralization was claimed as a way of introducing democratic participation at all levels of the system. In their turn, the provincial states also demanded the completion of the transference of the national schools, including secondary schools and the tertiary level (mostly teacher education institutions). The concept of decentralization shifted profoundly to articulate anti-authoritarian, anti-militarist, pro-juvenile struggles.

In the 1990s, "reform" spread as a "contagious discourse" (Schram, 2000) that brought into national debates categories that were not neutral nor innocuous. Decentralization, accountability, managerialism, professionalization, national standards, were all topics of the rhetoric of educational reform that were quickly adopted in Argentina as the road to success. It is important to take into account that these discourses involved ways of seeing the world, senses of selfhood and otherness, disciplinary knowledges, and power relations that were introduced in the local arenas along with the words used to describe the situations and prescribe the solutions. They were part of "régimes of truth" (Foucault, 1980) that established criteria for judgement and validation processes that had political and ethical implications. These rhetorics depicted an old-fashioned system, caught between struggles of interests and conservative tendencies. The participatory decentralization was seen as part of the problem and not the way out of it.

In a previous text (Dussel, Tiramonti, & Birgin, 2000), I have emphasized that the adoption of these reform policies produced hybrid discourses. It implied a translation process that put these new experiences and directions in relation to the ones that were available previously, and even if it erased and blurred the original markers, these older components remained as part of its texture, as when we find traces of previous writings in the palimpsest.[2]

The reform discourses were propagated by state-centered agencies, while the universities remained largely in the opposition.[3] Proposals such as the professionalization of teachers, unified curricular contents, site-based management of schools, and decentralization became the cornerstone of change and innovation. New legal and administrative frames were established. A compulsory general education of 10 years replaced the traditional 7-year long primary school, and a vocationally-oriented 3-year "Polimodal" education (with several orientations) took the place of secondary schools, traditionally structured, despite the technical or commercial-administration schools, by a humanist curriculum (cf. Dussel, 1997). The institutions that were in charge of teacher training were transferred to the provincial governments. The transference was accompanied by a deep restructuring of teacher education, including the reshaping of the teacher training system into a network with principal and subsidiary members, new standards for accreditation, and new content areas for the curriculum.

The provincial administrations were posed as the privileged sites of government of the educational system. Each province passed a new Law of Education that set their own principles and organizations for schooling. The new governing body of national education was supposed to be the Federal Council of Education, which included a representative for each province. From 1989, when it was created, to 2002, 195 resolutions and 22 general agreements were passed, whose contents range from primary and secondary education basic contents to compensatory programs to special and artistic education arrangements. A complex mechanism of transactions and negotiations between the national ministry and the provincial administration was established, which benefited the national ministry while it had access to foreign loans and could thus impose conditions on the provinces, but that ended by 1999 when international loans started to be scarce. The "provinces," a term which encompasses very different structures (Buenos Aires' province has a third of the school population of the country while other provinces have less than 50,000 students), gained political and financial relevance in their own territories, and the idea and the practice of a national educational system became much looser (Tiramonti, 2001).

Teachers and schools were also constructed as key actors in the decentralization policies. While the administrations that held office during the 1990s have diverged in their pedagogical orientations, some being more driven by the goals of participation and autonomy and others by managerial discourses, professionalization has remained a common thread among them. The notion that the teacher has to transform herself/himself into a different kind of practitioner, more academically oriented (i.e., with an updated knowledge purveyed by research findings) and more accountable in terms of her/his results, has received wide support.[1] The reforms have been oriented to give more weight to content areas and to "institutional knowledge" about how schools work. The notion of "institutional knowledge" has implied a new look at the life of schools in teacher education, which was significantly absent in the Normalist tradition—only requiring a small practicum at the end of the mostly theoretical training. But it has also implied the introduction of managerial language into pedagogy and curriculum. Schools are to be thought of as organizations that have to be managed, balancing inputs and outputs, controlling the flux of communications, and putting into numbers the daily interchanges and processes that take place in schools. These numbers will make teaching more accountable and thus, it is presumed, better.

The discourses of reform are related to shifts in the technologies and targets of power (Rose, 1999a). They are homologous to the ones involved in the reorganization of the workplace and the military, which focus on competency, flexibility, adaptability, and a re-education of the will ("the entrepreneurial self", as Popkewitz and Bloch (in press) define it). The individual is responsible for self-actualization, in a continual work upon the self in order to fully develop their potentialities.

In this new configuration of the social, "local" or "private" endeavors are seen as the most democratic and dynamic practices. The discourse on individual and community responsibility involves local institutions and individuals assuming what used to be done by the welfare State, and it links decentralization and democratization in a way in which each educational institution is the primary constructor of the new social agenda rather than the educational system as a whole. One central province, San Luis, has started six charter schools, although they remain as a limited experiment until now.[5]

But responsibility and accountability have permeated other areas as well. The French sociologist Alain Ehrenberg provides an interesting take on the categories and distinctions introduced by this therapeutic-economic discourse. In a book on depression and society, Ehrenberg points out that the new patterns of governance stress performance and success as the "normal" outcomes of conduct, and produce a new pathology of insufficiency and incapacity (Ehrenberg, 2000). All those who are incapable or unwilling to discipline themselves in line with the kind of performance needed to succeed will be considered a failure, and will enter into the realm of therapeutic technologies to redeem the self. These changes have deeply transformed the experiences and practices of the self. Ehrenberg points out that the psychological illness of our time is no longer Freud's neurosis but depression, "being tired of being oneself," of lacking sufficient initiative or responsibility. Pharmacology and the sciences of conduct will come to the rescue, helping the individual to cope with this incapacity—although, Ehrenberg argues, they have been complicitous in the production of the pathology. Ehrenberg's work is important because it shows to what extent the new patterns of governance are centered on the self, and imply new languages, new categories and new actions to be taken for/against the self.

Sanford Schram, portraying how welfare reforms have focused on a notion of "responsibility" that is defined in an economic as well as in a therapeutic register,[6] stresses that this kind of responsibility has reinscribed liberal ideals about the subject in terms of new race, gender, and class relations. For Schram, a discourse on personal responsibility defines citizenship and rights in relation to the ability to work and provide an income for oneself and one's family. Not being able to work is a consequence of bad habits (addictions, early pregnancies, inability to constitute a two-parent family) and of incapacity to discipline oneself (Schram, 2000, ch.1). The "welfare queen," an artifact produced by this discourse (Schram, 2000; Cruikshank, 1999), is the epitome of this deficiency: women, and particularly women of color, are seen as especially incapable of controlling their impulses, governing their selves, in short, of living as independent beings. This formulation encourages the idea that "women are more likely to be poor and the poor are more likely to act in a female-like fashion.... In this process, not only does poverty get feminized but personal responsibility is again reinscribed as a male phenomenon that women lack." (Schram, 2000, p. 41)

In Argentina, most of these discourses have circulated intensely, although with heterogeneous effects. Their dissemination poses interesting questions to think about the dynamics of the global and the local in the circulation and recontextualization of educational discourses. First, it should be noted that the discourses that focus on the empowerment of teachers and principals coexist with those that see the "provinces" as the key players of this new field, and both terms have been frequently pitted against each other (Tiramonti, 2001). At times of heated political struggle between the National Ministry and the provincial governments, the central administration has essayed a direct contact with the schools and the teachers via the production of educational journals or teaching guides. Discourses on professionalization have been juxtaposed, or even have contradicted, other discourses on decentralization as transference of educational services to the provinces.

Second, the recontextualization has implied negotiations and translations with older discourses as well. For example, the discourse on personal responsibility has been a central piece in educational reforms, providing arguments for changing the work of head teachers and supervisors, but it has crashed against a firmly entrenched teaching ethos that defines teaching as a wage-based work, subordinated to the central State. A case in point has been the unsuccessful attempts to reform the Teachers' Statute, a protective law passed on 1957 that grants stability and special privileges to teachers. Despite aggressive campaigns in the media, accusing teachers of being lazy and self-compliant, even corrupt, none of the three administrations that held office since 1990 have been able to change it.[7] It should be noted that, after the generalized political and social crisis that is taking place since December 2001, it is fairly obvious that these discourses on personal responsibility had very few chances to be efficacious when corruption and un-governability were widespread. However, they did produce some effects on how school principals and supervisors conduct their schools, having become more liable both in juridical and social terms.[8]

RESHAPING SCHOOL GOVERNANCE: THE NEW ROLE OF COHABITATION RULES

In this section, I will pay a closer look to the patterns of governance that are being put in place in schools. As it has been mentioned before, the restoration of democratically elected governments in 1983 brought about new concerns about democracy and participation throughout the educational system. School discipline became a heavily charged topic in the national agenda due to the repressive experience of the dictatorship. One of the first measures of the new administration in 1984 was to derogate the disciplinary regime for secondary schools, which dated from 1934. Throughout the 1980s and the beginnings of the 1990s, the life of schools changed dramatically. Parents' associations became again important in primary schools management, also due to the financial crisis and the economic needs of schools, and students' associations gained momentum in secondary and tertiary schools, contributing to a renewed political participation of youth.

At that time, there were some essays to introduce school governing bodies that included teachers, parents and students, which were not successful (cf. Tiramonti, 2001). By the early 1990s, these bodies were accused of bureaucratization, corruption or excessive politicization; also, there was a more general decline in civic participation which was especially felt in the human rights movement. The decentralization reforms, as have been noted above, seldom spoke in terms of increased communitarian participation. School councils persisted in some schools but became much less important in terms of the power strategies that were designed at that time.

By the end of the 1990s, however, there was a renewed interest in school discipline and governance, this time fueled by concerns about the crisis of adults' authority and the loose boundaries of permissions and prohibitions in schools as well as in the broader society.[9] The discourse on discipline and security constructs an association between the relaxation of norms and the crisis of adults' authority, on the one hand, and the rise of juvenile delinquency and school violence. Expert discourses on autonomy and responsibility have provided a language for dealing with these new situations, and new rules are being set in place in most provincial administrations.

In the city of Buenos Aires, the new rules were approved in 2001, under the name of "School System for Cohabitation" (Sistema Escolar de Convivencia). They establish that each school has to decide their own rules, constituting a Cohabitation Council. Despite its openness, it prescribes that the Council will have teachers, students, preceptors (disciplinary assistants), representatives of Students' Associations, and parents, and lists a set of sanctions that range from oral reprimand to separation from school.

The change from a centralized rule to a decentralized one, in which each school has a considerable degree of autonomy, is remarkable, and is one of the few aspects in which schools can exercise their autonomy—which, in other spheres such as curriculum design, monetary resources, or decisions on school personnel, is severely impaired by present conditions and regulations. In a study currently under way at FLACSO, we reviewed the statutes of 20 secondary schools in order to analyze what schools have made with that autonomy.[10] While we are still completing the research, some preliminary ideas will be summarized in what follows.

One of the most striking features of the statutes is that they are generally written in terms of the responsibilities that students have, and only two of them speak the language of rights and obligations. For example, one of the statutes states that, through cohabitation rules, students learn several important things: that conflict is an integral part of life; that problems can be solved through dialogue; that all situations can be improved; that each student has to assume her/his own responsibility; that anger and irritability have to be expressed through respectful language and so on.[11] Others are more concise but share the assumptions (i.e., in the definition of a technical school, the cohabitation system is a conflict-management strategy and entails permanent self-reflection[12]). The politico-legal language of rights and obligations is replaced by a psychological, even cognitive (problem-solving strategies) discourse.

The "responsibilities" listed in the school rules include: mutual respect, attention, respect for school property, and respect for patriotic symbols (flag, national anthem), among others, and are generally related to students' behavior and not to that of the teachers'. One school discourages students to bring along money or costly items and makes it explicit that the school will not be liable for lost items on school premises. Some schools opt for a "group ethics" that stresses the weight of the collective self of the school community. In this case, the idea of harmony and consensus inside the school community is so prevalent that transgression becomes much more serious. Only four of the 20 schools mention that the adults have some kind of responsibility or obligation, while the others assume that the statutes are intended to control students' behavior.

This last point can be noted in the importance, in all statutes, of the regulation of "proper attire" and conduct in schools (no smoking, no drinking alcohol, no violent games). Proper attire and conduct is primarily a responsibility of students (no reference is made to what would happen if a professor smoked in class). As it happens in other school systems, the "presentation" of the self is a relevant aspect of school interactions (cf. Dussel, 2001). In Argentina, while until 1984 secondary school students had to wear uniforms, the liberalization of vestimentary codes has become a conflictive point in the relationships of students and adult authorities. Most of the school rules/statutes list the kind of clothing items that cannot be worn in schools: teams' T-shirts, baseball caps, leggy pants, shorts or miniskirts. Young women cannot wear earrings or make up, and young men, if long-haired, have to wear it in a ponytail. Vestimentary codes, then, include a more or less short list of what cannot be worn in schools, and general claims about wearing "adequate, proper clothing." What is interesting is that the regulation of clothing has to include some openness or flexibility, as it stands as a flexible form against the rigidity of uniforms.

The notion of "proper attire" and "style," then, becomes much more powerful. It can be argued that "proper attire" is a regulation that has been in effect at least since the end of the 19th century. In Argentina, before uniforms were donned, teachers insisted on the idea of "proper attire" as a way of disciplining the bodies of children. However, the notion of what is "proper" and "improper" is much looser today than it was in the 1880s, its boundaries being continually redefined by marketing strategies and youth subcultures among others (i.e., the notion of hipness or coolness as perpetually changing—in fact, there is no other way of being "cool" than perpetually looking for the latest trend). I claim that the fact that the one who has to define what is "proper" and "improper" is the self, implies a careful and attentive work upon oneself, a continual monitoring of the self and others.

The education of "passions," to borrow Nikolas Rose's idea, through the intervention on people's lifestyles is a substantial change in the way power is affected and the technologies it brings into play. The very idea of "lifestyle" points in a different direction than the liberal technologies of the self, and introduces new practices of identity formation through "the active and practical shaping by individuals of the daily practices of their own lives in the name of their own pleasures, contentment's, or fulfillments." (Rose, 1999a, pp. 178–179). Again, as with the professional teacher, the individual is responsible for self-actualization, in a continual work upon the self in order to fully develop her/his potentialities.

But it is in the sanctions that issues of responsibility come out strongly. Some schools have a credit system for sanctions, which implies losing points each time a transgression is made. For example, students start the school year with 100 credits, and lose 15 credits if they miss a class without justification, 5 credits if they throw garbage in an inappropriate place, or 10 to 50 credits if they do not show respect for patriotic symbols. The goal is to produce the student as a calculating subject, a speculative person who can manage her/his credits adequately. The schools that do not have a credit system propose gradual increases in the penalties, a graduality that can also produce speculation and calculating strategies. However, parents are to be notified of each sanction and remain ultimately responsible, in most cases, for their children's behavior, reinstituting the notion of adolescents as minors incapable of self-regulation and autonomy.

The regulation of school discipline as it appears in the schools' cohabitation rules, then, combines old and new themes and strategies. It is formulated in terms of responsibilities and consensus, and emphasizes flexibility, adaptability, and a re-education of the will necessary to learn how to live together. It proposes dialogue and conflict-resolution strategies, in a similar way to what new managerial discourses are doing for other areas (Rose, 1999a). But, on the other hand, most of the statutes still see the child as incapable of self-government, and stress an idea of "responsibility" that resembles the old topics of school discipline (as in, i.e., "the student is responsible for obeying the rules"). The production of a calculating subject is counterbalanced by the weight of obedience and traditional sanctions. Reiterating an old relation between the state and marginal children (Guy, 2002), the cohabitation rules, most of the time, place the children and adolescents as "subjects-of-paternalism," incapable of self-monitoring responsibly, yet obliged to do it in many other aspects of school life.

Again, as it has been said in the previous section, governance is the result of hybrid discourses that combine the old and the new in unpredictable ways, and that can not be accounted for in terms of a "single will to power." Interestingly, most schools agree in establishing the disrespect for patriotic symbols as a severe fault, even leading to separation from school. That this consensus has gone unchallenged despite the wane of nationalisms and the crisis of the Argentinean state is remarkable, and constitutes an evidence of the complex translations that social and cultural dynamics have when they affect the school setting.

CONCLUDING REMARKS: THE PRODUCTION OF HYBRID PATTERNS OF GOVERANCE

Throughout this chapter, I have tried to unfold the many nuances and inflections that the discourses of reform of educational governance have

taken in the Argentinean educational field. The local translation of discourses on responsibility and autonomy is a powerful example of the
assemblage of several discourses and strategies that constitute the patterns
of governance. Mitchell Dean has argued that régimes of government
always put together features that are heterogeneous, some paternalistic,
some liberal, or simply authoritarian (Dean, 1998). As I have said before,
these regimes are not the expression of a single "will to power" (Rose,
1999a) but rather have to be considered as a "combinatory repertoire"
(Hunt, 1999) that adapts and relocates different discourses and strategies
in the process of governing schools, teachers, and students.

I have argued that we need to develop a renewed theoretical and political reading of the educational reform in Argentina that goes beyond the
uncritical stance of managerial reforms but also beyond the usual accusations of neo-liberalism or neo-colonialism. I have focused on the multiple
discourses that are being mobilized to structure new patterns of governing,
discourses that are not easily reduced to a single entity, be it ideology, political party, or policy. I have argued that they combine heterogeneous elements that have different dynamics inscribed in them, and that are
produced in a field of relations that have their own dynamics too.

Another point of the chapter has been to illuminate the ways in which
the translations made by reform strategies have implied adopting "foreign"
discourses to local arenas. Following Appadurai's work, I have tried to show
the importance of looking at the circulation of global cultural forms and
educational discourses and their translation into local practices. For example, the "import" of professionalization discourses and the construction of
the teacher as the privileged site of regulation has coexisted with another
movement, that of transferring educational services to the provinces and
constituting the provincial governments into central players of the
reforms. This coexistence has produced a hybrid that includes old and new
ways of governing schools and teachers. This simultaneous account for the
global and the local in the production of cultures and knowledge seems
much more tuned to current dynamics than either/or frameworks that still
abound in educational research.

I have claimed that the introduction of notions of "responsibility" and
"autonomy" has had dissimilar effects in a field in which people are used to
act and think with different categories and languages. Teachers and principals are supposed to act responsibly, with the new language and managerial
practices provided by the reformers, in a movement that points to the development of self-monitoring and adjustment. However, both the system's
organization and the school organization build up on a different direction,
tied to political negotiations and flows, and to a more traditional ethics of
wage-work. On the other hand, it can be said that "cohabitation rules" have
combined new managerial discourses and strategies with old themes, such
as plain obedience to rules, respect for patriotic symbols, and a more verti-

cal, hierarchized relationship between adults and children than the idea of "cohabitation," conflict-resolution, and anger management promises.

In both cases, patterns of governance can be seen as simultaneously changing and stable. They introduce ruptures at the same time that negotiations with old discourses and strategies are performed. Going back to the arguments presented in the introduction of this chapter, I hope it is by now clear why I do not share the assumption that schools, as well as the broader society, have become lawless or totally un-governable. There is an organization of the educational system and of the school as an institution, with its rules and hierarchies. While its efficacy on people's conduct should be investigated through other methods than the ones I have used here, it could be argued that the hybridity of the technologies speak about multiple accommodations and translations made at several levels; in that respect it can be said that they are already having effects on teachers' and students' behaviors.

To reintroduce complexity and heterogeneity in the analysis of Argentinean educational policy is also to go beyond the reference to disparate mechanisms or entities. It is not enough to point out the "mix and match" of heterogeneity. I believe that there is an important point to be made about any practice of governing: that it is never totally coherent, and that the idea of self-identity and purity are nothing but myths (cf. Valverde, 1998). To look for a general rationality of governance behind all governance patterns, call it "neoliberal policy," an overwhelming disciplinary power, or neo-populism, would reproduce these myths of self-containment and coherence. Neither total dismantling, nor total efficacy and reproduction: as many post-structural scholars have argued, it is in this in-between that we have to navigate, humbly struggling for more justice and freedom in these turbulent waters.

NOTES

1. As it will be noted, "federal government" takes a different meaning in the Argentinean context than in the U.S., and comprises the action of the provincial administrations and not of the central, national-level government.

2. In a recent paper, I discuss the implications of postcolonial notions of hybridity for curriculum theory (cf. Dussel, 2002). Hybrid is etimologically linked to the Latin word hubris, injury. Although a more rigorous etimological inquiry is needed, it is important to point out that the association of hybridity to a wound, an offense, an incision done to the self, is a long one in Western culture history, and that to construct it as a positive, contested place is a gesture that turns metaphysics upside down.

3. A history of educational discourse in recent years is yet to be written. Southwell (2003) provides an enlightening account of the continuities and breaks between the different administrations (radicalism-peronism). Public univer-

sities have held the monopoly of critical discourse, but their personnel initiated research about "teachers as practitioners" or the relevance of subject matter content. Cf. Palamidessi, in press.

4. Interestingly, in the debate around the legacy of the Normal Schools, "profession" has been pitted against "vocation." The professionalists argue that Normalists have relied on the primacy of "calling" or "vocation" over "scientific knowledge," turning teacher training into a moralizing endeavor instead of focusing on the content-knowledge that teachers have to impart. What this argument forgets is that "profession" shares the same religious roots of "calling": profession meant initially a public declaration of one's faith, an ideal of faithful service rendered to the community (La Vopa, 1988). This "forgetting" conveniently helps construct an image of the teacher as a neutral practitioner, one whose knowledge and role is prescribed by the objective sciences of teaching. No longer an "agent of the Republic," as the Normalists defined themselves, the teacher has to consider herself/himself as a professional whose task is to impart content knowledge.

5. It is remarkable that the experience has mobilized a strange coalition of hard-core rightist liberals and leftist libertarians. One school has been named after Eduardo Galeano, the author of an anti-imperialist best-seller in the '70s, "The Open Veins of Latin America."

6. Here Schram follows Nancy Fraser and Linda Gordon's distinctions about the idioms used to speak about dependency in their seminal article (1998).

7. Cf. Llach et al., 1999, for a pro-government account of why the Teachers' Statute should be changed. Llach was the Minister of Education in 1999–2000.

8. It is common to hear school principals complain about parents' increased demands on schools. Several districts have implemented meetings with parents on a regular basis, more on the spirit of client/consumer basis than on the traditional way of relating to parents (paternalistic, civilizing, redemption-oriented).

9. These discourses can be traced back to conservative and nostalgic views as well as to more progressive, humanistic ones. For an interesting account on the changes of parental authority, see Delumeau & Roche, 2000. For a discussion of the prevalence of discourses on youth violence and the criminalization of poverty, especially of the young, male body, in Argentina, see Kessler, 2002; Isla & Míguez, 2003.

10. There are 40 public secondary schools in the city. Seventeen schools denied the researchers access to the document, argumenting that it is not a public text, and 3 still have to answer.

11. Cohabitation School Project, Secondary School No. 1, 2002.

12. Cohabitation Statute, Technical School No. 6, 2002.

REFERENCES

Anderson-Levitt, K. M. (Ed.). (2003). *Local meanings, global schooling. Anthropology and world culture theory.* New York & Hampshire: Palgrave MacMillan.

Appadurai, A. (1996). *Modernity at large: Cultural dimensions of globalization.* Minneapolis & London: University of Minnesota Press.

Braslavsky, C., & Krawczyk, N. (1987). *La escuela pública. [The public school]*. Buenos Aires: Miño y Dávila Editores.

Cruikshank, B. (1999). *The will to empower. Democratic subjects and other subjects*. Ithaca, NY: Cornell University Press.

Dean, M. (1999). *Governmentality: Power and rule in modern society*. London & Thousand Oaks, CA: Sage Publications.

Delumeau, J., & Roche, D. (Eds.). (2000). *Histoire des pères et de la paternité* (2nd ed.). Paris: Larousse.

Dussel, I. (1997). *Curriculum, humanismo y democracia en la enseñanza media (1863–1920). [Curriculum, humanism, and democracy in secondary schools, 1863–1920]*. Buenos Aires: Oficina de Publicaciones del CBC-UBA/FLACSO.

Dussel, I. (2001). School uniforms and the disciplining of appearances: Towards a history of the regulation of bodies in modern educational systems. In: T.S. Popkewitz, B. Franklin, & M. Pereyra (Eds.), *Cultural history and critical studies of education: Dissenting essays* (pp. 207–241). New York: Routledge.

Dussel, I. (2002). El curriculum híbrido. ¿Domesticación o pluralización de las diferencias?. In A. C. Lopes et al., (Eds.), *O campo do curriculo. Novas perspectivas* (pp. 55–77). [*The curriculum field. New perspectives*] Sao Paulo: Cortez Editora.

Dussel, I., Tiramonti, G., & Birgin, A. (2000). Decentralization and Recentralization in the Argentine Educational Reform: Reshaping educational policies in the '90s. In T. Popkewitz (Ed.), *Educational knowledge: Changing relationships between the state, civil society, and the educational community* (pp. 155–172). Albany, NY: State University of New York Press.

Dussel, I., & S. Finocchio. (Eds.). (2003). *Enseñar Hoy. Una introducción a la escuela en tiempos de crisis. [Teaching Today. An introduction to schools in times of crisis]*. Buenos Aires: Fondo de Cultura Económica.

Ehrenberg, A. (2000). *La fatiga de ser uno mismo. Depresión y sociedad [Tired of being oneself: Depression and society]* (R. Paredes, Trans.). Buenos Aires: Nueva Visión.

Foucault, M. (1980). *Power/Knowledge: Selected interviews and other writings, 1972–1977* (C. Gordon, trans.). New York: Pantheon Books.

Franklin, B., Bloch, M., & Popkewitz, T. S. (2003). *Educational partnerships: The paradoxes of governing schools, children, and families*. New York & Hampshire: Palgrave MacMillan Press.

Fraser, N., & Gordon, L. (1998). Contract versus charity: Why is there is no social citizenship in the United States? In G. Shafir (Ed.), *The citizenship debates* (pp. 113–127). Minneapolis & London: University of Minnesota Press.

Grüner, E. (2003). Del experimento al laboratorio, y regreso. Argentina o el conflicto de las representaciones. *[From the experiment to the laboratory and back. Argentina, or the conflict of representations]*. Sociedad. Revista de la Facultad de Ciencias Sociales, 20/21, pp. 27–54.

Guy, D. (2002). The state, the family and marginal children in Latin America. In T. Hecht (Ed.), *Minor omissions: Children in Latin American history and society* (pp. 139–164). Madison, WI: The University of Wisconsin Press.

Hunt, A. (1999). *Governing morals: A social history of moral regulation*. Cambridge, UK and New York: Cambridge University Press.

Isla, A., & Míguez, D. (Eds.). (2003). *Heridas urbanas: Violencia delictiva y transformaciones sociales en los noventa [Urban wounds: Delinquent violence and social transformations in the '90s]*. Buenos Aires: Editorial de las Ciencias/FLACSO.

Kessler, G. (2002). Entre fronteras desvanecidas. Lógicas de articulación de actividades legales e ilegales en los jóvenes [Between blurred boundaries. Logics of articulation of legal and illegal actitivies in young people]. In S. Gayol & G. Kessler (Eds.), *Violencias, delitos y justicias en la Argentina [Violence, crimes and justice systems in Argentina]* (pp. 339–354). Buenos Aires: Manantial/Universidad Nacional de General Sarmiento.

La Vopa, A. J. (1988). *Grace, talent, and merit: Poor students, clerical careers, and professional ideology in eighteenth-century Germany.* Cambridge, UK & New York: Cambridge University Press.

Llach, J. J., Montoya, S., & Roldán, F. (1999). *Educación para todos. [Education for all].* Córdoba: IERAL.

O'Donnell, G. (2002). Las poliarquías y la (in)efectividad de la ley en América latina. [Poliarchies and the (in)efficacy of the law in Latin America] In J. E. Méndez, G. O'Donnell, & P. S. Pinheiro (Eds.), *La (in)efectividad de la ley y la exclusión en América latina [The (in) efficacy of the law and exclusion in Latin America]* (pp. 305–336). Buenos Aires: Paidós.

Palamidessi, M. (in press). *La investigación educacional en la Argentina: Una mirada al campo y algunas proposiciones para la discusión. [Educational Research in Argentina: A look at the field and some propositions for discussion].* Buenos Aires: FLACSO.

Popkewitz, T. (Ed.). (1993). *Changing patterns of power: Social regulation and teacher education reform.* Albany, NY: State University of New York Press.

Popkewitz, T. (1998). *Struggling for the soul: The politics of schooling and the construction of the teacher.* New York & London: Teachers' College Press.

Rhoten, D. (1999). *Global-Local conditions of possibility: The case of educational decentralization in Argentina* (Ph.D. Dissertation, School of Education. Stanford University: 354.)

Rose, N. (1989). *Governing the soul: The shaping of the private self.* London: Routledge.

Rose, N. (1999a). *Powers of freedom. Reframing political thought.* Cambridge, UK & New York: Cambridge University Press.

Rose, N. (1999b). Inventiveness in politics. *Economy and Society, 28*(3), 467–493.

Rose, N., & Miller, P. (1992). Political power beyond the State: problematics of government. *The British Journal of Sociology, 43*(2), 173–205.

Sábato, H. (1992). Citizenship, political participation and the formation of the public sphere in Buenos Aires, 1850s–1880s. *Past and Present,* 136.

Schram, S. (2000). *After welfare. The culture of postindustrial social policy.* New York: New York University Press.

Southwell, M. (2002). Una aproximación al proyecto educacional de la Argentina post-dictatorial: el fin de algunos imaginarios [Educational projects in Post-Dictatorship Argentina: The End of Some Imaginaries]. *Cuadernos de Pedagogía Crítica, 10,* 53–70.

Tiramonti, G. (2001). *Modernización educativa de los '90. ¿El fin de la ilusión emancipatoria? [Educational modernization in the '90s. The end of the emancipatory illusion?]* Buenos Aires, Ed. Temas.

Valverde, M. (1998). *Diseases of the will: Alcohol and the dilemmas of freedom.* Cambridge, UK & New York: Cambridge University Press.

CHAPTER 2

THEORIZING THE GLOBAL CONVERGENCE OF EDUCATIONAL RESTRUCTURING

Fazal Rizvi
University of Illinois at Urbana-Champaign

INTRODUCTION

In a landmark paper published more than a decade ago, one of the architects of the study of international and comparative higher education, Philip Altbach (1991) suggested that the restructuring of educational systems around the world showed an unmistakable trend toward convergence. Similar pressures, procedures and organizational patterns everywhere, he argued, increasingly governed educational systems. Almost ten years later, Daniel Schugurensky (1999) insisted that this trend toward global convergence was intensifying, accelerated by the developments in communication technologies and the increasing movement of capital, media and people. Schugurensky maintains that "what is most striking about the current higher education restructuring is the unprecedented scope and depth of changes taking place as well as the similarity of changes

Educational Restructuring: International Perspectives on Traveling Policies, pages 21–41
Copyright © 2004 by Information Age Publishing
All rights of reproduction in any form reserved.

occurring in a wide variety of nations having different social, historical and economic characteristics." He adds that although the actual dynamics and pace of change has varied across national systems, any review of recent policy changes implemented by governments throughout the world shows the direction of change to be unmistakably similar. So, for example, there is an almost universal deepening of shift from social democratic to neo-liberal orientations, manifested most clearly in the privatization policies, which assume reliance on market dynamics to be the most appropriate way of responding to the various crises facing states responsible for governing education.

Altbach (1991) has argued that despite its considerable durability as an institution, the modern university has, in recent years, been subjected to intense pressure to change, from government authorities, students, employers, professional associations and other external stakeholders. This pressure has resulted partly from the rapid growth in demand for higher education, especially with the broadening of its class, gender and ethnic base, creating conditions for a new politics of difference, which has included political demands for cultural recognition and distributive justice. As universities have become larger and more complex, new requirements of policy and governance have emerged, resulting in the corporatization and marketization of higher education. This has involved greater demand for accountability, which in turn has resulted in increased surveillance and bureaucratization of institutions, creating new pressures on academic work. In most western countries, as public resources for universities have declined there has been a growing emphasis on increasing the role of the private sector in higher education.

Yet, in the midst of all this change, and despite pressures on higher education systems around the world to diversify and restructure—to meet the needs of the global economy and the new requirements of the labor market—universities and educational higher educational systems have, somewhat paradoxically, tended to mimic each other, pursuing a common set of solutions to their fiscal and organizational problems. Indeed they have even interpreted the requirements of reform itself in a broadly similar fashion.

In a paper focusing on issues of university finance and governance, Bruce Johnstone (2000) has also spoken of "the worldwide university reform agenda," arising from a sense of crisis facing higher education in countries as culturally and politically diverse as the United States, Russia and South Africa. Johnstone suggests that this sense of crisis has been produced by extreme financial austerity and overcrowding, extending to deficits in quality and appropriateness. Within the public sector of higher education, questions about the fundamental purposes of higher education have been asked. There has been strong demand for both greater accountability and quality improvement. In this context, market orientations and solutions have gained ascendance, with the relentless search for other-than-government revenues to support expansion and growth. Yet, for all the "supplementation" by non-government revenues, most universities have remained dependent on public funding. This has led to a range of reforms in the ways in which public sector finances are allocated and managed. These reforms have included the introduction of performance management and other forms of incentive-sensitive funding; the removal of restrictions that impede the optimal allocation and utilization of public revenues; new more flexible forms of conditions of employment of faculty and staff; and the devolution of system governance and organizational management (Johnstone, 2000). Universities have been encouraged to view themselves within the market paradigms. In short, they have been asked to mimic styles of governance and management borrowed from the corporate sector.

This approach to restructuring involving the global ascendance of market thinking has not however been confined to higher education systems facing financial crisis. Even those educational systems of the newly industrialized countries, which have not confronted fiscal crises to any great extent, have pursued a broadly similar range of neo-liberal educational reforms. So, for example, despite its wealth and strong centralist traditions (Gopinathan, 2001), Singapore has pursued a restructuring agenda, which encourages the privatization of its higher education, on the one hand, and emphasizes greater corporate accountability in the use of public expenditure, on the other. As a result, a large number of educational entrepreneurs have emerged in Singapore over the past decade; some like the Singapore Institute of Management around commercially driven international education, while others, like Informatics, interested in the commercial delivery of education through e-learning. Hong Kong has also instituted a neo-liberal agenda based on corporatist conceptions of devolution (Rizvi, 1997), enabling each of its public universities to pursue commercial activities through its centers of continuing and life-long education. In both Singapore and Hong Kong, the state has, in effect, assumed an arms-length approach to the commercialization of higher education, while keeping intact its oversight role which is designed to preserve the traditionally core functions of its public universities. While newly developed systems like Singapore and Hong Kong have pursued neo-liberal reforms in order to fund expansion, at the other extreme, the least developed countries have viewed such reforms as necessary to their survival. As Bray and Lee (2001, p. 7) argue, while in some Asian countries privatization and cost-recovery has been an overt policy, in many poorer countries privatization has chiefly been by default. Furthermore, in Latin American and African universities, policies of neo-liberal restructuring have become a core component of a new discourse of development, driven largely by market principles.

What appears clear then is that the restructuring of higher education everywhere is informed by a similar set of neo-liberal market ideologies. But this account of the global convergence of educational restructuring raises a number of important questions: how should we understand the nature of this trend and explain its acceptance around the world? how is this convergence possible? how extensive is its scope? is it inevitable? and how can this trend toward policy homogenization be resisted? In this paper my main focus is on the question of the extent to which this convergence is a product of the broader contemporary processes of globalization. I want to examine some of the processes through which this convergence is achieved, since it is only through this understanding that we can identify the possible sites of critical intervention where some of the more destructive effects of globalization can be resisted and where we can work more creatively with its possible productive potential.

RESTRUCTURING AND THE IDEA OF "THE GLOBAL CONTEXT"

Much of the recent critical literature in policy studies seeks to explain recent attempts at restructuring higher education in terms of the seemingly ubiquitous idea of the "global context." Apple (2000, p. 58), for example, argues that "it is impossible to understand current educational policy in the United States without placing it in its global context." Thus "behind the stress on higher standards, more rigorous testing, education for employment, and a much closer relationship between education and economy in general" he suggests, "is the fear of losing in international competition..." Similarly, Kenway (2001) seeks to explain Australian educational reforms in terms of the imperatives of the emerging global knowledge economy. Peters, Marshall and Fitzsimons (2000, p. 110) locate the rise of neo-liberal educational reforms in New Zealand within the predominant ideology of globalization. And in Britain a similar explanation has been put forward by leading policy scholars like Whitty (1999).

This use of the idea of global context is not restricted to English-speaking countries, however. Samoff (2000) discusses the global diffusion of western ideas about education. In late twentieth century, he argues, education has become totally dominated everywhere by the idea of economic progress, with notions of human capital and development becoming part of a broader discourse of capitalist triumphalism. Through borrowing and imposition, the broader processes of economic, cultural and political globalization are now interpreted in similar ways across the globe, tending to steer national educational policies into the same neo-liberal direction. Samoff (2000, p. 53) maintains that "with few exceptions, the direction of influence is from European core to southern periphery. Institutional arrangements, disciplinary definitions and hierarchies, legitimizing publications, and institutional authority reside in the core, which incorporates students and professors from the periphery, of whom many never return home."

In their book, Academic Capitalism, Slaughter and Leslie (1999) argue that policy makers in most English-speaking countries—the United States, Britain, Canada and Australia—interpret the real or imagined implications of globalization for the restructuring of higher education in remarkably similar ways. So much so, that "despite the very real differences in their political cultures, the four countries have developed similar policies at those points where higher education intersected with globalization of the postindustrial political economy." Globalization, Slaughter and Leslie (1999) argue, has destabilized patterns of university cultures everywhere, requiring the development of new structures, incentives and policies within a framework of fiscal constraints and pressures on nation-states to hold universities accountable. As a result, higher education in each of these four countries has moved towards policies that emphasize academic capitalism, towards curricular policy that focus on science and technology and fields closer to the market requirements, toward greater value for public money and toward greater accountability of academic institutions and faculty.

Burbules and Torres (2000, p. 4) suggest that educational endeavor is now increasingly affected by the processes of globalization that "are threatening the autonomy of national educational systems and the sovereignty of the nation-state as the ultimate rule in democratic societies." Globalization, they argue, is changing the fundamental conditions of an educational system, threatening to weaken education's links to the imperatives of a community, while making stronger its relationship to the requirements of the global economy. Under the conditions of globalization, not only the purposes of education but also the modes of its governance are converging around the underlying notions of global interconnectivity and interdependence.

Perhaps a stronger link between the cultural logic of globalization and higher education reform has been drawn by Currie and Newsom (1998), who suggest that the global convergence of policies is an outcome of the structural conditions under which they are developed; and that these conditions are anchored in a global economy that shapes most of the educational policy options nation-states have. They speak of unstoppable "globalization" and its tidal wave force. Currie and Newsom define globalization as "a material set of practices drawn from the world of business," combined with a new liberal "market ideology." operationalized through a managerialism, the impact of which is evident in systems around the world. Their main argument is that this managerialism has altered the nature of academic work and has led to the transformation of university systems into commercial entities, robbed of their traditional role as sites of cultural debate and catalysts of social change.

LOGIC(S) OF GLOBALIZATION

There is clearly a great deal of truth to these claims: neo-liberal restructuring has indeed transformed the nature of academic work everywhere, within the framework of the broader changes in policy and governance. Nor can it be denied that the changing "global context" has had an impact on the manner in which educational institutions are financed and managed. However, what this assertion does not show is how this impact occurs; and what the nature of the relationship between the idea of "global context" and educational change is. Often, this relationship is assumed as self-evident; and the notion of "context" itself is not problematized. For as Taylor and others (1997) have pointed out, what counts as context can be articulated in a variety of different ways; and what is fore grounded as "the global context" is often ideologically constituted. If this is so then an adequate explanation of the global convergence of educational policies demands an account not only of globalization but also of the processes through which convergence is achieved.

Yet, much of the recent educational literature views the relationship between globalization and educational policies in functional terms, assuming global processes to be somehow outside the cultural and educational terrain. In so assuming, many educational writers follow the influential analyses of globalization provided by such authors as David Harvey, Saskia Sassen and Manual Castells. Each of these authors has sought to examine the changing structural conditions under which social life is arranged and public policy is formulated. Each has drawn our attention to the complex workings of the global economy, and the ways in which it affects local priorities and invites responses to problems that involve macro-economic and geopolitical transformations.

For Harvey (1989) the condition of globalization is a postmodern one. He argues that the last three decades have witnessed "an intense period of time-space compression that has had a disorientating and disruptive impact on political-economic practices, the balance of class power, as well as upon cultural and social life." In this new era a more fragmented global capitalism is acquiring hegemony across the planet, as time and space are reorganized by the dictates of multinational capital. The rigidities of Fordism have been bypassed in favor of a new organizational ideology that celebrates flexibility as a foundational value, expressed most explicitly in ideas of subcontracting, outsourcing, vertically disintegrated forms of administration, just-in-time delivery systems and the like. These are obtained through improved systems of communication and information flows and rationalization in the techniques of distribution, making it possible to circulate capital and commodities through the market system with greater speed. At the same time, there is a shift away from the consumption of goods and into the consumption of services—not only business, educational and health services but also entertainment and life-style services. In the realm of commodity production, argues Harvey, the primary effect of this transformation has been an increased emphasis on instrumental values and the virtues of speed and instantancity.

Writing from a related perspective, in her analysis of global cities, Sassen (1991) assumes a similar set of attributes as characteristic of economic globalization. These attributes include the increased economic transgression of national boundaries, heightened capital mobility, the shift from manufacturing to business and financial services, the control of economic activity from a distance, and hierarchical organization of economic activity in a global system of accumulation, command and movement of international capital. Underlying this description of the key attributes of economic globalization is the core assumption concerning the logic of global integration, which implies no specific limits to the reach of multinational capital, even though it is concentrated in just a few global cities. Sassen treats this logic to be foundational, which can supposedly be used to understand the changing nature of social life and cultural priorities everywhere.

In an analysis that is less determinininistic, Castells (1996) also speaks, in relatively naturalistic terms, of the ways in which cultural and political meanings are under siege by global economic and technological restructuring. He represents late modernity as an "informational mode of development" through which global financial and informational linkages are accelerated, converting places into spaces and threatening to dominate local processes of cultural meanings. He argues that networks constitute "the new social morphology of our societies, and the diffusion of networking logic substantially modifies the operation and outcomes in the processes of production, experience, power and culture." The new economy, he maintains, is "organized around global networks of capital, management, and information, whose access to technological know-how is at the roots of productivity and competitiveness." From these networks, capital is invested in all sectors of activity, from information and media industries to tourism, culture and entertainment.

What this argument suggests then is that education is best understood as an industry trapped within the networking logic of contemporary capitalism, subject to the same economic cycles, market upswings and downturns and segmented global competition. It is therefore not surprising that recent educational restructuring has involved attempts to become highly dynamic systems, open to innovation; flexible and adaptable, since these are the attributes most directly linked to the requirements of the networked global economy. Indeed it is not hard to see how this epochal shift has implications for educational policy, since education is a site which is not only affected by time-space compression and the way in which contemporary capitalism has increased the pace of life and overcome spatial barriers to capital accumulation by globally reorganizing processes of production and consumption, but which is also the location where new ideologies are imparted to the new generation.

While the arguments presented by Castells, Sassen and Harvey focus on different aspects of the logic of globalization, they share a set of epistemological and methodological assumptions. Writing about issues of urban politics, Smith (2001, p. 6) points out that they each draw our attention "disproportionally upon the global economy, reified as a pre-given "thing," existing outside of thought" whose developmental logic not only "explains the development of cities but even determines the subjectivity of their inhabitants, without ever interrogating them about what they are up to." In explaining change, each of Castells, Sassen and Harvey privileges economic over socio-cultural and political processes. Smith adds that because such accounts of globalization give "scant attention to the discursive and material practices by which people create the regularized patterns that enable and constrain them, these discourses lack an effective theory of political agency, or any other kind of agency."

Thus, Harvey's account ultimately posits a functional theory of capital accumulation, with its super structural conceptualization of "culture, which radically separates economic from cultural practices and subordinates cultural dynamics to economic generalizations." For Harvey, it is the deeper economic logic of globalization that produces the social conditions he refers to as "postmodernity." He assumes that it is the time-space compression that causes people, independently of their historical and social location, to experience a sense of insecurity that often expresses itself in the various forms of identity politics. Harvey thus views culture not as an ever-changing product of human practices but as an expression of the deeper logic of economic imperatives. As Smith points out, Harvey's political theorizing fails to "come to terms with people's situatedness in the world—the situatedness of their knowledge as well as there unique positionality…" Not surprisingly therefore Harvey privileges class over all other possible relations of race, ethnicity and gender, overlooking the social significance of social networks and political institutions.

The globalization narrative in Sassen's work is also largely devoid of historical actors. What is presented instead is an account of what Smith terms "structural potential of global command and control of economic production and exchange." Her analysis of global cities is based on an account of the processes of economic globalization, which are located somehow outside the wider political and cultural contexts. As a result, key differences in the ways different cities approach economic relations within specific historical context are elided. As Cox (1997, p. 19) argues, the globalization debate has to take into account not just deterritorizing forces that reduce the policy options that nations have but also the ways territorizing conditions that exit in all communities which render local political particularities more significant than is often assumed in the functionalist accounts of globalization.

What this critique of the structuralist logic of globalization suggests is that globalization is a historical construct rather than a naturalized economic process operating in a reified fashion. As McMichael (1997) points out some aspects of globalization have pre-dated not only the contemporary period but also capitalism as such. And if this is the case then why has today's grand narrative of economic globalization acquired the status of a universalistic logic that supposedly propels and legitimizes such practices of managerialism as downsizing and state deregulation and privatization, as if they were a natural and inevitable response to the steering logic of globalization? The fact is that the origins of the contemporary ideology of globalization are historically specific. It is an ideology that serves a set of particular interests on behalf of powerful social forces, including transnational corporate and financial elite. I am not suggesting here that globalization is merely an ideology but rather that its particular form and impact needs to be understood historically through a perspective that connects the macro-economic global processes to the actual networks of social action that people create, move in, and act upon in their daily lives. Globalization thus needs to be located within specific sites.

What this analysis implies then is not any rejection of the thesis concerning the global convergence of educational restructuring but the need to describe the multiply diverse and complex ways in which the pressures toward convergence occur and must therefore be understood historically. Convergence should be viewed as the work of human actors and institutions, constituted by everyday practices that are historically specific and locally articulated. Thus the idea of networks is useful, but not as a universal economic logic but as a concept that describes a set of social practices through which policy actors and institutions influence each other. The idea of convergence itself needs to be understood as a set of historically specific social processes articulated through various power configurations.

PROCESSES OF GLOBAL CONVERGENCE

In what follows I discuss some of these processes through which convergence is achieved in a number of historically specific ways: through the global circulation of ideas and ideologies; through international conventions and consensus guiding educational reforms; through cooperation and competition inherent in the international practices of trade in education; through formal bilateral and multilateral contracts between systems which can sometimes involve a high degree of coercion of systems by international lending organizations such as the World Bank. Each of these processes involves a different pattern of political activity and power play, and has varied consequences for particular educational systems. Through advances in modes of communication and travel, circulation of ideas and ideologies through social and policy networks has become a noted feature of the global community. Conventions involve agreements in which educational systems expose their own policy practices to external scrutiny, agreeing to subscribe to an ideological consensus forged multilaterally. In a globally inter-connected order, both cooperation and competition can generate similarities in educational policies, which different systems might pursue to achieve market advantage. A contract is an agreement between two or more parties to pursue policies that have been negotiated bilaterally or multilaterally. And finally, coercion involves an imposition of policies upon a weaker system under threat of sanctions.

CIRCULATION OF IDEAS AND IDEOLOGIES

With the developments in transport, communication and information technologies, international mobility of people has never been greater. People are mobile for a wide variety of purposes from tourism and immigration to education, trade and work. Moving groups of people create new diasporas and now constitute an essential feature of the world, and affect the cultural politics of and between nations to an unprecedented degree. New technologies enable people to move at high speed across various kinds of previously impervious boundaries. An inevitable consequence of all this mobility is the increased circulation of ideas, images and ideologies across spaces. Conferences that were once local and national now strive to be international, inviting participants from all parts of the world. Anyone who has regularly attended the annual meeting of the American Educational Research Association (AERA) will not have failed to notice how international the conference has now become. At this conference ideas are exchanged, but often in ways that are asymmetrical given the sheer size and influence of the participants from the United States.

Circulation of ideas and ideologies does not of course always require the physical movement of people. Media capabilities now exist to produce and distribute information instantaneously to large audiences. The dominance of American media networks, such as CNN and FOX, now ensure that a certain range of ideas and images dominate throughout the world. Appudarai (1996) has spoken of ideoscapes, which are constituted as "concatenations of images," which circulate throughout the world in a directly political fashion. This circulation is frequently affected by the ideologies of states and the counter-ideologies of movements opposed to them. In the contemporary period, educational policies seem to be converging towards a particular concatenation of neo-liberal ideas we have discussed above, despite opposition from a wide variety of sources. The concatenation Appudarai speaks of is produced by policy borrowing, modeling transfer, diffusion, appropriation and copying which occur across the boundaries of the nation states and which, as Halpin (1994, p. 204) has argued, "lead to universalizing tendencies in educational reform." At conferences and in journals where educational ideas circulate, it is often difficult to determine the extent to which there has been free exchange of ideas, or indeed where policy debates have already been constructed by the dominant neo-liberal assumptions. But the point that needs to be emphasized here is that the circulation of educational ideas is not a function of globalization but involves actual historical processes; human agents, with capacity to accept, resist or reject them. Convergence of ideas is a consequence of political processes that demonstrate particular configurations of power and hegemonic dominance.

In a research report produced by Henry, Taylor and Lingard and I (2001) have shown how the Organization of Economic Cooperation and Development (OECD), traditionally a site for the free exchange of educational ideas, has become a policy player in its own right, influencing, cajoling and directing member states towards a pre-determined neo-liberal educational ideology. The OECD (1985, p. 3) never viewed itself "as a supranational organization but a place where policy makers and decision-makers can discuss their problems, where governments can compare their points of view." But in more recent years, it has evolved as an instrument of the globalizing world economy, which it seeks to promote through communicating its central message and maximizing its influence on policy. (OECD, 1996, p. 16). Over the past decade, the OECD has spent much of its efforts on debates about restructuring of public sector to meet the requirements of the global economy. It has argued that: "The common agenda that has developed encompasses efforts to make governments at all levels more efficient and cost-effective, to increase the quality of public services, to enable the public sector to respond flexibly and more strategically to external changes, and to support and foster national economic performance." In this way the OECD's role and sphere of influence has changed from being a "think actor to a policy actor in its own right." Through its conference and reviews, it has promoted a clearly identifiable set of neo-liberal proposal for the restructuring of education in all its member countries and beyond.

However, it would be a mistake to assume that the OECD's audiences throughout the world have received, interpreted and experienced its ideas and images in the same way. Indeed the processes of reception have been complicated and interconnected, creating a politics that is profoundly mixed. So, for example, while the English-speaking countries have largely embraced the OECD's dominant ideology, the Scandinavian countries have resisted many of its educational prescriptions. Around the OECD's Indicators project, for example, there was much dispute around the meaning and significance that should be accorded to cross-national comparison of educational achievements, and around the question of what impact they might have on attempts at pedagogic reform. Similarly, Japan and Korea have actively filtered the OECD's recommendations for reform through the prism of their own distinctive history and priorities. These varied interpretations of neo-liberal ideas have created significant ideological tensions within the OECD around shifting discourses of equity, quality and internationalization. What is hard to refute however is that the OECD has been enormously successful in generating a marked degree of consensus among its member countries and perhaps beyond.

CONSENSUS AND CONVENTIONS

Of course, this success has occurred against the backdrop of a range of international and regional settlements, both formal and informal, which have institutionalized, to a large extent, neo-liberal ideologies. These settlements often involve agreements and commitments that expose the domestic policies of nation-states to some kind of external scrutiny. In this way, consensus and conventions reduce the policy autonomy that states have over their own policies. Examples of conventions include liberal conceptions of human rights, democratic elections and social benefits and educational opportunities. While conventions are supposedly entered into voluntarily, there is often a great deal of pressure on countries to conform to particular ideologies. In recent years, almost all conventions have been framed in ways that make them both consistent with and supportive of the imperatives of neo-liberalism and conduits of the global economy.

Perhaps the best recent example of a consensus in line with the assumptions of neo-liberal economic and social order is the Washington Consensus. The term, "Washington Consensus" was coined by John Williamson in

1989 to refer to "the lowest common denominator of policy advice being addressed by the Washington-based institutions to Latin American countries as of 1989" (Williamson, 1990). Williamson viewed Washington Consensus as a product of "the intellectual convergence" which led countries in most of Latin America and elsewhere to accept to a set of common assumptions about economic reform. George Soros (1998) refers to these assumptions as "market fundamentalism;" and much of their acceptance worldwide has been in no small measure due to its persuasive rhetoric in the battle of policy ideas. Thus most Washington based development institutions have sung from the same sheet, preaching relentlessly the values of macro-economic discipline, trade openness and market-friendly micro-economic policies. In the field of education, this has implied fiscal discipline about educational funding, a re-direction of public expenditure policies towards fields offering both high economic returns and the potential to improve income distribution, such as primary education, as well as privatization and deregulation.

Through most of the 1990s, the Washington Consensus acquired the status of a mantra forged in order to persuade debt-ridden countries of the South that they had no other choice but to follow its dictates. Most Structural Adjustment Programs (SAPs) assumed its validity, promising levels of poverty reduction and economic redistribution considered impossible without their implementation. And despite the doubts expressed by many Non-Government Organizations (NGOs) and some governments, Washington Consensus reigned supreme in the field of development. It served to institutionalize everywhere the neo-liberal notion that governments no longer had the capacity to tame markets, promote growth and keep social inequalities within reasonable limits. It served to promote the ideology that only markets can solve the intractable problems facing societies. The markets thus defined the limits of politics, and exerted unprecedented influence in shaping policies not only in relation to aid programs, but also in industrialized countries. They redefined the role of the nation-states which were no longer expected to play a role as effective managers of the national economy and of social and educational policies.

However, the Washington Consensus was never complete. There were always those who doubted its untested economic claims and contested its social and political prescriptions for human endeavors and organization. Indeed, even within the field of development many people, organizations and governments have now begun to view the Washington Consensus as a relative failure. Williamson (2000) himself has spoken of the need to develop a new understanding of policy as involving a renewed emphasis on the institutional dimension, in addition to the sort of assumptions embedded in the original version of the Washington Consensus. A new discourse of post Washington Consensus is now emerging which admits some of the limitations of the Structural Adjustment Programs but refuses to accept the need to reframe the broader ideologies that impelled their development. As Jayasuriya (2001, p. 1) maintains, post Washington Consensus (PWC) "should be more properly viewed as an attempt to develop a political institutional framework to embed the structural adjustment policies of the Washington consensus." In this way, new thinking complements rather than replaces the Washington consensus. However, Jayasuriya (2001, p. 1) insists that "the politics of PWC is a distinctive form of anti-politics which seeks to cleanse economic institutions of the assumed debilitating effects of political bargaining." This analysis shows the terminology of consensus and conventions to be highly ideological, especially with respect to its attempts to divorce itself from the murky terrains of political contestation: the discourse of consensus is produced in a set of tacit assumptions that are assumed to be beyond critical scrutiny and challenge.

Indeed this is also the underlying logic of the Bologna Declaration, a process reflecting regional convergence. Signed by twenty-nine European countries in 1999, it pledges to reform their higher education system in a convergent way. The Declaration insists that the reform process it prescribes is not a path towards standardization or uniformization of European higher education but "reflects a search for a common European answer to common European problems," and recognizes the value of coordinated reforms, compatible systems and common actions. Its action program is designed to enhance the employability and mobility of citizens, conditioned by globalization. It builds upon the programs of the European Union such as ERASMUS and SOCRATES, and views itself as an important program in the process of European integration. The Bologna process involves the development of a common framework of readable and comparable degrees; the introduction of undergraduate and postgraduate levels in all countries; comparable credit system of courses and learning activities; a Europe wide system of quality assurance and the elimination of all remaining barriers to student mobility.

While claiming to be entirely transparent, as a consensus, document the Bologna Declaration masks a number of assumptions. Despite its insistence upon the principles of diversity and national autonomy, it nonetheless assumes the importance of European convergence, weakening national control over degrees and diplomas, and de-linking education from powerful political sentiments in the field of national culture, language and social emancipation. But more importantly the Bologna process barely hides its more fundamental economic rationale: its preference for the marketization of higher education. While it does not completely support liberalization and deregulation of higher education, its main objectives are informed by a market logic—the need for the European system to become a more effective and efficient player in the highly competitive global market in higher education. The course of the Bologna process is thus heavily influenced by dominant neo-liberal perceptions of globalization, the trade issue, and more specifically GATS negotiations. One of the main ambitions of the Bologna process is to strengthen the competitiveness of the European higher education in the global marketplace so that it can more effectively compete with the American and Australian universities who have been more active and successful in the export of higher education. Convergence in degree structures, the development of a credit transfer system, a comprehensive quality assurance system is considered to be essential in the international trade of higher education. But in accepting this commercial logic the Bologna Declaration in effect embraces the global trends towards commodification, privatization and commercialization of higher education, sidelining higher education' traditional commitment to the "public good." So despite recent policy discourses in Europe that highlight ideas of social inclusion, the Bologna Declaration remains embedded with the neo-liberal assumptions about higher education.

COMPETITION AND COOPERATION

What this discussion of the Bologna Declaration indicates is that international trade in higher education involves both competition and cooperation: competition for the recruitment of students and faculty and for profits and prestige and cooperation because outside the compatible products, services and structure competition becomes a meaningless concept. The architects of the Bologna Declaration recognize that European universities cannot compete with other regions unless it is restructured in a consistent and coherent fashion within the region. But beyond this, international trade in education does not only require cooperation at the regional level but also at the global level. This realization is of course the basis of the current talks on education in the General Agreement on Trade in Services (GATS) within the World Trade Organization (WTO). GATS are designed to specify a range of conditions under which the global trade in education is to be pursued. These conditions include such matters as transparency of rules; liberalization of markets; elimination of practices acting as barriers to trade and student mobility; and the development of rules for resolving disputes.

The main assumption underlying GATS is that education is a commodified service like any other business and that therefore its international trade should be encouraged, especially in a globalized economy. Against this assumption, full-fee paying student mobility across national boundaries has increased markedly. International mobility to the OECD countries has doubled in the past decades. In Australia, the number of full-fee paying students in higher education has risen from nearly 40,000 to 135,000 through the 1990s and now constitutes almost 15 per cent of the student population in universities. In higher education in the United States the number of international students in 2000 rose to a half a million, generating more than $10 billion in revenue. A recent report published by IDP Australia (2003) has forecast the global demand for international higher education to increase from 1.8 million students in 2000 to over 7.2 million in 2025. Much of this growth is likely to come from India and China and the major beneficiaries are expected to be the United States, Europe and Australia. These projections are highly significant for they reveal a changing landscape of higher education in which commercial concerns will become even more dominant.

Jane Knight (2002) has called this phenomenon "trade creep" in higher education—driven more generally by the increased emphasis on trade and the market economy in an era of globalization, and enmeshed with other issues and trends in higher education. Knight suggests that:

> these trends include the growing number of private for-profit entities providing higher education opportunities domestically and internationally; the use of information and communications technologies (ICTs) for domestic and cross-border delivery of programs; the increasing costs and tuition fees faced by students at public and private institutions; and the need for public institutions to seek alternate sources of funding, which sometime means engaging in for-profit activities or seeking private sector sources of financial support.

These trends appear well entrenched in most higher education systems around the world, raising important issues of student access and opportunities, modes of funding and student support, regulation of private and public cross-border providers, recognition and transferability of credits and quality assurance. These issues cannot be addressed within national boundaries but require rather the kind of global collaboration that GATS is seeking to provide. Somewhat paradoxically, GATS is both encouraging, in an ideological manner, international trade competition in higher education but also seeking to define its form and scope, laying out the ground rules to tame its unfettered expansion and its unexpected consequences.

But this convergence towards privatization has not remained uncontested. The 2001 Porto Alegre Declaration, signed by Iberian and Latin American universities, is radically opposed to international trade in educational services, citing fears that further deregulation in the higher education sector would lead to the removal of legal, political, fiscal and educational quality controls, and that it may also mean national governments abandoning their social responsibilities for combating social inequalities. The Declaration maintains furthermore that deregulation is likely to weaken national sovereignty and to erode some of the cherished ethical and cultural values that define and sustain community life. Competition, the Declaration suggests, invariably leads to standardization, and benefits only those who already possess power and prestige and the resources to access education abroad. This also means the flight of not only much needed resources but also the academic talent, which is often essential to maintain a university's research culture. Added to these legitimate concerns is the view that international trade in education serves to create a tension between public good and market commodity approaches to education, which in the long run has the potential to further weaken the sovereignty of the nation-states.

CONTRACTS AND COERCION

The Porto Alegre Declaration, it is clear, is based on a perfectly understandable fear that international trade in education has disproportionally harmful consequences on developing countries. Indeed it is widely recognized that further international mobility of talented students is likely to intensify the phenomenon of "brain drain." A study conducted by the Department of International Development in the UK has found that three quarters of Africans studying abroad do not return home, and that roughly half of Asia's and South America's emigrants have university degrees, almost sixty per cent graduating from a university in the West. While there is a debate concerning the contribution that these emigrants are still able to make to their home country through remittances, what is beyond doubt is that their departure makes the development of higher education systems in the developing countries much more difficult, due largely to the lack of resources and talent pools in critically significant numbers. Moreover, those who do return home bring back with them ideas that are often foreign to their communities, inapplicable to the local conditions.

Most of the returnees work for either transnational corporations or government bodies dealing with international organizations such as the World Bank. In these dealings the ideas they learnt in western universities and the ideologies of the international organizations often converge. They seldom have the community resources to be able to challenge such coercive ideologies as those embedded in the Structural Adjustment Programs (SAPs). These programs, as has already been noted, are developed ostensibly because developing countries are unable to meet the payment schedules on their debts to the international banks, such as the World Bank and the International Monetary Fund (IMF). But before these countries are permitted to renegotiate schedules of debt repayment they are forced to meet a range of conditions, in order to "better manage their economy" and "get their house in order." And while these conditions are often assumed to have the status of contracts, they are negotiated under the coercive demands of the banks, which are invariably accepted by the western trained economists advising the governments of the developing countries.

According to Faraclas (1997, p. 147) "far from being mechanisms of debt reduction and economic recovery SAPs have often resulted in the consolidation of neocolonial power," and the institutionalization of a series of new Enclosures. These Enclosures have a transparently global character, involving a common set of ideological beliefs about the capitalist path of accumulation and appropriation of new resources and new labor power. To the policy makers in the developing countries, the coercive SAP contracts represent a major dilemma. On the one hand, it is almost impossible for the developing countries in severe economic difficulties to reject the offer of help, yet the experience of SAPs has meant having to pursue alienating and exploitative policies with little chance of success. Ultimately, SAPs require nation-states to concede some of their autonomy, and pass legislation designed to create conditions more conducive to international investment in the country than to the improvement of the social conditions and educational opportunities.

Of course it is not only the international lending agencies that demand neo-liberal restructuring of their educational systems from the developing countries as a condition of loans, the transnational corporations (TNC) offering to invest do as well. The relationship between TNCs and governments is a complex one, involving dynamics of both conflict and cooperation. Dicken (1998) argues that sometimes governments and TNCs may be rivals but they may collude with one another at the same time. In the global economy, the governments need TNCs to help them in the process of material wealth creation, while TNCs require the nation-states to "provide the necessary supportive infrastructures, both physical and institutional, on the basis of which they can pursue their strategic objectives" (Dicken, 1998, p. 276). TNCs and governments are often involved in a bargaining process as each tries to get maximum advantage from each other. As Dicken (1998, p. 276) observes, "states have become increasingly locked into a cut-throat competitive bidding process for investments; a process which provides TNCs with the opportunity to play off one bidder against another." Some of this bargaining involves the demand by TNCs that education be restructured, with policies more conducive to creating a human resource pool to meet the labor needs of the TNCs.

CONCLUSION

In this paper, I have assumed that the facts about the increasing global convergence of educational policies with respect to the institutional practices of restructuring require cannot be denied. Restructuring everywhere, so it seems, is informed by a similar set of neo-liberal market ideologies. Indeed, even a cursory glace at comparative policy documents produced by international organizations appears to confirm the emergence of a new policy discourse, which promotes commercialization on the one hand and new mangerialism, expressed in such ideas as "value for money," accountability, performance management and functional decentralization, on the other. This discourse preaches an increased reliance on private sources of revenue, links with the business sector, growth of private institutions, user-pays systems and entrepreneurialism.

In recent years, a range of scholars has theorized this convergence of educational restructuring in terms of its functional relationship with the contemporary processes of globalization. It is assumed that this convergence is an outcome of the global economic processes. I have argued that this functionalist explanation is largely flawed. Functionalist explanations run the risk of ultimately reducing educational politics to the requirements and logic of capital accumulation. By this I do not mean to imply that issues of capital accumulation are not relevant to educational restructuring but to suggest instead that functionalist explanations divert attention away from historical and situational contingencies as well as political processes through which influence is achieved and power is exercised. The global convergence cannot be adequately explained within the grand narrative of economic globalization. Globalization needs to be understood as a historical construct rather than a naturalized economic process operating behind our backs. If this is so then global convergence of educational restructuring needs to be viewed also as historically contingent, as well as locally articulated by actors and institutions working within the framework of particular pressures, some of which are global and transnational while others are national and local. We need to understand the actual empirically grounded processes of convergence.

Without suggesting that they represent an exhaustive list of the processes of convergence, I have discussed how global convergence of educational restructuring is driven through a number of processes involving global circulation of ideas and ideologies; consensus and conventions; cooperation and competition; and contracts and coercion. Increasing transnational movement of people have created conditions in which people can exchange ideas; but this circulation of information has not entirely neutral with respect to the ideologies that become dominant. Neo-liberal ideologies have been promoted multilaterally not only by organizations like the OECD but also by the network of state employed policy analysts. Governments have seldom developed their own policy solutions to educational crises they confront but have borrowed and copied heavily from each other. Both regionally and globally, they have signed conventions that have reduced the scope of their policy options. Increasing trade in higher education in particular has demanded common modes of instruction and credit recognition policies; and has encouraged other practices of cooperation, as well as competition. Within the developing countries, convergence has been achieved through imposition of conditions and other forms of coercion. This paper has thus stressed the need to examine the processes of convergence through which power is exercised with the global education system. It has also shown the contingent effects of the neo-liberal convergence, benefiting some systems and interests while depriving others of educational and cultural opportunities.

REFERENCES

Altbach, P. (1991). Patterns in higher education development. *Prospects, 21*(2).

Apple, M. (2000). Between neoliberalism and neoconservatism: Education and conservativism in a global age. In N. Burbules & C. Torres (Eds.), *Globalization and education: Critical perspectives* (pp. 57–78). London: Routledge.

Appudarai, A. (1996). *Modernity at large: Cultural dimensions of globalization*. Minneapolis: University of Minnesota Press.

Bray, M, & Lee, W.O. (Eds.). (2001). *Education and political transition: Themes and experiences in East Asia*. Hong Kong: The University of Hong Kong, Comparative Education Research Centre.

Bologna Declaration. (1999). *On the European space for higher education.*

Bohm, A., Davis, D., Meares, D., & Pearce, D. (2002). *Global student mobility: Forercasts for the global demand for international higher education.* Sydney: IDP Australia.

Bonal, X. (2002). Plus ca change: The World Bank education policy and the post Washington consensus. *International Studies in Sociology of Education, 12*(1).

Burbules, N., & Torres C. (Eds). (2000). *Globalization and education: Critical perspectives.* London: Routledge.

Castells, M. (1996). *The rise of the network society.* Oxford: Blackwell Publishers.

Cox, K. (1997). *Spaces of globalization.* New York: Guildford Press.

Currie, J., & Newsom, J. (Eds). (1998). *Universities and globalization: Critical perspectives.* Thousands Oaks: Sage Publications.

De Wit, H. (2000). The Sorbonne and Bologna Declarations on European higher education. *International Higher Education, 18*(5).

Dicken, P. (1998). *Global shift: Transforming the world economy.* London: Paul Chapman Publishing Ltd.

Gopinathan, S. (2001). Globalization, the state, and education policy in Singapore. In M. Bray & W.O. Lee (Eds.), *Education and political transition: Themes and experiences in East Asia* (pp. 21–36). Hong Kong: Comparative Education Research Centre, The University of Hong Kong.

Halpin, D. (1994). Practice and prospects in educational policy research. In D. Halpin & B. Troyna (Eds.), *Researching educational policy: Ethical and methodological issues.* London: Falmer Press.

Harvey, D. (1989). *The condition of postmodernity.* Oxford: Blackwell Publishers.

Held, D., & McGrew, A. (Eds). (2000). *The global transformation reader: An introduction to the globalization debate.* Cambridge: Polity Press

Henry, M., Lingard, B., Rizvi, F., & Taylor, S. (2001). *The OECD, globalization, and education policy.* Oxford: Pergamon Press.

Jayasuirya, K. (2001). *Governance, post Washington consensus, and the new politics* (Southeast Asia Research Centre Working Papers Series No. 2). Perth Australia: Murdoch University.

Johnstone, D. B. (2000). *Worldwide reforms in the financing and management of higher education.*

Krasner, S. (2000). Compromising Westaphalia. In D. Held & A. McGrew (Eds.), *The global transformation reader: An introduction to the globalization debate* (pp. 124–135). Cambridge: Polity Press.

Knight, J. (2002). Trade creep: Implications of GATS for higher education policy. *International Higher Education, 28*(2).

McMichael, P. (1996). Globalization: Myths and realities. *Rural Sociology, 61*(1), 25–55.

OECD. (1996). *Globalization and linkages to 2030: Challenges and opportunities for OECD countries.* Paris: OECD.

Peters, M., Marshall, J., & Fitzsimons, P. (2000). Managerialism and educational policy in a global context: Foucault, Neoliberalism and the doctrine of self-management. In N. Burbules & C. Torres (Eds.), *Globalization and education: Critical perspectives.* London: Routledge.

Rizvi, F. (1994). Williams on democracy and the governance of education. In D. Dwokins & L. Roman (Eds.), *Beyond the border country: Essays in honour of Raymond Williams.* London and New York: Routledge.

Samoff, J. (1999). Institutionalizing international influence. In R. Arnove & C. Torres (Eds.), *Comparative education: The dialectic of the global and the local* (pp. 51–90). Lanham, MD: Rowman & Littlefield Publishers.

Sassen, S. (1991). *The global city: New York, London, and Tokyo.* Princeton, NJ: Princeton University Press.

Sassen, S. (1995). *Losing control in an age of globalization.* New York: Columbia University Press.

Schugurensky, D. (1999). Higher education restructuring in the era of globalization: Toward a heteronomous model? In R. Arnove & C. Torres (Eds.), *Comparative education: The dialectic of the global and the local* (pp. 283–304). Lanham, MD: Rowman & Littlefield Publishers.

Slaughter, S., & Leslie, L. (1997). *Academic capitalism: Politics, policies and the entrepreneurial university.* Baltimore: John Hopkins University.

Smith, M. P. (2001). *Transnational urbanism: Locating globalization.* Oxford: Blackwell Publishers.

Soros, G. (1998). *The crisis of global capitalism.* Boston: Little, Brown.

Taylor, S., Rizvi, F., Lingard, B., & Henry, M. (1997). *Education policy and the politics of change.* London: Routledge.

Williamson, J. (2000). What should the World Bank think about the Washington consensus? *The World Bank Research Observer, 15*(2), 251–264.

CHAPTER 3

CHANGING PATTERNS
OF POWER

Rethinking Decentralization in the
Educational Reform in Taiwan[1]

Yang-tien Chen
Taipei Municipal Teachers College

The aim of the chapter is to reexamine the meaning and the role of the concept of decentralization in current educational reform and education restructuring in Taiwan.[2] Decentralization has been regarded as one of the most prominent global reasons, which orders and guides the direction of current reform and education restructuring on the small island since the 1990s (Huang, 1997). It is believed that the decentralization of education is something "good" and "right" and ought to be carried out during the reform. People in Taiwan also think that current educational reform is merely a unidirectional process from a centralized educational system to a decentralized one. Education restructuring, in this sense, is just the objectification of the decentralization of the educational institutions.

When the concept of decentralization is viewed in this way, its opposite concept, the educational actors and agencies, naturally view centralization, to be "bad" or "wrong". A centralized government as well as a centralized educational system is conceived of "the evil of evils" or the source of problems that prevent the modernization of education (Huang, 1997).

Educational Restructuring: International Perspectives on Traveling Policies, pages 43–68

This chapter interrogates the educational restructuring that places centralized government in opposition to a decentralized system. The concepts of cultural hybridity and social inclusion and exclusion are applied to explore the complexity of the appearances of the concept of decentralization in current reform and education restructuring. I will argue that whether the centralized government is an evil or not depends on the discursive practices formed by the scaffoldings in historical, cultural, political, and social contexts. It is the effect of power.

CULTURAL HYBRIDITY AND
SOCIAL INCLUSION/EXCLUSION

Cultural hybridity allows us to think of a cultural mixture of the global and the local. The concept of the global refers to ways of thinking or the rationality about the objects of reflection and action in education that circulates among multiple contexts around the world. Its real meaning, however, depends on the local contexts in which particular discursive spaces are formed about educational actors. The cultural mixture of the global and the local involves an objectification of a local scenario through the inscribing of global rationalities. To fully fit the local story in Taiwan, the appearances of the global reasons become complex and elusive in educational reform and education restructuring. By exploring the relation of the global and the local, it is possible to think about the two cultures as not pure and distinct. Rather they overlap and hybridize which is more than a cultural mixture.

The concept of cultural hybridity directs the educational reform and education restructuring in Taiwan, and can not be reduced to either a process of Westernization or Americanization as argued or criticized in current literature (Huang, 1999; Yang, 2001), or to a notion of walking our own way through understanding how particular global rationalities are brought into and "fit" into Taiwanese reforms. This does not mean I neglect the consequence of the processes of globalization. I agree that the interrelationship among countries has changed a lot through multiple, different historical trajectories as evident in the discussions related to cyberspace and global issues like SARS, environmental protection, and anti-terrorism. Further, while talking about globalization as an important process in Taiwan's educational reform, I do not see that the role of the state has been lessened or declined on the island. What I can say at this moment is that global discourses are realized within the nation for the ongoing retelling of the national story and the ongoing new social reconfigurations.

I use the term social inclusion/exclusion. As with centralization and decentralization, the processes of inclusion are always linked with processes of exclusion. There is a continual insertion of a we/them, us/other in which to think about the progress and modern character of Taiwanese culture, education, and political forms. My concern is not to simply point out the social inequality and injustice expressed by the marginalization of certain minority groups in Taiwanese society, but to uncover the system of reasoning that makes their changes in social inclusion/exclusion possible. Analytically, cultural hybridity and social inclusion/exclusion are two separate issues but sometimes they are tied together in practice.

My main task in exploring the educational restructuring is to think about the twin processes of globalization and localization as producing and reshaping national imaginaries formed in the specific political, social and cultural contexts in the island. I pay attention to a group of people called Tai Wan Yi Sh Luen Zhe (Taiwanese Nationalists) who play a crucial role in this process. What the Taiwanese Nationalists have been doing is to subvert so-called Great China ideology in order to rebuild the national imagination by making-up people through specific categorization and differentiation related to class and ethnicity. The historically constructed evil of the island are all governments, that have ever ruled Taiwan in the past four centuries. Under such a historical construction, the debate over the notion of the Taiwanese now is given concrete form through the redefining of the concept of centralization that reforms the current construction of we/otherness.[3]

Finally, this chapter should not be read as a rejection of particular reforms and restructuring that is occurring. Some changes incurred by the reforms and the restructurings are helpful to clarify the complicated appearances of the reform and the restructuring. My purpose is to question what we have taken for granted so as to open up new possibilities to further rethink the reforms and restructurings.

FABRICATING CENTRALIZATION: MUST IT BE AN "EVIL"?

Until the very end of the 1980s, Taiwan had maintained a centralized government. The decision of educational policies had been thoroughly made by the government, either a central, or a provincial, or a local government, depending on the level of the education. According to the literature, this top-down pattern for educational decision-making had been operated for centuries in this island since the sovereignty of the Dutch (1624–1662). Perhaps from the viewpoint of most people today in Taiwan, a centralized government is an evil for educational practices. But historically, a centralized government could mean a good thing in education. What is important here is to analyze how a centralized government is fabricated as an evil for education. To do so, we will need to take into account the historical context that forms the power relation at that moment.

The Dutch built the first "centralized" government in Taiwan. The aim of their occupation of the island was to find ways to trade with China and Japan at the beginning of the 17th century. The literature gives us an idea as to why and how the Dutch had maintained their centralized governing in this island during their almost four decades' rule.

> ...From their trading base in Taiwan, the Dutch imported Chinese from Mainland China to teach the aborigines about agriculture among other things. Taiwan thus became a place to export sugar, rice, and the skins of deer from which the Dutch greatly profited. The Dutch...converted them [the aborigines] to Christianity by force...Although most natives converted to Christianity, those who refused to convert were persecuted. Of the 250 Inibs, the native priestesses who were banished, not more than 48 returned. The remaining 202 Inibs died by either reason of old age or of destitution. (Lee, 1995, p. 28)

Won't you call a regime, which exercises its power through brute force, even for religious conversion, a centralized government? But a centralized government is not necessarily a bad regime in implementing education and in maintaining aboriginal culture in Taiwan.

> ...Initially, the preachers who came to Taiwan learned the native dialects, then Romanized them, compiled dictionaries and then translated the bible. They also translated "The Door or Portal to Language" written by Commenius, and used it as the textbook to teach the natives Dutch...Owing to the success of the linguistic education, in 1813, the aborigines were still using their Romanized words to record the contracts of land sale 152 years after the Dutch left Taiwan. These legal manuscripts still survive and are called "Sinkan Manuscripts"... (Lee, 1995, pp. 28–29)

The Dutch built the first school in the island. They used it as a means to inculcate the aborigines for the purpose of increasing the unit production of crops to enhance commercial exchange. The first teacher named Georgius Candidius was appointed by the Dutch government in 1627 to engage in religious and educational work. The government offered students rice and clothing for the continuity of school education. The curricula were taught by the aboriginal dialects. With the increasing demands on a small number of teachers, the first teacher education program was implemented for the training of the aborigines as local teachers. It is believed that until 1645, there were seven to eight villages in aboriginal societies which had schools and totally about six hundred boys and girls attending schools (Lin, 1929/2000).

The Dutch's centralized regime contributed a lot to cultural preservation and the cultivation of the aborigines, which no authority over Taiwan has ever done. A similar situation happened in the sovereignty of Imperial China. Ming was the first Dynasty of Imperial China, which ruled this island. Governor Zhen Chen-Gung, who was the surviving official of the Ming Dynasty, brought Han culture and institutions into the island. Due to the strong military tension between Ming and Cheng Dynasty, Taiwan had been governed in a very centralized way for the recovery of the Mainland China. Even though the government was centralized, according to the literature (Xu, 1995), Zhen Chen-Gung had earned high respect from the people in Taiwan. The educational institutions established during this period were also influential. For example, every village, including Chinese and aborigine, had at least one class with one teacher. Once family member(s) attended the village class, the compulsory labor service for the government was waived.

A Confucian temple with an Ethics-learning Classroom (min-lun t'ang) was established at Ch'eng-tien, the capital in 1666. This was the Grand School (T'ai-hsueh), the earliest Confucius' school in Taiwan. This temple and school was called the Taiwan Prefecture School during the Ch'ing Dynasty, and has been repaired and enlarged many times since. It is the Confucian Temple in the city of Taiwan and is scrupulously preserved by the government. (Lee, 1995, pp.31–33)

Ming is the first government in Taiwanese history to establish the educational institution of the entrance exam, the impact of which on Taiwanese society has lasted until now. At that time, the entrance exam to the Grand School was held twice every three years. The students took the tests step by step—the Chou Test, the Prefecture Test, and the Yuan Test, in order to become formal students at the Grand School. Then students needed to stay for three-year study and to be tested every month so as to be qualified for the 'final exam'. The students could serve in the government after passing the final exam (Lee, 1995).

In short, Zhen family committed themselves to the issue of education during their "centralized" government over this island, and their endeavor had earned their high respect from the people in Taiwan. Even under the rule of Qing Dynasty, there were some rebellions, which advocated "the recovery of the Ming Dynasty." The recovery of Ming, in fact, involved an imagined homeland that inserted the notion of we/otherness between Ming and Qing, between Han and non-Han, since the Ming rebels had to be unjustly ruled by the "savage" Qing.

Some Taiwanese Nationalists, who have been trying to reshape the national imaginaries in this island for the past few decades, have reinterpreted the government of Zhen and his successors to be a kind of "colonialism." They assert that what Zhen and his successor did is just like what KMT did for Taiwanese people. Both had maintained dramatically centralized authorities for "their own" national recovery regardless of Taiwanese people's needs. Their common neglect of the actual demands of the Taiwanese has been labeled as colonial regimes. This kind of feeling, in fact, is merely a projection of cultural displacement[4] embedded in the Taiwanese Nationalists. If we check on the literature, it is hard to find evidence to show that the Zhen family's centralized government and the educational policies being carried out at that stage were an evil to the people in Taiwan. Even in Qing Dynasty, Zhen and their family were cited for what they did for the Taiwanese by the emperor as he thought this kind of personal manner was necessary to the sustenance of the new empire.

Qing Dynasty is another example of illustrating the necessity of a centralized government for the building of a new society. It is believed that Taiwan had undergone a social transition from a frontier and immigrant society to a fully settled one under the rule of Qing Dynasty. The majority of people who came to this island from Mainland China were to seek for a means of existence since their hometown could not offer enough jobs or could not provide enough food. When they arrived in this island, unfortunately they were facing another problem. The struggle for the land as a means of existence from the aborigines became their new challenge. At this moment, a centralized government to fulfill their economic need (to protect them from the invasion of the otherness, the aborigines) was important to them. Later, the sustenance of social order among various ethnic groups in Han society became another issue for the ancestor because the constant fighting between these groups had made Taiwanese society unstable.

The strong local or hometown identities residing in the ethnic groups embodied the multi-layered imaginaries among the Han. At times, the notion of we/otherness was demarcated between the aborigines and the Han. At other times, it was demarcated between Hakka and Holo, or between Zhang and Quan within Holo, or between even finer nuances within each group.

The notion of we/otherness, in this case, was historically, socially and culturally flexible and flowing, depending on their economic and social needs. So, the continual conflict among and within ethnic groups was inevitable. No social order could be guaranteed under such circumstances. A more centralized government then was necessary to deal with the chaotic situation for the public good, such as the need for agricultural and commercial prosperity.

Further, the cultural image of moving from "barbaric" to civilized had made it urgent to these ancestors when the process of tu zhu hua (indigenization) was finished. Here the concept of tu zhu hua means an identity switch from the original hometown to the fully settled society. It is a normal

process for the establishment of the new immigrant societies of the diasporas of the Han people (the Chinese people). Usually it involves the ongoing importation and transplanting of the "mother culture" of the
inhabitant. Once this happened, the de-barbarization of Taiwan became
the hot issue for the gentry in the island. A centralized government could
facilitate the civilization (Sinoization) of the people on the island effi-
ciently and effectively.

In the second half of the 19th century, Taiwan began to face new invad-
ers from another wave of imperialism and colonialism, compared to the
imperialism and colonialism of the Dutch. A centralized and efficient government with strong military force and with the continual technological
innovation from "modernization" imitated the Western to protect their
homeland.

According to the preceding analysis, we are unable to argue that a centralized government under the sovereignty of Qing was necessarily an evil.
Similarly, we are unable to argue that the educational institutions carried
out by the centralized government of Qing were necessarily an evil.

> In fact, education and examination were very successful in Taiwan during the
> Ch'ing Dynasty. Guided by the influence of government political power,
> inspired by the economic advantage and high social status, and encouraged
> by religious belief, most of the scholars closed their doors to study for the
> examinations through all their lives...They learned from Confucian "truth"
> and taught the common people with it. People should be loyal to the emper-
> ors and should endure everything unjust or not, accepting and following
> their duty, maintaining the society... (Lee, 1995, p. 284)

In Qing Dynasty, education functioned as means to maintain social
order through inscribing the Confucian systems of reasoning onto the
school subjects. Educational literatures also show that a centralized government is significant for the modernization of education in the era of Imperial China. For example, during the whole period of sovereignty of Qing
Dynasty, public educational institutions had played a more influential role
than the private in cultivating Sinoization in the people of the island (Lee,
1995). The government in the last decade of the rule of Qing Dynasty also
established the first modern school. The number was few. The aim of the
establishment of modern education in Taiwan at that time was to cope with
the inescapable diffusion of Western imperialism and colonialism in Asia,
especially when a couple of harbors in the island were forced to be open to
the western world under the unequal treaties made among Qing Dynasty
and the western countries.

Japanese occupation is another example to illuminate the necessary
advantage of a centralized government. Due to the shortage of the knowledge of modern hygiene and health care, the infant mortality rate was very

high in the beginning of occupation. This indicator was thought to be the decline of the national strength by the government. To rescue the declining national power, a variety of vaccines and modern knowledge of hygiene were imposed on the child. As Tsurumi said:

> Overall, Japanese goals for education in Taiwan were fairly well met. Although the common schools probably convinced more Taiwanese of the importance of boiling water and washing one's hands after visiting the toilet than of the majesty of the Japanese emperor, by the end of the colonial period common schooling touched the lives of even rather humble Taiwanese. Certainly it had gained widespread acceptance...(Tsurumi, 1991, pp. 69–70)

Gender issues were encountered in the centralized educational system. Girls could go to the same school and study the same curricula with boys. The notion of gender equity was widely inculcated in schooling, whereas it was almost impossible to implement under Chinese traditional school systems as gender inequality was commonly accepted and tacit among Chinese people. At the very end of the Japanese occupation, the notion of gender equity began to prevail after the long time spent cultivating it in the schools. In fact, more than 50 percent of girls at elementary school age received the compulsory education. As Tsurumi analyzed,

> ...The effort to get girls as well as boys to attend common school was eventually rewarded: by 1935 one-quarter of the Taiwanese female elementary school-aged population was in school, and nine years later this percentage has jumped to 60. These school girls studied the same curriculum as their brothers, and although textbooks did deal with differences in boys' and girls' roles, a surprising amount of the books' didactic content was addressed to both sexes equally...(Tsurumi, 1991, p. 70)

The impact of the occupation of the Japanese centralized government on Taiwan is overwhelming. It is more than an institutional transformation but the changing systems of reasoning among the people on the island. Not only had the traditional notion of social division of labor and of gender in family been changed, but also the traditional notion of career planning by gender in the labor market had been switched. This result should also be attributed to a centralized educational system carried out by a centralized "colonial" government.

> ...Increased school attendance for girls was related to two other new directions for women: an end to the Chinese custom of foot binding and entrance into the colony's industrial work force. It also paved the way for the emergence of Taiwanese women as white-collar workers and as professionals with careers in medicine, commerce, science, and pedagogy. Of course, many more Taiwanese men trained for such careers and found employment as

white-collar workers. The colonial government's early attention to the training of native doctors and teachers left post-colonial Taiwan with a small army
of experienced physicians and educators. (Tsurumi, 1991, p. 70)

To summarize, it is "dangerous" to argue that a centralized government
and a centralized system of education are necessarily bad or wrong. It is
also "dangerous" to argue that a centralized government and a centralized
system of education necessarily bring in an unequal or unjust society.

NATIONAL IMAGINARIES AND MEMORY/FORGETTING

When the national story is being retold, a reformulated memory and forgetting occurs. The reconstructed colonial memory of Qing Dynasty over
Taiwan and the purposive forgetting of the "contribution" of Qing government to Taiwanese society are expected and understandable. Similarly, the
re-evaluation of Japanese colonialism on Taiwan, which disturbs the former
story told under the Great China ideology, is also understandable. In the
sentiment of anti-Sinoization and de-Sinoization, the educational modernization of Taiwan is traced back only to Japanese occupation, rather than
the sovereignty of Imperial China. It is a cultural amnesia! But their effort
to reconstruct the Taiwanese story, in my view, should have ironically
pushed the intellectual community to rethink whether or not a centralized
government or a top-down pattern of government is necessarily an evil to
education and, if so, how.

The reshaping of national imaginaries and the memory/ forgetting
incurred allow us to rethink the historical uncertainty and ambiguity of the
use of the concept of centralization. This derives from these Taiwanese
Nationalists, on the one hand, emphasizing a colonialized authority of the
Qing Dynasty (an over-centralized and authoritarian government), but, on
the other hand, complaining about the diminished intervention of the
Qieng government (an under-centralized government) in this island since
it is said that "the government did not take good care of the people on the
island due to their less administrative intervention." Similar irony has been
found for their critique of KMT government.[5] KMT authority is thought to
be a centralized and an unjust regime due to its total "domination" of the
society (for example, the re-articulation of the memories of "Two Two
Eight Incidence" in 1947, "White Horror" in 1950s, and the declaration of
martial law, which deprived Taiwanese people of the freedoms of speech,
press, and association). In the meantime, it is also argued that KMT regime
is working inefficiently and ineffectively because of severe bribery and corruption. We can ask that if the state apparatuses of KMT government are
inefficient and ineffective, how they can totally dominate the society?

The contradiction in the superficial level uncovers the deeper meaning embedded in the language for the retelling of the national story. In other words, the evil is not the type of government, either centralized or decentralized. The evil now is viewed as KMT regime, which ruled the island in light of the Great China ideology. The evil has also been further applied, inevitably under their theoretical framework to rebuild the national imagination, to all regimes in the modern history of Taiwan which have ever governed this island but analytically been categorized as the dominant, ruling group, whether it is centralized or not. In the following exploration, the reader will see the close relationship between the issue of national imaginaries and the practices of educational reform and education restructuring in Taiwan. Decentralization or deregulation is not "negotiable" only in specific educational discursive spaces such as NICT.[6] My feeling is that the people in Taiwan seem to strongly support the concept of decentralization or deregulation overtly but simultaneously they tacitly tolerate or ironically support the concept of centralization in some cultural practices without interrogation, or even without being aware of it. I will elaborate it later in this chapter. But I wish that the reader could keep in mind that this cultural debate embodies, from its beginning, the historical and cultural ambiguity of the fabricated concept of centralization and decentralization due to the intimate relationship between educational reform and education restructuring, and the reconstruction of a national imaginary.

With regard to the KMT authority, undoubtedly it is the target of the attack during the educational reform because people here gradually think the KMT government is "the source of the evil of the evils." Compared to the government of the United States, the KMT government is rhetorically a centralized one. When the former salvation story, however, was prevailing, KMT's role of rescuing this island was relatively undoubted and viewed as progress. For example, the land reform, economic miracle, the extension of compulsory education and the expansion of technical and vocational education, and so forth, which embodied the notion of Taiwanese Exceptionalism, had been thought to be a contribution to the modernization of Taiwan. During the past two decades, all the stories told by KMT before began to be questioned, reexamined and reevaluated. The imposition of the Great China ideology on schooling, for instance, has been reinterpreted as an indicator of the evil of KMT's centralized government. The concept of centralization or the centralized government as an evil is a specific historical construction of the "truth" in Taiwan.

THE DISCURSIVE SHIFT IN THE 1980s

Social Base

Regarding how the redefining of the notion of centralization could happen in Taiwan in the 1980s, we have to first pay attention to the discourse about Taiwan's withdrawal from the United Nation in 1971 and its following impact on Taiwan's diplomatic relationship with "democratic political campaign." People begin to consider KMT as a "foreign regime" or an "authority of outsider," a conceptual opposite of an "indigenous regime," which has political legitimacy of sovereignty over Taiwanese people. The drastic uncertainty that this discourse of withdrawal from the United Nation had embodied, e.g., the direct and immediate military threat from the Chinese Communist after the diplomatic suspension with most countries in the political democratic campaign, including the United States and Japan, made the former salvation story and cultural redemption no longer plausible for the people in the island. The masses panicked, selling out their estate, emigrating from Taiwan to other countries. The emerging and continual global "uncertainty," i.e., energy and economic crises in the 1970s, worsened that situation. This is the social base from which the discourse of political democratization prevails in the 1980s.

Cultural Base

The cultural base that paves the way for political democratization in 1980s is the interrogation of KMT's Great China ideology after its diplomatic defeat in the 1970s. The Great China ideology had an intimate relation to the salvation story told by KMT. As mentioned earlier, KMT's salvation story embodied a cultural imagination of the notion of the civilized/the savage and the concept of we/otherness. The duality of the salvation story involved a double-layered imagination, i.e., the imagined civilized/the savage between Taiwan and the advanced countries, and the imagined civilized/the savage between Taiwan and Mainland China. These dual aspects in salvation story had been intertwined together and mutually strengthened in cultural practices related to education and other cultural institutions. The salvation story embodying the cultural admiration of the advanced countries gave the people in Taiwan a sense of certainty of the future, which in turn enhanced the one embodying the cultural redemption of the Communist China.

The notion of democracy as an imagined we/otherness was embedded in this salvation story, which made a moral distinction between KMT authority and Chinese Communist authority. The way in which KMT fabricated their international "democratic image" is through the alliance with "political democratic campaign" whose leader is the United States during The Cold War period. (Along with the notion of democracy are the notions of industrialization and of science for the uncertain future embedded in the notion of democracy.) Once KMT government lost the diplomatic support from the political democratic campaign, the imagined we/otherness and the civilized/the savage constructed by KMT could no longer be plausible enough to give people certainty and hope and simultaneously the salvation story they told became faded, too.

The example of the societal shift in cultural imagination as well as salvation story was the fashion of native literature. In the past, Chinese literature and the study of Mainland China were the mainstream in the intellectual community. The study of the "Taiwanese" culture had never been emphasized. The use of dialects was viewed to be "the savage." The discourse changed in the second half of the 1970s. Indigenous cultural literature began to circulate in the turning of the sixties to the seventies and has been blossoming since the second half of the 1970s (Lu, 1995). Nowadays, Taiwanese literature and the study of Taiwan have inversely become the mainstream in discursive practices. In the field of humanity and social science, the department or graduate institutes of local language and local culture have been constantly established.

All these educational restructurings in Taiwan in the past decade embodied the redefining of the meaning of a centralized government in the island. However, it also involves a new way of social inclusion and exclusion as scholars rethink the question: what is local culture(s), or what is Taiwanese culture(s)? Reformers had a hard time to find a clear distinction between Taiwanese culture and Chinese culture. Ironically, what they have done is to include the very "local" culture such as a city or a township to be Taiwanese culture, which usually has no common ingredient among them. It turns out to be a deconstruction of the notion of Taiwanese culture.

Political Base

The political base that enhances the movement of political democratization in the 1980s is the prevailing notion of unequal allocation of political resource between two ethnic groups, so-called the Taiwanese, the dominated group, and the Mainlander, who dominated. The circulating slogan of "the ten-thousand-year congress" in political arenas embodied the reinserting of the concepts of the social inequality and social injustice in Legislative Yuan and the National Assembly. This slogan tells of the previous national imaginary of Great China Consciousness on which the reelection of legislators and National Assemblymen were not possible since the representatives from other thirty four provinces in Mainland China were impossible under the political reality after 1949.

Embedded in this slogan was the differentiation and classification of the people through the notion of class and ethnicity. When these two notions were analytically interwoven together in the study of social entity, a new imagination of we/otherness was engendered. It came from a redefining of the concept of social inequality and social injustice among the newly constructed "Taiwanese people."

When the notion of Great China was prominent, social equality and social justice were defined as equal political representation and the equal allocation of the political resources among all alleged legally owned "provinces" governed by KMT authority.[7] Once the discourse of a Great China was no longer persuasive, social equity and social justice were rearticulated to be an equal share of political resource between the newly fabricated categories, i.e., the Taiwanese and the Mainlander. Due to the high inter-marriage among various ethnic groups and the use of Mandarin as official language in the island, the distinction between these two groups was not clear. Xio (1998) indicates that there is no difference between these two groups in the issue of "love Taiwan" or "care for Taiwan" except for the abstractive national imaginaries. The heterogeneity within each group was much bigger than the homogeneity when an analytical tool such as "class" was applied and when the concept of "the dominant" and "the dominated" was assigned to each group. The redefining of the notion of social inequality and social injustice also involved the new type of social inclusion and exclusion when it was intertwined with the new concept of the Taiwanese. This occurs as the newly fabricated notion of Taiwanese was not only a spoken exclusion of the so-called Mainlander but also an unspoken exclusion of all other ethnic groups except for the Holo, the largest ethnic group in Taiwan.[8]

Furthermore, the slogan of the 'ten-thousand-year congresses' embodied the problematic of the maintaining of the political sovereignty of the culturally imagined territory. This previously imagined territory was reconsidered to be inadequate and unrealistic by the public opinion. It is mainly because conceptually the notion of the Taiwanese began to be segregated from the notion of the Chinese. The emerging Taiwanese consciousness also began to stand in opposition to the notion of Chinese consciousness. Under such a cultural reconstruction, Mainland China belonged to the motherland of the Chinese and was no longer the hometown of the Taiwanese.[9] The real Taiwanese should "love Taiwan," identify Taiwan," and put Taiwan in the first priority of any concern. The retelling of the salvation story and the reshaping of the national imaginaries embarked on by the Taiwanese nationalists made possible the interrogation of the formerly imagined homeland by arguing that the "not reelected" Legislators and National Assemblymen should "go back to China to seek for your electorate."

The social, cultural, and political bases discussed above allowed what I called the discursive shift in Taiwan from which we can begin to think about the restructuring processes of education. The centralized government began to be viewed as an evil, although the term decentralization and deregulation had not been imported yet. The languages of educational reform were the "indigenization" of curriculum, the "nativization" of curriculum, or the "Taiwanization" of curriculum, which strongly implied a decentralized government to realize the social "equity" and "justice." The notion of social equity and social justice were contingently tied to the notion of multiculturalism[10] which gave the voices to the previous "minority" or "marginalized" groups that in effect were the majority of the people on the island.

This discursive context gave historical meanings to the notion of decentralization or deregulation in the 1990s. It meant Taiwanization, which appealed for a decentralized KMT government whose leaders was the traditional elite group of the Mainlander. It also involved a new social inclusion and exclusion about who or what group needed to be decentralized. For example, not all members in KMT government were the evil. The phrases of "Taiwanese KMT" and "Chinese KMT" made a distinction about what group of people in the KMT needed to be politically dismantled. As long as one was categorized as "the Taiwanese," such as former President Li Deng Huei and his followers, she/he was still not an evil even within the "dominant group."

FROM "DECENTRALIZATION OR CENTRALIZATION" TO "DECENTRALIZATION AND CENTRALIZATION"

Processes of centralization coexist, co-develop or are produced in the ongoing educational reform movement, where the concept of decentralization is advocated. The concept of decentralization embodies a dual relation of governing that is applied to specific actors or agencies that were culturally and discursively defined to be an evil. In the meantime, centralization could co-exist whenever it was needed for "public good" or for carrying out "social justice" in the re-visioning of the citizen embodied in the phrase "Taiwanese culture" as social aspirations were constructed in the new salvation story and new national imaginaries. It is interesting that the public opinion only carefully keeps an eye on the pace of the decentralization in specific educational actors or agencies, which tie to KMT's "conservative group" but simultaneously neglects the opposite process of centralization occurring in the reform.

The re-visioning of evil and good in centralization/decentralization is found in three elements of the 1990s reforms: the changing role of the National Institute for Compilation and Translation (NICT), teacher's redefined role for curriculum design and curriculum planning, and the relation of ability-grouping and multiculturalism in the education restructuring. They had a common feature related to the removing of the symbol of KMT's unjust rule.

NICT, a branch of the Ministry of Education, used to be the only official institution in charge of writing and screening textbooks. It is considered now as a representation of KMT's authoritarian rule due to its monopolistic role in producing the official version of textbooks' knowledge and its role as the agency to carry out the ideology of Great China. To decentralize the role of NICT was to decentralize the Great China ideology in school practices, i.e., a reshaping of national imaginaries. For example, once NICT is no longer the only institution to produce the knowledge, the diversity and multiplicity of knowledge, especially the knowledge of the indigenous culture(s), which embodies the ideology of Taiwan Priority, could be actualized. The decentralization of NICT was thought of as a way to reshape national imaginary by giving teachers' the right to freely choose the textbooks embodying the notion of Taiwan Priority or the right to edit the textbooks and design the curricula in their own way. In so doing, the concept of Taiwan Priority can be included in the textbooks or in the curricula design and planning.

The reshaping of a decentralized/centralized textbook also involves new patterns of the social inclusion and exclusion. In fact, in the 1980s, the ideology of Taiwan Priority prevailed in counties whose chief executives belong to KMT as the ideology of Taiwan Priority either in textbooks or in curricula are not required. Dichotomy and conceptual contradiction between the ideology of Taiwan Priority and Great China ideology were engendered. This results in a choice of "either/or" in the use of textbook. Finally the ideology of Taiwan Priority becomes prominent in the production of school knowledge as the ideology of Great China is reinterpreted as a mentality and the potential behavior of "the betrayal of Taiwan." It is seemingly apparent, in this case, that what it wanted to include, the Taiwanese consciousness, and what it wanted to exclude, Chinese consciousness. However, as I mentioned earlier, if we look more carefully at the material practices such as the establishment of the Act of Language Equity, the unspoken exclusion is all other ethnic groups except for the Holo who is composed of about 75 percent of the inhabitant in the island.

The recovery of teacher's professional autonomy in curriculum design and curriculum planning is one important element of the restructuring that relates to the textbook revisions. The professional autonomy could be read as a way for teachers to get rid of the Great China ideology embedded in the textbooks in order to include native and local materials for classroom teaching in which the stories about the land, the population, and the culture are retold. But the global language of "professionalism" or "professionalization" is another way to reshape the national imaginaries. This may sound contradictory—professionalization is a global discourse about transcending the local and national values and the stories and images of the textbook are about national imaginaries. But they are not contradictory.

The meaning of teacher's professionalization or professionalism is historically based on the salvation story and the national imaginary, which involves what must be decentralized and what not. In the first four decades of the postwar period, teacher's professionalism related to teacher's professional knowledge and the capability of inculcating national spirit (Chinese nationalism). Current notion of teacher's professionalism or professionalization is contingently intertwined with the notions of individual liberty, indigenous concern, and some fashionable global reasons in education. What is included and excluded here tells what needs to be decentralized. The notions of individual liberty and indigenous concern are, in fact, tied to the concept of "the subjectivity[11] of the teacher" in the current reform context, a concept that travels from the cultural and political terrains. In other words, "the subjectivity of the teacher" does not mean a teacher can do whatever she/he wants but includes something else—the "indigenous concern," collaborative teaching, constructive instructing, curricula integration, and so forth. This process of re-centralization in teacher's professionalism or professionalization engendered a big contradiction between the reformers and the teachers as the latter thought de-centralization, i.e., an "absolute autonomy" without any kind of "centralized" or "top-down" intervention, should be the right representation of "the subjectivity of the teacher."

I think what the teachers neglect is the co-development of the twin processes of decentralization and centralization. The populist opinion of "the subjectivity of the teacher" circulating among teachers assumed a fixed and universal notion of individual liberty, but it was not. The second reform consummation happened on Teacher's Day in 2002 and embodied the polarized cognitive differences of the notion of teacher's professionalism or professionalization between the reformers and the teachers. The notion of teacher's professionalism or professionalization, in effect, refers to the dual twin processes of the decentralization and centralization as well as social inclusion and exclusion.

The ambiguous and complex appearances of the concept of professionalism of the teacher embody the cultural re-imaginary that re-constructs a we/otherness, the civilized/the savage, and the rescuer/the rescued. The teacher as a "rescuer" should be free (rescued) from the previously "distorted" ideology in advance (a process of decentralization or individual freedom) by inscribing the Taiwanese consciousness and the concept of Taiwan Priority in the teacher education program (a process of centralization or social administration), which are now arranged under the courses of "indigenous education" or "multicultural education" in teacher education programs. The child must learn "indigenous material," "native material," "local material" or "Taiwanese material," including local dialects, in order to be rescued and disciplined as a civilized being. It is also an irony that the alleged aim to lessen the pressure of students advocated by the reformers turned out to be an extra burden imposed on students' language learning. It means current first graders are learning local dialect(s), Mandarin, and English[12] together at a time while they just needed to learn Mandarin in the past.

The debate over the recovery of NICT was not a simple matter of the decentralization of state government. It also involved a new commercial mechanism among new textbook publishers in Taiwan. NICT has a factual monopoly in the textbook market. As parents could not afford the tremendous, constant, and rapid increases in textbook prices, parents NICT could offer more competitive prices of textbook with better quality in material and in content then before. Parents' nostalgic reaction entailed a huge debate over whether reviving a symbol of dictatorship in Taiwan was adequate or not. The global rationalities like decentralization, deregulation, social equality, and social justice were readdressed to resist the restoration of authoritarianism. Compared to the lack of a reaction to the centralization of the Ministry of Education in the management of the private school system,[13] the public opinion seemed to be "emotional" and sensitive in the recentralization of the cultural symbol of KMT's authoritarianism through the publication of textbooks.

School ability-grouping involves a case of centralization as government reform actualizes social equity or social justice. The concept of ability-grouping used to be thought of as a good or right in Taiwan that enabled efficient and effective use of resource in teaching and learning. Ability-grouping operationalized one important educational principle in Confucianism called Yin Tsai Shi Jou, i.e., to teach by virtue of students' capability, potential and performance. Later, the concept of equality and justice was evoked through the problematic of the social labeling of students' performance that eventually was officially prohibited. However, it never perished. According to Confucianism and traditional Chinese culture, receiving good and higher education is important to a person and her/his family to move upward in the social hierarchy and to provide honor both for family and for her/his own person. In school practices, to be placed in a high performance class means to receive higher quality education and to have a greater chance for advanced study. Plus, the success or failure of a child is thought to be the parents' responsibility in Taiwanese society, which roots in Confucianism again. Inevitably, the parent will "do whatever they can" to help with the child's class placement.

Multicultural education was to replace the ability grouping that became viewed as an evil. The notion of multiculturalism was to give equal respect to high performance and low performance students, which made it possible to think about its illegality among the folk, especially when the notion of evil was linked to KMT's corruption of placing some students of low performance into high performance groups through subtle and tricky strategies.[14] Public opinion seemed to tacitly support county government's decision to centralize the "public authority" to remove the "evil."

The new teacher selection system is another example of the irony of the concept of centralization re-incarnated through an education restructuring named decentralization. The initial teacher selection system required the city or county government to hold tests for new teacher selection. During the reform period, the policy to hold tests for new teacher selection is devolved to the Selection and Screening Committee of Teachers at each individual school. However, this educational "good" has been widely questioned by the masses under the shadow of previous authoritarian rule of KMT in educational system. The worry about the decline of the quality of new teachers produced in the new policy (the era of decentralization) emerged as soon as the "back door" culture and strategies derived from the prior corruptive rule of KMT surfaced. The issues of social equity and social justice were re-addressed. The concept of centralization was requested for carrying out social equity and social justice while the delegation of authority is proceeding. The re-centralization of the authority in a city or county government to re-host the tests for teacher selection for elementary and secondary education teachers in that area is desired by more and more areas on the island. The concept of centralization, instead of the concept of decentralization advocated by the reformers, becomes the tool to remove the evil, the culture of lobby and bribery deriving from KMT's unjust rule. No blame has been evoked for the centralization of the county or city government. Centralization is socially tacit and is, to some degree, encouraged by the reformers and the society.

A NATIONAL RE-IMAGINARY FROM "OTHERNESS"

Perhaps Douglas Clifford Smith's viewpoint can give us more insights in the issue of the fabrication[15] of the concept of decentralization. Smith is an American scholar who taught and did research in Taiwan for a long time. His approach not only touched the surface issues such as the comparison of educational institutions among countries but also the deeper concern of the culture. Confucianism, as one of the most influential rationalities in Chinese culture, was re-examined to show how a modern school system in Taiwan could be successfully maintained through it. In 1991, just after the discursive shift emerging in the 1980s, he edited *The Confucian Continuum: Educational Modernization in Taiwan*. Although this is only one of the seven books he wrote about Taiwan, Smith's argument here is sufficient for rethinking the twin process of the decentralization and centralization (or recentralization) in current educational reform and education restructuring.

Smith recognizes the binary between the East and the West, the Eastern culture(s) and the Western culture(s), and the Oriental civilization and the Western civilization, a reinsertion of the construction of "we/otherness." He also recognizes the cultural imaginations built as "the civilized" and "the savage," and "the rescuer" and "the rescued." What he has done is to disturb what we used to think of as natural or right by interrogating the Western as "the civilized" and "the rescuer" for the Oriental. He points out the decline of the Western civilization recently in world marketplace, especially from the concern of the performance of global competition of the Western countries, to call for the cure from Confucianism, the cultural foundation for Oriental societies, which used to be thought of as "the barbarian." He reverses the "the civilized" and "the rescuer" into "the savage" and "the rescued," and hopes the people growing up in the West civilization, "the progeny of Greco-Roman civilization," can humble themselves to learn from the Oriental civilization, the formerly imagined "savage," to better educate their young and old.

Smith depicts the educational chaos happening in "the Western societies" as if they culturally lag behind the Oriental societies and are waiting to be rescued. Moreover, he further reconstructs the concept of "centralization" which we now thought as an evil, and attributes to it the success of educational systems implemented in Taiwan. In his view, the implicit notions of social equity and social justice have been successfully carried out through these centralized institutions such as exam systems and the family institution.

> As with family life, the tradition of centralization is a major part of Chinese society and the educational process. Language, the traditional and modern examination system, the views of Confucianism, and the Chinese family with its pyramidal structure all reflect the emphasis that China [Taiwan] places on centralization. The United States prides itself on being highly decentralized...In the homogeneous civilization of China [Taiwan], centralization of all institutions has been the pattern that has proven most successful. (Smith, 1991, p. 33)

It is interesting to compare current reformers' viewpoint with Smith's. While Huang Wuxiong, the leader of the demonstration of education reform in April 10th in 1994, is arguing "decentralization" as the remedy for current educational symptoms (Huang, 1997), Smith thought that "centralization" has made Taiwan what it is today, i.e., the amazing "Taiwan Experience." While Huang is arguing that KMT's centralized government is "an evil," based on the context in which national imaginaries are being reshaped in Taiwan, Smith is arguing that KMT's centralized government is "a virtue," based on the context in which educational a "Dark Age" is occurring in the West world.

My concern is not to appraise who is right or whose approach is better. What I want to explain here is the puzzling and elusive feature of the concept of decentralization. Our solutions to educational problems depend on our cultural imaginaries. The reexamining of the shaping of national imaginaries allows us to question what we thought to be "true" and to denaturalize what we thought to be "right." It also gives us a better understanding of the character of "fabrication" of educational reform and education restructuring.

CONCLUSION

Though the global rationality of decentralization has been undoubtedly accepted, both decentralization and centralization in government authority operate for the removing and inscribing of the evil of injustice and inequality. The point is, how it is possible to think of what is "an evil" and "good"? Current educational reform and education restructuring are interwoven with the reshaping of national imaginaries. KMT's corruptive authority was thought to be the origins of lobby, bribery and other unequal and unjust cultural phenomena prevailing on the island. There is today a rebuilding of national imaginaries to relocate Taiwanese culture (local culture) in a cultural hierarchy to revise or remove the pathological symptoms. For the KMT government, Great China ideology, social inequality, and social injustice and cultural pathology are historically interwoven together to form the notion of "evil" in school practices which need to be reformed. The ideology of Taiwan Priority has replaced the one of Great China as a new national imaginary. Centralization, in fact, is not the real target of the reform. The target of reform is KMT regime, which advocates the Great China ideology. Global rationality as a world-wide bible is just a means to embody the scenario of the local film. The notion of social equity and social justice are redefined and are objectified simultaneously through the twin notions (and the twin processes) of decentralization and centralization.

The complexity of appearances of the concept of decentralization and centralization embodies the historical continuity and discontinuity of the indigenous cultures. As found in Smith's analyses (Smith, 1991), the actualization of the concept of centralization is given as the reason of success in school practices in Taiwan. The co-existence of centralization in the alleged process of decentralization in educational arenas shows the historical continuity of the Chinese culture rooted in Confucianism. In another sense, the factual but ambiguous appearance of the concept of decentralization in schooling projects the historical discontinuity of cultural re-imagination beginning in the 1980s.

Our solutions to educational problems are tied to our cultural imaginations. The notion of centralization could be a poison or an antidote, an evil or a virtue, depending on the way we construct "the civilized/the savage" and "the rescuer/the rescued." Current reformers think decentralization is the remedy to cure the educational illness, but the positive functions of the concept of centralization manifested through the historical journey shown earlier in the chapter help us de-naturalize what we have taken for granted. It opens up new possibility for us to rethink the reform and to re-examine the restructuring rhetorically addressed by the reformers.

The reshaping of national imaginaries so far I have discussed in the educational reform was tied to the notion of de-sinoization, which redefined the notion of social equity and social justice and reconstructed a Taiwanese salvation story. It was related to the discursive shift in the 1990s. The decline of economic condition, the ethnic tension for the allocation of political resources and the missile threat from Mainland China, among others, were the most influential. The notion of Taiwanese Exceptionalism indicating the self-confidence and self-identity of Taiwanese people switched its focus to political silent revolution. The contestation of national imaginaries embodied in the ethnic tension and contradiction within the island was intertwined with the discourse of anti-China derived from the missile threat of Chinese Communist government to form a new Taiwanese salvation story and the emerging conception of de-Sinoization. In the 2000 Presidential election, KMT was defeated by DPP and it also brought tremendous impact on Taiwan society. Decentralization was no longer the prominent issue in the educational reform and education restructuring except for the minute debate because it was thought that the "evil" had already been removed. Ironically, the Taiwanese people had chosen another authoritarian, President Chen Shuei-bian, in the name of a democratic country in the 21st century. Whether decentralization is still the goal of the reform and the structuring or not is getting more and more elusive and ambiguous in Taiwan. Conversely, the concept of 'Taiwan priority' has provided the solid mental ground for the re-centralization in material practices.

NOTES

1. The original draft of this article was presented in ECER 2002 at Lisbon, Portugal. I owe special debt to Thomas Popkewitz for his invaluable comments and patient assistance during the entire process of writing. Without his encouragement and careful guidance, it could not be produced. I would also like to thank Sverker Lindblad and Wang Ta-Chi for their productive feedbacks on an earlier version of this article; and conversations with Shen Yi-ying, Yang Shen-Keng, Wang Chiou-Rong, Inés Dussel, Noah Sobe, and Gau Huey-tyng.

2. Its formal and official name is the Republic of China (R.O.C.), a different country from China, whose official name is People's Republic of China (P.R.C.). The former, whose sovereignty was over Mainland China, retreated to Taiwan after the defeat in the civil war in 1949. The Chinese Nationalist Party (the Kuomingtan, or KMT) had substantially maintained its one party ruling over R.O.C. until the defeat of Presidential election in 2000 by the Democratic Progressive Party (DPP), an emerging political party in 1980s.

3. Please see my analysis below.

4. For some Taiwanese Nationalists, KMT government's goal is to build a 'model of province' of 'Three Principles of the People' for the recovery of Mainland China. This quasi-religious mission is analogous to what Zhen and his successors had intended to do on this island for the recovery of Ming Dynasty.

5. See previous footnote number 2 for detailed explanation of KMT.

6. Its full official name is National Institute for Compilation and Translation. See the following analysis in this chapter for further discussion of its changing role and meaning.

7. Until the first half of 1990s, KMT government had alleged that The Republic of China, the official name of Taiwan, legally owned Taiwan and the Mainland China, though the latter had never been under its sovereignty since 1949. This unrealistic story could be maintained because the concept of democracy had been historically tied to and intertwined with the cultural imaginations embedded in the salvation story through the inscribing of Great China Consciousness onto school subject in all levels of education.

8. The enactment of the Language Equity Act by the Ministry of Education in Taiwan in 2002 is an example of the new ways of social inclusion and exclusion. The initial officially 'spoken' aim of this act is to give equal respect to 'all' dialects spoken on the island by giving them equal status as the official language Mandarin. Unfortunately, it results in the social re-inclusion of thirteen dialects only. The dialect spoken by the people in Mazu, Lian Jiang Hsian, and a variety of dialects spoken by multifarious groups within the notion of the Mainlander, have been socially and culturally excluded, though they both used to be included in the notion of the Chinese under the rule of KMT government. See Chen (2003) chapter four for detailed discussion.

9. In fact, some of the Taiwanese Nationalists had ever argued that several small islands politically belonging to Taiwan but just next to Mainland China could be counted as the territory of China. Of course, the habitants of these islands were discursively excluded in the notion of the Taiwanese.

10. The other example for the actualization of the concept of social justice through the practice of the concept of multiculturalism is the establishment of New System of Multiple Channels for Admission in joint entrance exam. This new method is supposed to take into account the former marginalized group of students who cannot show their normal performance through written exam.

11. The term 'subjectivity' when used by Taiwanese nationalists refers to the cultural and political autonomies from the ideology of Great China.

12. The elementary school students are not supposed to learn English until the third grade as announced by the Ministry of Education but the notion of 'Do not let your child lose at the starting point' has made the impossible become possible at most elementary schools.

13. I will elaborate it in the following text.

14. One of the strategies being used is to represent 'the average' through placing the students who have best performance at a grade and the students who have least performance at a grade together in one group (class).

15. The notion of fabrication implies a rejection of the concept of ultimate truth of the knowledge of the natural or social world. Conversely, it focuses on the surface construction of the knowledge in historical contingency. The concept fabrication also indicates its doubles in 'fiction' and 'making'. For example, nationalism, one of the most powerful discourses in the 20th century, is regarded as 'imagined' for scholars (Anderson, 1991). In material practices, it has already engendered huge impact on social action and participation around the world regardless of its 'imagined' feature. For instance, the notion of 'the Taiwanese' does not refer to all people who live on the island but people who have identity on this island no matter where they live. It involves people you have never seen and have never met before. Although it is imagined, it could become an object which you die for. Similarly, the concept of modernization is a fabrication, but it has already produced dramatic influences in Taiwanese educational history. It has ordered and guided the directions for the past and current educational reforms and education restructurings.

REFERENCES

Anderson, B. (1991). *Imagined communities: Reflections on the origin and spread of nationalism.* London: Verso.

Bhabha, H.K. (Ed.). (1990). *Nation and narration.* New York: Routledge.

Bhabha, H.K. (Ed.). (1994). *The location of culture.* New York: Routledge.

Baker, B. (2001). *Perpetual motion: Theories of power, educational history, and the child.* New York: Peter Lang.

Chen, P.C. (1995). Knowledge and control: Reflection of rationality and legitimacy in the Institution of Joint Entrance Examinations. *Chinese Education & Society, 28*(4), 7–14.

Chen, Y. (2003). *Modernization, governing the soul, and cultural hybridity: A problematic of educational reform in Taiwan.* Unpublished doctorate dissertation, University of Wisconsin-Madison.

Chung, Y. (2001). Taiwanese identity in a global/local context: The use and abuse of national consciousness in Taiwan. In C. Aspalter (Ed.), *Understanding Modern Taiwan: Essays in Economics, Politics and Social Policy*. Burlington, VT: Ashgate.

Copper, J.F. (1997). *The Taiwan political miracle: Essays on political development, elections and foreign relations*. Lanham, MD: University Press of America, Inc.

Dean, M. (1994). *Critical and effective histories: Foucault's methods and historical sociology*. New York: Routledge.

Elias, N. (1978). *The history of manners*. New York: Pantheon Books.

Ferguson, R.A. (1997). *The American enlightenment, 1750–1820*. Cambridge, MA: Harvard University Press.

Foucault, M. (1978). Governmentality. In P. Rabinow & J.D. Faubiou (Eds.), *Power: Essential works of Foucault, 1954–1984* (Vol. 3). New York: The New Press.

Foucault, M. (1988). The political technology of individuals. In P. Rabinow & J.D. Faubion (Eds.), *Power: Essential works of Foucault, 1954–1984* (Vol. 3). New York: The New Press.

Gilroy, P. (1993). *The black Atlantic: Modernity and double consciousness*. Cambridge, MA: Harvard University Press.

Gold, T.B. (1986). *State and society in the Taiwan miracle*. New York: M.E. Sharpe.

Gold, T.B. (1991). *Civil society and Taiwan's quest for identity*. New York: M.E. Sharpe.

Hacking, I. (1999). *The social construction of what?* Cambridge, MA: Harvard University Press.

Huang, H.S. (1999). Educational Reform in Taiwan: A Brighter American Moon? *International Journal of Educational Reform, 8*(2), 145–153.

Huang, W. (1997). *Taiwan Jiao Yu Di Chong Jian*. Taibei Shi: Yuan liu chu ban gong si.

Hughes, C., & Stone, R. (1999). Nation-building and curriculum reform in Hong Kong and Taiwan. *The China Quarterly*.

Huyssen, A. (1995). *Twilight memories: Marking time in a culture of amnesia*. New York: Routledge.

Latour, B. (1999). *Pandora's hope: Essays on the reality of science studies*. Cambridge, MA: Harvard University Press.

Law, W. (2002). Education reform in Taiwan: A search for a "National" identity through democratisation and Taiwanisation. *Compare, 32*(1), 61–81.

Lee, H. (1995). *Education in Taiwan during the Ch'ing Dynasty, 1683–1995: A case study of cultural colonialism?* Unpublished doctoral dissertation, The University of Connecticut.

Lin, M. (1929/2000). *Riben tong zhi xia Taiwan de xue xian jiao yu; qi fa zhan ji you guan wen hua zhi li shi fen xi yu tan tao (Public education in Formosa under the Japanese administration: A historical and analytical study of the development and the cultural problems)* (Lin Yueng-Mei, trans.). Taibei Shi: Third Nature Publishing Co., Ltd.

Lin, W., & Wang, C. (1995). The institutional aspects of education reform: The mechanism of its function and dysfunction. *Chinese Education & Society, 28*(4), 22–40.

Lu, Zhenghui (1995). *Wen Xue Jing Dian Yu Wen Hua Ren Tong*. Taibei Shi: Jiu Ge Chu Ban She.

Mao, C. (1997). Constructing a new social identity: Taiwan's curricular reforms of the nineties. *International Journal of Educational Reform, 6*(4), 400–406.

Pollock, S., Bhabha, H.K., Breckenrighe, C.A., & Chakrabarty, D. (Eds.). (2000). Cosmopolitanisms. *Public Culture, 12*(3), 577–590.

Popkewitz, T.S. (1998a). The culture of redemption and the administration of freedom as research. *Review of Educational Research, 68*(1), 1–34.

Popkewitz, T.S. (1998b). *Struggling for the soul: The politics of schooling and the construction of the teacher.* New York: Teachers College Press, Columbia University.

Popkewitz, T.S. (2000a, October 18–20). *Constituting the American school in the turn of the 20th century: Nation-ness, the citizen, cosmopolitanism and "the others."* Paper presented for the seminar, Philosophy and History of the Discipline of Education. Evaluation and Evolution of the Criteria for Educational Research. University of Leuven, Belgium.

Popkewitz, T.S. (2000b). Globalization/Regionalization, knowledge, and the educational practices: Some notes on comparative strategies for educational research. In T.S. Popkewitz (Ed.), *Educational knowledge: Changing relationships between the state, civil society, and the educational community.* Albany, NY: State University of New York Press.

Popkewitz, T.S. (2000c). Rethinking decentralization and the state/civil society distinctions: The state as a problematic of governing. In T.S. Popkewitz (Ed.), *Educational knowledge: Changing relationships between the state, civil society, and the educational community.* Albany, NY: State University of New York Press.

Popkewitz, T.S. (2000d). National imaginaries, the indigenous foreigner, and power: Comparative educational research. In J. Schriewer (Ed.), *Discourse formation in comparative education* (pp. 261–294). Frankfurt am Main: Peter Lang.

Popkewitz, T.S. (2001). Rethinking the political: Reconstituting national imaginaries and producing difference. *Inclusive Education, 5*(2/3), 179–207.

Popkewitz, T., & Brennan, M. (Eds.). (1998). *Foucault's challenge: Discourse, knowledge, and power in education.* New York: Teachers College Press, Columbia University.

Popkewitz, T., & Fendler, L. (Eds.). (1999). *Critical theories in education: Changing terrains of knowledge and politics.* New York: Routledge.

Rose, N. (1999). *Powers of freedom: Reframing political thought.* Cambridge: University Press.

Schafferer, C. (2001). Liberalization and democratization in Taiwan. In C. Aspalter (Ed.), *Understanding modern Taiwan: Essays in economics, politics and social policy.* Burlington, VT: Ashgate.

Smith, D.C. (1988). *Lessons from the past: The Confucian legacy in Taiwan pedagogics— An Eidetic interpretation.* In International Symposium on Confucianism and the Modern World (1987). Taibei Xian Xinzhuang Shi: Guo Ju Kong Xue Hui Yi Da Hui Mi Shu Chu, Min Guo 77 (1988).

Smith, D.C. (Ed.). (1991). *The Confucian continuum: Educational modernization in Taiwan.* New York: Praeger.

Smith, D.C. (1997). *Middle education in the middle kingdom: The Chinese junior high school in modern Taiwan.* Westport, CT: Praeger.

Spivak, G.C. (1992). The politics of translation. In M. Barrett & A. Phillips (Eds.), *Destabilizing theory: Contemporary feminist debates*. Stanford, CA: Stanford University Press.

Tsai, C. (2002). Chinese-ization and the nationalistic curriculum reform in Taiwan. *Education Policy 17*(2), 229–243.

Tsurumi, E. P. (1991). The non-Western colonizer in Asia: Japanese educational engineering in Taiwan. In P.G. Altbach & G.P. Kelly (Eds.), *Education and the colonial experience*. New York: Advent Books Inc.

Wald, P. (1995). *Constituting Americans: Cultural anxiety and narrative form*. Durham, NC: Duke University Press.

Wagner, P. (1994). *A sociology of modernity: Liberty and discipline*. New York: Routledge.

Xio, Xinhuang (1998). *Taiwan Yu Xianggang Di Ji Ti Ren Tong: 1997 Qian Di Bi Jiao*. Xianggang: Xianggang Hai Xia Liang An Guan Xi Yan Jiu Zhong Xin.

Xu, Zongmao (1995). *Wu Shi Di Taiwan Ren*. Taibei Shi: Tian Xia Wen Hua Chu Ban Gu Fen You X.

Yang, S. (2001). *Dilemmas of education reform in Taiwan: Internationalization or localization?* Paper presented at the Annual Meeting of the Comparative and International Education Society, 45th, Washington, DC, U.S.A.

Yang, S. (2002). *Educational research for the dialectic process of globalization and localization*. Paper presented at the 2002 Conference of European Education Research Association (ECER). Lisbon, Portugal.

Yang, Y. (1994). Education and national development: The case of Taiwan. *Chinese Education & Society, 27*(6), 7–23.

Ying, Y. (1994). Reform of secondary education for the equality of educational opportunities. *Chinese Education & Society, 27*(6), 42–56.

Young, R.J.C. (1995). *Colonial desire: Hybridity in theory, culture and race*. New York: Routledge.

CHAPTER 4

EDUCATION RESTRUCTURING

Governance in the Narratives
of Progress and Denials

Sverker Lindblad and Thomas S. Popkewitz
Uppsala University and *University of Wisconsin-Madison*

INTRODUCTION

Our discussion draws on a European Union study of eight countries. The research focus was on education governance and social inclusion/exclusion.[1] In this paper, we examine the various cases of the study to consider its broader significance to recent controversies in education often labelled "restructuring." What are the discourses on education restructuring in texts and talk of actors within the political and school arenas as they relate to education? What arguments are put forwards and what are the alternatives?

Our approach considers schooling comparatively and theoretically as part of a world system. The focus on schools as part of world system is to consider how policy and education system knowledge (what we call "the systems of reason") circulate among various institutional settings to create patterns of social cohesion and collectivity that simultaneously produce

Educational Restructuring: International Perspectives on Traveling Policies, pages 69–94

divisions related to social exclusion. Our focus on policy and governance is to historicize the manner of thinking and "seeing" educational reforms.

The first section explores the salvation narratives of education related to our studies in the European Union. The restructuring discourses of reform embody salvation narratives about social welfare and the future that ties the well being of the individual to that of collective commitment and belonging. The salvation narratives of progress, rescue and redemption are not recent but are part of the worldwide institutionalization of schooling since the 19th century (Meyer et al., 1997). In the second section, we focus the ways in which different restructuring practices of school management and individualization overlap to produce governing practice that, to play with the rhetoric of reform, restructures who we are and should be. The third section examines how the narratives and images of school reform construct distinctions that normalize and divide those outside of the pall of progress and thus to be rescued and redeemed. In the fourth section our attention is turned to statistics as a cultural practice that creates kinds of people. The kinds of people are those whose actions and values lay outside of an unspoken normalcy and whose deviancy is managed as a practice of rescue/redemption.

Our study continues yet departs from existing studies of world systems and traditions in the sociology of education in at least two ways. First, it makes the knowledge about educational change as a concrete phenomenon amenable to empirical investigation. Second, it differs from previous studies through giving a particular historical specificity to the changes. That specificity is related to our focus on the European Union space and our emphasis on interviews with multiple layers of policy texts and actors in the political as well as educational arenas. Third, the study also broadens the focus of existing studies of education and world systems through its detailed discursive analysis to consider how educational knowledge not only describes and explains the phenomena of, for example, the social exclusion of youth, but is also a social 'fact' in the construction of norms and distinctions that links the inclusion and exclusion of youth. In this way we consider the relation of educational governance and social inclusion/exclusion as related in the study of restructuring. Our ambition is to explore the system of reason that functions as a governing practice through producing principles that qualify and disqualify individuals for action and participation.

Our approach to restructuring involves thinking about restructuring as embodying an amalgamation of social, economic and cultural practices that changes the relationship of government and individuals. Changes in institutional and organizational practices in current reforms entail, for example, relations to the principles of action and participation that connects the individual to collective rationalities and national "destinies." This second notion of restructuring is related to the notion of all modern states as a welfare state meant to care for their populations, including the making of the rules that govern the conduct of conduct. The modern state is a welfare state, in this second sense, meant to ensure progress through the production of the self-responsible and self-motivated citizen. The study of restructuring is to focus on the changing rules and standards of "reason" that order the conduct of the citizen.

Our data is drawn from different state systems as they relate to education. National cases from three Mediterranean states—Greece, Spain, and Portugal—and three Nordic welfare states under reconstruction—Finland, Iceland, and Sweden. To this is added the UK cases—England and Scotland, and Germany with links to Eastern as well as Western Europe. The set of researchers from each context carried on multi-layered analyses that included text analyses of significant texts ($n = 56$) dealing with the reconstruction of the education governance system; interviews with politicians and administrators in the education field ($n = 136$); and interviews with actors in different local sites: head-teachers, teachers, school nurses and so forth in compulsory and post-compulsory education ($n = 360$). The study also surveys adolescents in five cases—Finland, Sweden, Portugal, Spain and Australia—of a sample of students ($n = 3,008$) at the last year of compulsory education in the sites studied.[2]

NARRATIVES OF PROGRESS AND SALVATION: GOVERNING FOR EQUITY AND INCLUSION

We use the word "narrative" to think about how "the things" of the world are formed through the distinctions and categories that circulate in public policy and in the statements of educational actors. The narratives of education are salvation stories. Policies and research about school reforms "tell" about saving or delivering the nation through the education of the child. The narrative of redemption is an informational society. The themes are about the restructuring of education as producing democracy, equality and economic progress. Educational attainment and child development become tales about "finding the better life," fulfilling one's own and national destiny, and joining of the progress and development of the individual with collective hopes and desires of the nation. Progress is told as change in the curriculum and teaching that ensures the future of democracy in the new global, informational world. The mechanisms of inclusion are access to differential integration into labour markets, inclusive cultural representation in the curriculum, and democracy promoted by decentralizing decisions and improving all children's achievement and performance.

The narratives of salvation are stories of redemption. The saga of progress is told through a political system that is continually vigilant in working toward a totally inclusive society. The stories are about disintegration (moral, economic, political) and salvation narratives decry the fall of the nation and the prophesies of progress. The new paths to redemption are through globalization, and individual choice and privitization to prevent anyone from falling outside the narratives of progress. This narrative of redemption is told today with new categories of the marginalized but through previous storylines of the state making the educational system as a more efficient and effective credentialing system. In our review of the literature (Popkewitz & Lindblad, 2000), certain categories pointed to the problem of "equity" across nations. These include: (1) economic inclusion in which education is related to labour markets, with issues of class and social stratification privileged; (2) cultural inclusion in which issues of group access are broadened to include cultural representations of gender, race, ethnicity and religious minorities; and (3) inclusion of the disabled.

The salvation narratives involve particular elevator words that are topoi. Topoi are banalities that appear as seemingly universally accepted truths that do not need to be questioned. The phrase "improving all children's achievement" is one common topoi in restructuring efforts, such as the topoi "life long education and training" and "knowledge society" (Nóvoa et al., 2001). These words are accepted as universal truth that "everyone" accepts without explanation. The British reforms deploy related topio expressed as "Social exclusion is about income but it is about more. It is about prospects and networks and life changes." The phrase, "zero tolerance" is another topoi that supports reasoning about those who do not fall in the consensus and who are outside of the norms that enable success and stability (Alexiadou et al., 2001).

The topoi has no author as it appears as a truth born of a universal consensus. The consensus of the present crisis and its solutions appear as authorless, but with progress narrated through the new subject of reform who is to act responsibly and with self-motivation (Ladwig & Gore, 2001). The Finnish case study of governance and inclusion, for example, talks about the invisible clients who make rational choices, but with the image of rational choice directed toward the 'good' pupils and families and no one speaking about the poor and the ill at ease in such a manner (Simola et al., 2001).

We can locate salvation narratives in the descriptors in public policy and statistics of a nation and international organizations. The saga is of the European Union as collective normative site that has made great strides toward equity but which has to be continually vigilant in relation to its political and social commitments. The vigilance is in the identification of new populations that require state attention, which is both an expression of the dream of progress and of the need for its ideals as yet to be fulfilled. The comprehensive school, for example, is offered as a universal example of this progress, but with variations in the ways in which streaming and tracking occurs. The saga of progress is expressed, for example, as the percentage of the citizenry that has access to schooling. (In Sweden, it is 100% in the comprehensive school; 98% in upper secondary school, and 35% in higher education in 1999). In Greece, Spain, and Portugal, the identification of progress through high educational rates is tempered with numbers that tell of the degree of ruralization and gross-national income that are lower than those of the northern tier.[3] Even the distinctions among nations seem to point to a salvation theme related to efforts to close the gaps in schooling and its finances (for Germany, see Keiner, 2001). The almost universal school is linked to indicators of the economy to suggest a relatively good climate since the early 1990s. Statistics are continually interjected into the stories of the progress of the nation, telling of high enrolment rates and graduate rates and of relation of educational finances to gross national products.

The salvation narratives of current restructuring can be thought as having particular characteristics. One is a myth structure of consensus produced through participation. The centrally planned, vertical strategies of legal and R&D rational-empirical model of the State is now articulated as progress of the future built through a new consensus on public values born of local networks of groups. In the Finnish and Icelandic case study, for example, it was reported that system actors thought of the educational reforms as existing within a "remarkable political consensus." The consensus embodied a feeling of the inevitability of the change being produced through globalisation and the new economics, the need to respond to individual needs through a language that is deployed as decentralising, and responding and creating markets. In the different State traditions of Scotland and England, policies emphasise consensus models of decentralisation, and devolved government. The consensus is an article of faith to overcome challenges to the sagas of the nation. These challenges, as we will argue later, are encapsulated in stories of a perceived lack of coherence and cultural and social disorganisation that relates to juvenile delinquency, single parent families, and students unskilled for the new work world.

The salvation narratives of policy and system actors are not "merely" fictions or "talk" about the world. The narratives embody a field of cultural practices through which sets of distinctions and differentiations order the objects of reflection, generate principles for action and participation, and provide boundaries that shape and fashion the possibilities of our human conditions and its progress. That is, the ways in which people speak and write in the policy documents and interviews embody particular rules and standards of "problem-solving" that generate principles of action and participation.

MANAGEMENT AND INDIVIDUALIZATION AS SYSTEMS OF REASON GOVERNING INCLUSION/EXCLUSION

In this section, we will examine some of the discursive practices that organized the ongoing policy agendas within the different countries of this study. We focus on certain narratives of participation and democracy that overlay with those of school management and new strategies of evaluation. The redemption of state policy and education is in individualization. This construction of the subject is not one of overt policy but of the overlapping of multiple discourses through which the problem solving of school reform is engaged.

These narratives of salvation and redemption occur in a world that is relatively unstable. By that we mean that the European Union has, as has other places of the world, encountered dramatic changes in its economy, movements from rural to urban societies in certain member countries, and immigration in and outside of the European Union. This has placed great demands on the welfare state structures and particularly education.

THE "MAKING" OF THE NEW CITIZEN THROUGH SCHOOLING: THE PACT AND THE PARTNERSHIP

In this section, we argue that restructuring can be thought of as not only institutional and organizational changes, but changes in the system of reason that orders the management of schools, its principles of individuality, and the relation of the state and the citizen. But to approach this problematic of restructuring, we first need to consider political theory of the relation of the citizen and the state. The modern citizen is one produced through a dual relation that is expressed in the phrase of the American Declaration of Independence, We, the People. The "We" refers to the participation of the citizen who acts with others in forming the rules and practices of a democracy. This is the Lockean notion of the polity formed through a partnership or social contract. As the same time, the "We, the People" locates the rule of government as the collective representation or Pact to express the people's "will." The elected representatives of government act in the name of the Pact with the citizens to maintain order and bring progress. The doublings of government/governing is also expressed by Hommi Bhabha (1990) as the writing of the nation. The nation is not merely a unity but involves a "double time," as people are both historical "objects" that construct a memory of a constituted historical origin and the "subjects" of a process of signification through which national redemption and reproduction occur. Further, the production of new memories of the "self" embodied forgetting as new feelings of attachment and identity inscribe anxieties and displacements.

This doublings of "the We" of the Pact and "the We" of the Partnership provides an initial entrance to consider the governing patterns of the restructuring. The salvation narratives of reform embodied notions of the Pact as school reform is to embody the collective obligation of the state to ensure the well-being and progress of its citizenry. The reforms are narrated through the metaphor of promise about the future: the promise of national development, social mobility, and more equity through the individual who engages in partnerships. The promise is mediated through a relation of the state obligations to construct the citizen who can participate with self-responsibility and success in an equitable society. And at the same time the school assumes an active role in constituting a labour force that is inherently differentiated.

The strategies of rescue and redemption involve a double-time: the administration of the state in the making of the citizen and the citizen who makes the governing through participation. The two are mutually formed rather than distinct ends of a pole of values. The dual relation is expressed first in the assumption of the Pact that the state ensures all in society have adequate conditions for participation, social justice and equity. If the Pact is the collective and central obligation of the state, the Partnership seems to move to a different relation of a strong civil society where social groups work together to produce the common good and progress. In most political theories, the idea of the welfare state is seen as having a strong institutionalization of the state's obligation to society—the notion of the Pact. In liberal states, there is a weaker articulation of the Pact in favour of a stronger civil society where voluntarism provides for the common good. Our analysis, however, is to place the Pact and Partnership in a relation to each other in the production of governing. That is, restructuring involves a "writing" of the school in which people are both historical "objects" of governing and "subjects" of a process of signification through which redemption and reproduction occur.

The relation of the Pact and Partnership is evident in multiple case reports. In Finland, for example, the development of a less centralized public sector of the school is to produce local efficiency and effectiveness in flexible, decentralized management; while at the same time, strengthening the strategic capacities of the centre through performance oriented resulting. Portugal has no culture of participation while giving focus to democratization of educational systems, teacher training and educational reform. Participation resides particularly with parents and local authorities, and participation focuses on institutional participation on school governance exclusively.

The relation of the Pact and Partnership is embedded in the saga of the professionalization of teachers. The story is of different combinations of schools, parents and community organizations brought into the decision-making processes associated with the new reforms. In Britain, the pact has undergone modifications in the way that different social actors relate. British reforms to re-organize school decision-making are called a new partnership established in educational zones. The educational zones involve a seeming devolution of decision-making through the collaborative working of businesses, local government, local parent groups and the State for the improvement of schools. The Partnership is told as a story about parents who have duties and obligations to their children's learning, and responsibility for discipline and attendance at school.

These changes are in the changes of the state vis-à-vis the individual in defining the public good. The British 1944 Educational Act saw public education as a public good that is part of the entitlement of citizens in the new welfare state. It was previously a partnership between professionals, state officials and politicians. Now the partnership is with business and clients, with differences with Scotland where the administrative class was closer to schools and teachers. This is in contrast to the situation in England where one is educated in private schools, with a policy of trust and deference, and corporatist approach that had mutually reinforcing relationships. But the story of a partnership appears not only in Britain, but also in Portugal and Sweden as part of renewing the Pact.

Such reform strategies for decentralization and partnerships put together discourses about (a) social planning that strives for greater control of change with the promise of social betterment and (b) a democratization that provides individuals and communities a greater say and preparedness to operate more flexibility and productively in the new worlds of global work.

The different agendas that on the face of it seems contradictory are not in practice. The educational zones of the partnership in Britain, for example, carry salvation themes that include a faith in schools to bring triumph to the nation and the individual through better planning. The state discourses are about poverty and normative claims about correcting social organisation/disorganisation (the single parent family, juvenile delinquency), and a plan for making for global competitiveness through the participation of multiple communities that make the new imaginary of the nation.

Our purpose in pointing to the different discourses in the areas where school reform occurs is to recognise management strategies, then, as not only a set of procedures and operations for affecting policy. They embody complex sets of rules that govern how problems are defined and the principles for engaging in solutions. Our intent in this and the following sections is to illustrate linkages that circulate through management narratives to stories that individualise the problem of inclusion and exclusion. The management strategies embody multiple and overlapping practices that inscribe principles about particular kinds of people with particular capacities and capabilities that qualify and disqualify others for participation and action.

MANAGEMENT AND GOVERNING

The relation of the Pact and Partnership is embodied in the restructuring of school management. To say that management is a governing practice might sound like an oxymoron. Management is to provide the procedures and processes that rationalise and order the phenomena and people of the world to bring change and progress. But the management procedures that articulate the Pact of the State in the name of a common good overlap with other discourses of individualization and social exclusion to produce governing principles that are embodied in the restructuring that is occurring.

We can think of the changes in school management as related to changes in the State in relation to civil society. For example, the State functioned through monopoly paradigm, in the Nordic countries of Finland, Sweden, and Iceland. The principles of management embodied a centralism, a universalism, a social engineering and a myth structure of national consensus. System management told of the progress of the nation through distinctions of social differentiation defined as categories of class, generation and geographical origin. State management of education and its research communities were to correct these differentiations through chronicling inequality, domination and subordination. The comprehensive school system became a saga that narrated the State as opening the school to all social classes in a crucial step toward social equality and justice.

Changes in the welfare state begin in the European contexts in the last two decades of the 20th century (with variations among different states) with new stories of progress and democracy. The changes bring to governing patterns of the "Planning State" to the "Evaluation State" into the characteristics and conditions of individuality. In the Portuguese case, they argue that the current situation returns to an optimistic state, one that moves from that of the Regulating State to that of the Educating State (steering rather than rule). This entails a process of decentralization, with central political decision-making to play a role in normative regulation and a transference of competencies and transference of problems in the phrase "acting locally."

It is in this context of an evaluation state and educating state that the management narratives of the state vis-à-vis education appear. They are a mixture of centralised and decentralised practices that involve social specialisation. The stories are of greater local control, more parent school choice, changing in budgetary funds (lower funds or reallocation of resources), changes in evaluation mechanisms (greater central monitoring in relation to outcomes such as achievement tests and more local and teacher evaluation), and in the professionalizing process of teaching, more local and teacher autonomy. In some instances, the salvation narratives involve the establishment of independent schools, the introduction of vouchers, and the provision of State subsidies as lump sums to the municipalities, such as in Sweden. In Iceland, contract management appears in budget reforms and schools receive money in proportion with the number of students and credits they finish.

The narratives of evaluation are constructed as an administrative task of managing the educational system. System, local community, and professional evaluation practices are to work in tandem and replace the old task of the normative steering, control and inspection system through a system of governing by results. The Swedish respondents saw, for example, that there was a greater need to develop networks to find the necessary money for pupils with special needs. At the same time, there were new social networks in which to negotiate—with local actors of politicians, principals, and teacher becoming increasingly powerful.

But the model of decentralization places management in the forefront. New sets of standards are set from the centre as goal steering for teachers. In Iceland, for example, the saga of progress is built around the school, with indicators (referring to e.g., to TIMSS[1] comparisons) making it a national project to revise the curriculum and make the country the best in the world through making the school as the best in the world (Ingólfur Ásgeir Jóhannesson et al., 2001).

Evaluation is a practice of managing the decentralization. New Icelandic laws, for example, make evaluation as one management strategy that relates decentralized and centralized practices. A new law stipulates school-based self-evaluation that coincides with the Ministry creating a special unit to evaluate the school evaluations. The new systems of evaluation are justified through topoi of democratization and management: for professional development, monitoring of school practices, and self-evaluation making it easier for adjustment for children's individual needs. In Portugal, Teaching Career Statute not only involves how often teachers need to attend professional programs, but also introductions of performance evaluation mechanisms that reveal both a distrust of teachers and conflict among different objectives.

The focus on outcomes, consumer services, and concern with prevention (not cure) we find in Scotland and England. Progress, freedom and wealth are key words. Standardization of the national curriculum is meant to allow for parents to make informed choices, teachers to be trained properly, and inspectors to judge improvements, thus placing responsibility for improving in hands of the local school. But the discussion is mostly technical rather than a discussion of what make for good goals and objectives.

The different management practices are related to elevator words of national economic progress and social equity. Decentralization processes, notions of marketization, and local school autonomy are such management schemes that provide procedures that govern social interactions and that are assumed to bring better conditions for the citizens of a nation. It is also clear that the rhetorical strategies in reform seem to offer a reduction of school change to meeting economic goals. For example, achieving a more general higher level of schooling and changes in teaching and teacher education are to link schooling to the industrial skills and knowledge that will reduce unemployment and at the same time produce national economic growth.

The changing management that moves decisions to local contexts is not only about management and planning. They overlap with discourses about the individualization of pedagogy and the control of uncertainty. For example, we can look at the new strategies for school-based management that are being instituted as a narrative of progress. In multiple case studies, the decentralization of state policy is to give local municipalities and regions greater control that, in turn, will bring new efficiency, flexibility, and effectiveness through the self-managing of the school. The rhetoric of such changes is often expressed as one of a new partnership in which groups that have direct interests in the school and communities should be directly involved in the choices taken, instead of a central bureaucracy far away from the local conditions. The decentralization strategies are made through contrasting logics of modernity that entail a democratic devolution and a management for efficiency.

THE SUBJECT OF INCLUSION: INDIVIDUALISATION OF SOCIAL PHENOMENA

The new strategies of evaluation are themselves related to the individualizing process that we discussed earlier. It occurs without a formal evaluation but as part of a discourse about management quality that focuses on results or outcomes and not inputs. In Finland, it is seen as encouraging children's individual learning, developing personality and socialization, awareness of abilities and skills, and selection for further studies.

The "good" pupil is one of an individualization. The discourses no longer place the school in socio-historical and cultural contexts in discussing issues of equity and justice. Few teachers or system actors in Finland, for example, mentioned structural characteristics of social exclusion. In place of structural concerns are images and narratives about the individual who participates or is excluded. The patterns of individualization are also embodied in the narratives of a decentralized school.

The subject is produced through an individualization focus on the capabilities and capacities of the child who is successful. In most of the case studies, the different system actors describe the characteristics as what is demanded of young people, teachers, and school leaders in order to be successful. Success is formulated in the Sweden study, for example, as following similar pathways to the other cases: the individual is to be autonomous, feasible, communicative, information-seeking, and problem-solving. The Portugal case illustrates participation as related to discourses of decentralization, efficiency and effectiveness, with congruence to the market as creating "spontaneous order" in which individuality can develop. The Finnish case focuses on the shift in teachers' responsibilities to developing programs for individual choices, with the discourse about the "lone rider looking for a suitable niche in an uncertain world." The characteristics of the child that now appear across the case studies involve new dispositions: not only virtues of diligence, punctuality, regularity, reliability, trustworthiness and good behaviour, but also independence, flexibility and adaptiveness.

In Britain, the state, community, and individual are thought of as networks connected through the activity of government/governance. Governance, in the Pact side of obligation, is to provide networks of individuals, sites and institutions to sustain projects. The Pact though is related to individual outcomes that are not only achievement, but also the dispositions of the child and parent. These dispositions are to enable the individual to enter into private relationships that ensure obligations are met. For the school, these dispositions are to mirror the successful enterprises in England, as a "mosaic of learning" that is of loose networks; in Scotland it is the idea of the nation and the people that become expressed through myths of the commitment and ingenuity of the people and the mythical fair minded and close-knit community supported by the Scottish government.

Different discursive strategies overlap to order the characteristics of the child who is successful. First, difficulties in school are more and more seen as qualities of individuals. Second, these difficulties are more and more seen as cemented in the "learning history" of the individual pupil and thus beyond the influencing effect of the school. Third, pupils with difficulties are isolated and "sit alone" with their problems without any connection to others with similar "difficulties." Finally, with school organized to treat its pupils individually, teachers are to offer individual treatments to different pupils.

A similar conclusion is expressed in the Iceland case: The documents focus on the education of the individual; therefore, there is little space in them for inclusion policy based on the definition of groups, such as gender, rural-urban, or culture. Does this mean that boys and girls, if not diagnosed, are out of the map? Does the focus on the individual mean that rural children or the children of socially disadvantaged groups are not included? Who is included anyway? Immigrant children seem to be knocking on the door in terms of the discourse on the national level. And the municipalities are made responsible for the inclusion of rural and village children and teenagers. What we are saying is not that the needs of boys and girls, or the needs of rural children or any other needs are deliberately excluded; we are simply saying that the focus on the individual favours technically diagnosable differences but not those that are social or economical.

The individualization focuses on the need of a special person rather than on special competencies. In Swedish policy texts by the late 1990s, inclusion/exclusion is put on the agenda through discussions about the lack of motivation and the self-governing of the students, teachers, parents (Lindblad et al., 2001). The shift in narratives of individualization in the Finnish case study moves from comprehensive school discourses of previous decades that focused on teaching as the organizer of education who defined pupil's aptitudes and development. By the 1990s, students were seen as the active subjects or clients making individual choices without regard for social background or cultural heritage. Individualization also embodied clinical models drawn from medicine and discourses of pathology. In Iceland, for example, the child who is in special education is organized through clinical measures, the diagnosable child who is different and needs to adjust to school.

With a credo of individualism, the teacher is a "counsellor of learning," "designer of the learning environment," and the student engages in "individual study plans" and "personal curricula." New expertise is to work in pairs and teamwork, with "flexi-class." Individualization is also part of the saga of Iceland, told as stories about individual diagnosis by teacher, stronger individuals, and independent students. The teacher is to professionally investigate, map, classify, and work on the territories of individuality for "lifelong learning." The teacher's expertise is to engage individuals and communities so that they can be better managed and to "be healthier and happier." There is a paradox here that entails increasing autonomy in the diversification of roles.

But this focus on the individual involves certain anomalies. Teachers talk about and overvalue the social rather than to refer to the child as learner (Portugal). Teachers have two different meanings of exclusion—one is the old commonsense of children who are failing in school achievement and dropouts; a second group of teachers focus on what they "see" as a set of new social phenomena that disturb the teachers' ways of acting in school. The teachers talk about heterogeneity. The latter has different meanings, such as related to access of democratization, to migrations and the urban crisis, and thus a major obstacle to pedagogical work of teachers. In Finland, teachers see less risk of inclusion/exclusion than do state actors.

It is at this point that we can more fully identify the new salvation narratives of the school and its construction of the subject. First, the topoi of the new narratives emphasize the value of the individual who acts for equality but without any structural narrative about collective equality. Second, the placement of the individual is squarely in the national revival for global competition. Third, the salvation narratives embody a revising of the principles of participation. In multiple countries in our study, individual freedom is respect and participation that are organized through particular sets of rules about what constitutes participation. They entail individuals who work for cohesion, consensus, the application of the new management techniques of collaboration, and an individual autonomy related to an organization-enterprise model and culture. Fourth, the notion of participation is produced through multiple and overlapping discourses as they intersect to form school reform. The notions of consensus embodied in the new management practices intersect with particular pedagogical and psychological narratives about the productive characteristics and capabilities of the individual who is included.

The Iceland report summarizes the changes as an individualization that introduces new legitimating principles in the educational discourse. These entail a conjuncture of technological discourse (through, for instance, precise and measurable objectives, the emphasis on the clinical model), a decentralizing discourse (in, for instance, the transfer of the primary school to municipal authorities, school-based self-evaluation), a market discourse (in financial and budget reforms), and the seeking of consensus grounded in technical understandings of educational concepts and procedures. Moreover, we witness a moral discourse concerning a lack of discipline that is a part of this picture.

These changes are seen as a way to disentangle the various discourses—such as technological, child-centered humanism, and equality—that authorized educational discourse in the 1970s and 1980s. There is an absence of child-centered and humanistic views from the documents analyzed that was present in, for example, the 1970s. The individualism is connected to the new management narratives of decentralization/centralization discussed earlier. But they also intersect, as argued above, with changing systems of reason related to didactics and pedagogy that install a pragmatic outlook to the relations of children, teachers and school content teaching.

MANAGING UNCERTAINTY/CERTAINTY

Individualization is a nice elevator word that seems to be tied to individual freedom and autonomy. But individualization is a governing practice that orders a relation between uncertainty and certainty. At a system level, decentralization is a form of individualization that is organized to manage uncertainty. It promotes and orders local school development through new mechanisms of professional mentoring, supervision, and networking.

The uncertainty emerges at two layers. One is as an institutional disillusionment in the role of the school. The school is viewed as no longer able to appear as a fair institution in an unfair world. But the disillusionment occurs with the hope of progress as the inescapable promise of the school. For example, the school is to respond to increasing demands for access and longer school itineraries for studies to fulfil the hope of equity and justice. Teachers in Finland, for example, deploy a double register of complaint and fear with a saga of progress that seems inevitable and unquestionable. While a belief seems to exist in Portugal and Sweden that the schools are no longer seen as the "centres of knowledge and competence," policy actively legitimated the position of the school in the development of the nation.

The uncertainty is also embodied in the notions of change as inevitable. The restructured child and teacher are to be disciplined with the characteristics and capacities that will enable work in situations that require continual self-reflectivity and flexibility. The teacher is one who is personally responsible for "problem solving" in a world that is personally unstable. The professional teacher administrates the child who is flexible, ready to respond to new eventualities and empowered through the voices of local "communities" to construct and reconstruct one's own "practice," participation, and ways of reason.

But that uncertainty of the future and constant change is regulated by a certainty. The certainty in the uncertainty is forged through a relation between policy, science and schools that give regularity and a seeming consensus to the demands of a new global context. The salvation narratives embody the certainty of the rational ability to organize change and produce a more progressive and responsive world. While the categories of policy are imprecise and ambiguous, they continually give references to the new government policies and research "findings" that will provide corrective mechanism in the patterns in the spaces of schooling that enable the future to be guaranteed. For many of the respondents in our study, the school is a progressive institution brought by the certainty of science and rationality.

The certainty is also embodied in the system of reason that disciplines the new "person" to navigate the world of change. The deregulation that enables teacher autonomy and local responsibility in the case studies can be viewed as "governance-at-a-distance" or "governance without government," and "steering from behind." The stories of salvation are told of an uncertain system in which individuals are involved in local decision-making that brings governmental policies closer to the individual. But that local involvement is related to a more intrusive set of practices as the targets of policy are not only the external inputs and outputs of the school system. Policy targets the attitudes and norms through which individual goals and performance are formed and evaluated. Icelandic reforms that focus on the procedures of diagnosis of students in relation to state goals have become defined through greater and greater distinctions of the individual who succeeds or fails. New national, centralized test systems are installed to measure results. The code words of the reforms are input-output, accountability, diagnosis, and a clinical model that is instrumental, and which has experts who determine treatments rather than pedagogical processes.

The relation of certainty/uncertainty as a governing practice is expressed in the Portuguese case. The Portuguese case discusses the move from a policy context concerned with producing citizens to a pre-established civic model context to a new policy context in which there is a set of inherent stable values and uncertainties. This in turn involves three guidelines of action and participation:

1. Policy territorialization (rationalization of management modes that gives emphasis to the importance of evaluation processes and a quest for quality that relates to participation and partnership);
2. Diversification of offers that entails managing a tension between uniformity and heterogeneity; and
3. Inclusion policy.

The governing-at-a-distance embodies principles of certainty and uncertainty in the restructuring efforts. The teachers' work, to draw on the Portuguese study, is a kind of autonomy under tutelage. The certainty/uncertainty in the governing of the Portuguese teacher is a movement from a magister whose teaching derives from a central, absolute valued attributed to knowledge, to a pedagogue for whom knowledge's central place is replaced by the pupil's capacity and needs; and an animator, where the central value of the teacher is to renounce an external position as the core of the teaching profession. While the teacher feels nostalgia for the magisterial, the Portuguese teacher is to take into account what surrounds the child.

TALES OF THE STABLE AND THE UNSTABLE:
SAGAS OF PROGRESS, SOCIAL FRAGMENTATION
AND MORAL DISORGANIZATION

The individualization discussed earlier involved the double relation of inclusion and exclusion. With all of the focus on the problems of equity and social inclusion, there is remarkably little specificity to the character of the subjects excluded. At one level, teachers used a common vernacular to describe those who are excluded. They were called troublemakers, truants, and the child with learning difficulties. Embedded in the individual's characteristics of success are also the characteristics of the individual who is outside of that success and thus defined, at least practically, as deviant. In Sweden, the individualization involves organizational mechanisms that are designed to assist school dropouts. Young adults who leave the compulsory system without grades are assigned to individual programs in order to receive grades. These programs, however, have an over representation of children from low educated and immigrant families.

The narratives of progress and salvation, then, are also narratives of degeneration, those who are not capable of being "civilized" and thus need rescue. It is in the narratives of progress, salvation and degeneration that principles are produced that govern social inclusion/exclusion. The progress is told of those who will bring in the new futures and receive the promises of national and individual development. But the salvation narratives also tell of denials. The salvation narratives embody stories of fall, rescue and redemption. Restructuring reforms are stories about those who do not meet the demands of globalizations and/or the preventing of moral disintegration of the family, community, and nation.

The doublings of progress and its denial is told in Neoliberal policies of privatisation and marketization. Markets are to make a better world for the chosen people through challenging the bureaucracies of the institutions of the Welfare State and prompting individual involvement in the local agencies that directly affect their lives. But it is not only Neoliberalism that tells of salvation through revising the state's collective obligation. Welfare state commitments are articulated about promoting community involvement to empower previously marginalized groups. Decentralization is the elixir that rescues the poor and the immigrant by enabling the choices that move the poor into the realms of those of who the poor are not! The topoi of inclusion are related to producing (and sometimes consuming) a subject that has no reference other than that of the statistical qualities presented.

STATISTICS AND NARRATIVES OF SOCIAL EXCLUSION:
NEW KINDS OF PEOPLE

A central site for locating and rescuing the fallen is the statistical reporting of exclusion. The categories and quantities that report on exclusion identify the villains to be redeemed. In Finland, the villain of the school is the family: unemployment alcohol, drugs, role model parents, divorce, corrosion and fragmentation of family life, with an increasing picture of the seriously ill and disturbed pupils. The unsuccessful student in Iceland is one who lacks discipline in schools and society.

Discipline is regarded as the "glue" of society as a mechanism of integration, solidarity, and cultural reproduction and thus preventing dissolution and chaos. Moral and social disorganization and degeneration travel among in the different sites of the EGSIE study. The rhetorical strategies are to talk about economic problems of employabilities and meeting the needs of a global society. But the economic tales are quickly brought into narratives about those who do not succeed as cultural norms about family and social discipline are inserted into the narratives of restructuring. Stories among different actors are of declining discipline in social life that circulates in media as well. New pupils in Portugal's statistics are not the middle class but "drug addict" children, unstructured families, and more recently "the assured minimum income children." The categories place the phenomena of exclusion as outside of the school and at the same time, provide hope that the correct ensemble of activities and policy will bring redemption. The "plots" of teaching are to rectify the inequities and impurities of the system by rescuing the fallen through a new discipline.

The categories of statistical reports and statistical data are viewed as tools to capture educational realities as well as to make distinctions between individuals and groups so as to identify the populations that do not have adequate access to educational resources and attainment and are thus targeted for special attention.

Our interest in statistics, however, is its narratives of kinds of people who are classified as outside of the norms of social progress and thus in need of rescue. The significance of the quantification into numbers is not that the numbers exist or that they are good or bad, but that the inscribed systems of reason normalize and divide the characteristics of the child, the family, and the community.

Central in the management and individualization in the restructuring of schooling is statistical reasoning. In this sense, numbers are governing practices through the distinctions and divisions that circulate in educational statistics. Statistical categories divide and order the characteristics of people into groups or populations of what is normal and what is abnormal. Hacking (1986) studies of 19th century official statistics, for example, found that statistics becomes a means of ordering and administering deviance, from counting and categorizing "things" from murder and suicide to prostitution, drunkenness, vagrancy, and madness. What is important to the increased use of statistics is that it created new ways of ordering and classifying deviance through creating slots in which we "fit" people. But once the categories are there, people fit themselves in. Hacking writes:

> Social change creates new categories of people, but the counting is no mere report of development. It elaborates, often philanthropically; create new ways for people to be (p. 223).

According to Hacking there is a dynamic pattern here between people and their acting on one hand and the classification of these people and their acting on the other hand. That is why, in a way, categories make up people. In making up people, numbers embody the intersection of social, moral, and political discourses that establish a practical causality. The causality is not one of a formal logic but a practical one that forms in the patterns of categories, distinctions, and magnitudes of the "textual relations."

One can think of the way in which organisational changes influence the categories (and things) of inclusion and exclusion through looking at the Swedish comprehensive school. With the creation of the comprehensive school, and its serving as a transition point to the upper secondary school, there were also new markers of exclusion. This occurs, first, through identifying the numbers who are eligible (90%) and those who fail at least one subject (20%) and leave the school without any mark (1%). Also the creation of a new grading system can be understood as related to a rise in pupils who leave the upper secondary school.

The categories serve as the markers of targeted state governance to bring about the promise of an inclusive society. Policy and research focus on the degree to which social groups participate. The magnitude places the group categories is a comparative method that gives a functional standard of progress. Governance is the influence of activities on the magnitudes. The ideal of policy and research is exemplified in the problematic that we previously called "equity." That is, the salvation narrative of the modern state's care for its population is to eliminate (at least theoretically) the exclusion of targeted social groups through social policy. Such targeted groups are the categories of national and international statistics, such as those of poverty and social stratification, gender, race or ethnicity.

The making-up of people is an important element when considering the salvation narratives of education as practices that govern inclusion and exclusion. Let's explore this through current statistic reporting about the processes of schools in the European Union and their relation to social exclusion.

First, we find that in the past decade there has been an increase in the distinctions and differentiations to define the kinds of people who have missed progress and denied salvation. One of the "new" categories of state policy that appears in the 1990s is gender-based differentiation as they reflect gendered divisions of labour markets. There are also populations of people classified as immigrants and foreigners. The excluded in Britain are defined through categories of Asian, ethnicity, and those of non-English speaking background. Scotland and England is statistics of achievement and employment are that with same qualifications, ethnic minority has higher unemployment rates, but also regional discrepancies. A different set of categories of exclusion is related to special education. In the Swedish texts by the late 1990s, for example, inclusion and exclusion in education and society have moved from distinctions of class that existed in the 1970s to terms of the resources that children and young people dispose of or, inversely, are excluded from in four different respects: accessibility, division/integration, distribution, and participation.

The category of special education appears in all of the case studies. It is a field of schooling that expanded in Finnish comprehensive school in the 1990s. The Icelandic policy has targeted the inclusion of the physically and developmentally disabled child as well as the child diagnosed with specific reading difficulties. But this notion of inclusion/exclusion is different from those of the other categories as they focus on children of special education who are segregated or integrated with school classes.

Second, the different categories and quantities produce human kinds through establishing a practical causality. The different categories, charts and quantification in the statistic reports, for example, "make" a pattern of relations among the categories to describe and interpret not only the performance of educational systems across national and international reports of educational statistics.[5] The pattern of relations also establishes the kinds of people who are deviant. This is not done through formal logical definitions of causation but practically through the ways in which the categories form a family of common distinctions in the statistical texts.

International reports of education statistics, for example, focus on the relation of input and output contexts of education (Lindblad, 2000). The input context assumes that resources to education will produce good things or competent citizens (GNP, unemployment rates, life expectancy) such as combating illiteracy or social exclusion. The output context focuses on what happens as a consequence of given inputs. Education restructuring can be regarded as a transition from an input context to an output context. Here, the focus is on efficient use of resources, implying definitions of what are important outputs of education. These indicators, in turn, are placed in relation to educational indicators (enrollments, the percent spent on education), teacher/student ratio; and individual categories (gender, age, ethnicity, family background of the child in school, physical disability).

The magnitude of relations between input and output statistical categories inscribe a grid from which intelligibility is given to the problem of exclusion. With great similarities among the nations, social structural and demographic numbers concerning social segregation of class, ethnicity, race, poverty, rural/urban, crime) are related to other population groups of deviancy, such as children and families "at risk" and thus in need of special governmental targeted assistance to prevent their exclusion. The numbers of these two sets of categories about populations excluded are then placed in proximity to those of educational systems.

The practical causality of the categories and magnitudes of statistics embody the salvation narratives and its denials in modern educational practices. The numbers reconfigure overlapping boundaries of the political, the moral, the educational and the technical to form a single plane from which to fabricate the capabilities that lie outside of the norms of the citizen. The national reporting in Sweden, for example, relates statistics of economy and school organization and participation to other magnitudes of internal differentiation, such general problems of recruitment and retainment of teachers in order to establish a practical set of relations about schooling, economy and those who have not received the benefits of society, the poor, minorities, and other classifications of the excluded (Lundahl, in press). In Portugal, numbers about school populations serve a double purpose: to confer visibility to the distance that separates Portugal from its European centres, and as unquestioned norms of the inevitability of guidelines for integration and development in Europe. But the numbers are also technologies of government. Nicolas Rose (1999) relates the use of numbers, such as in statistics, to technologies of government. The finer distinctions of the internal groupings in schooling enable a more calculated population in which to work on and thus make possible the increased possibilities of governance of inclusion and exclusion. Besides the notions that numbers determine who will be in power and who will not, and that opinion polls quantify public feelings etc., we find the use of numbers makes modern government possible and judgeable:

> Possible, because they help make up the object of domains upon which government is required to operate. They map the boundaries and the internal characteristics of the spaces of population, economy and society. Judgeable, because rates, tables, graphs, trends, numerical comparisons have become essential to the critical scrutiny of authority in contemporary society (p 197f).

To this is added the fact that the numbers are important techniques for administration, taxation and so forth. Rose states that there is a reciprocal and mutual constitutive relation between numbers and politics in three ways: First, the choice of what to measure is a political choice as well as how to interpret and present results. Second, by means of numerical technologies, which "constitute the domains they appear to represent" (p. 198) the political domain is constituted by numbers. And third, numbers appear to depoliticise areas of political judgement. Based on these considerations, Rose argues that modern government is based on numbers in the ways political problems are stated and political programmes are evaluated. More precisely he puts forwards:

> There is a constitutive interrelationship between quantification and democratic government (p. 199).

Numbers are in a way to capture majorities as well as tendencies in the governing of democracies. Numbers tell us stories and about the ways these stories are received and acted upon by the citizens.

CONCLUDING REMARKS: RESTRUCTURING THE DISCOURSE OF RESTURCTURING

Salvation narratives are important elements of modernity that recognize both the boundaries and limits of the projects of progress. We sought to interrogate the salvation narratives as embodying systems of reason in European Union reforms that shape and fashion what is possible as the actions of reform. The salvation themes in the current reforms are not merely paths for redemption but governing practices inscribed in the rules and standards of reason. We explored how salvation narratives are embedded in educational restructuring to govern social inclusion and exclusion.

We would like to put forwards the following remarks as a conclusion.

- The European Union space is an unstable space that seeks to create consensus and harmony in contexts of continually ongoing cultural and social uncertainty.
- The restructuring embodies a restructuring of the governing principles that relate the individual and the state. We discussed these governing principles as the relation of the Pact and Partnership.
- We explored how salvation narratives in educational restructuring govern social inclusion and exclusion. Here we state:

    > The distinctions of the characteristics of individualization, for example, embodied a dual character. There were principles of the successful and "good" child who was the lifelong learner. And there were the distinctions of deviance.

The individualization involves a governing that brings together the uncertainties of change with the disciplining and regularities that are to enable change to be stabilized and harmonized.

An individualization has occurred that obscures the historical and social conditions in which that individualization is occurring.

New and finer sets of distinctions have appeared to order and classify those outside of the borders of success and in need of remediation. These categories moved from those of gender and "special needs" children to those who belong to particular groups such as minorities and ethnic groups. These categories embody doubleness as targets of inclusion and as categories that normalize the groups as outside of the values of normalcy.

- The politics of school reform is in the manner in which and the conditions in which current reforms have become naturalized so that they seem to be fatalistic. In looking at actor responses, for example, there is both a fatalism about the changes occurring and a fear of crisis in the discourses that circulate in the policy texts as well as among the actors. The narratives of reform seem as the production of necessary changes.

Restructuring, then, involves a complex set of relations about what a child and citizen is, should be, and who is not that "citizen." Inclusion and exclusion now can be seen as not only about who can enter the playing fields, but also in what constitutes the boundaries of participation. The participation and collaboration of the child in current reforms may reduce the spaces actually opened for "problem-solving" through the processes of naturalising the characteristics of the child who is a problem-solver or lifelong learner. This naturalisation occurs through the crystallisation and removal of the cultural/social moorings of school knowledge, particularly through the call for "useful" knowledge. What might seem as democratic and useful knowledge may not be either democratic or useful when its interments and enclosures are diagnosed.

A way to understand the narratives that we captured and analysed in our studies on education restructuring in Europe is that they are part and parcel of a cultural change in the construction of a modernised hegemony (Gramsci, 1973) producing new consents on education, society, and individuals. These stories deal with the necessities in adjusting to the globalization of economies and the safeguarding of cultures. The narratives work as elevating concepts (Hacking, 1999) in a time of transition. They make it possible to handle a transition period in ways that make alternative futures non-existent. But these narratives can be questioned as well as the categories in use.

NOTES

1. The research project Education Governance and Social Integration and Exclusion has been conducted with the financial support of the European Commission, Directorate-General Research, the Targeted Socio-Economic Programme. We would very much like to thank our friends and co researchers in the EGSIE project. In alphabetic order: Nafsika Alexiadou, Natália Alves, Mikko Aro, Ingólfur Ásgeir Jóhannesson, Rui Canário, Pablo J. Castillo, Sharon Cooper, Elín Dögg Guðjónsdóttir, Gunnar E. Finnbogason, Guðrún Geirsdóttir, Juan Carlos González Faraco, Germán González, Jennifer Gore, Thomas Griffith, Þorsteinn Gunnarsson, Katariina Hakala, Pia Hirvenoja, Christel Hus, Kristín Indriðadóttir, Magdalena Jiménez, Maria João Sucena, Ruth Kalaijan, Eleni Karadjia, Andreas Kazamias, Edwin Keiner, Joel Kivirauma, Manfred Kroschel, James Ladwig, Martin Lawn, Joakim Lindgren, Bob Lingard, Julián Luengo, Lisbeth Lundahl, Antonio Luzón, Angela Marliani, Carla Menitra, Regine Mohr, Kellie Morrison, Alexander Mühlberger, Pamela Munn, Sandra Muskat, Sigurjón Mýrdal, Athena Nikta, Antonio Novoa, Jenny Ozga, Miguel A. Pereyra, Katarina Podlech, Ólafur J. Proppé, Risto Rinne, Yiannis Roussakis, Diego Sevilla Merino, Farzana Shain, Hannu Simola, Joan Stead, Regína Stefnisdóttir, Rita Stolbinger, Johanna Strandberg, Kathrin Tietze, Mónica Torres, Ina Wittmeier, Paul Woolley, Gunilla Zackari, Evie Zambeta, and Annica Åberg.
2. Lindblad & Popkewitz (2001) are presenting the different studies and their results.
3. See Kazamias et al., 2001; Nóvoa et al., 2001; Pereyra et al., 2001).
4. Third International Mathematics and Science Study.
5. This commonality is a recent phenomenon, produced as international and inter-state agencies work on common categories by which to compare nations. This commonality in statistical categories is not only one of globalization founded by, for example, efforts of the European Union to develop identity through educational projects (Nóvoa, 2002), but also of national political debates of which, in the case of this discussion, education has become a measure of modernization for domestic consumption.

REFERENCES

Alexiadou, N., Lawn, M., & Ozga, J. (2001). Educational governance and social integration/exclusion: The cases of Scotland and England within the UK. In S. Lindblad & T. Popkewitz (Eds.), *Education governance and social integration and exclusion: Studies in the powers of reason and reasons of power (A report from the EGSIE Project)* (Vol. Uppsala Reports on Education 39, pp. 261–298). Uppsala, Sweden: Department of Education, Uppsala University.

Bhabha, H. K. (1990). *Nation and narration.* New York: Routledge.

Gramsci, A. (1973). *Selections from the prison notebooks.* London: Lawrence & Wishart.

Hacking, I. (1986). Making up people. In T. C. Heller, M. Sosna, & D. E. Wellbery (Eds.), *Reconstructing individualism: Autonomy, individuality, and the self in Western thought* (pp. 222–236, 347–348). Stanford, CA: Stanford University Press.

Hacking, I. (1999). *The social construction of what?* Cambridge, MA: Harvard University Press

Ingólfur Ásgeir Jóhannesson, Guðrún Geirsdóttir, Gunnar E. Finnbogason, & Sigurjón Mýrdal (2001). Changes in Patterns of Educational Governance and Social Integration and Exclusion In Iceland at The Beginning of a New Millennium.

Kazamias, A. M., Zambeta, E., Karadjia, E. with the cooperation of Roussakis, Y. & Nikta, A. (2001) Educational reform 2000: Toward a paideia of open horizons—the modern Greek Sisyphus. In S. Lindblad & T. Popkewitz (Eds.), *Education governance and social integration and exclusion: Studies in the powers of reason and reasons of power (A report from the EGSIE Project)* (Uppsala Reports on Education, 39). Uppsala, Sweden: Department of Education, Uppsala University.

Keiner, E. (2001). Germany education: Governance and social exclusion and integration. In S. Lindblad & T. Popkewitz (Eds.), *Education governance and social integration and exclusion: Studies in the powers of reason and reasons of power (A report from the EGSIE Project)* (Uppsala Reports on Education 39). Uppsala, Sweden: Department of Education, Uppsala University.

Ladwig, J. G., and Gore, J. M. (2001). Australia: The imposition of a schooled habitus. In S. Lindblad & T. Popkewitz (Eds.), *Education governance and social integration and exclusion: Studies in the powers of reason and reasons of power (A report from the EGSIE Project)* (Uppsala Reports on Education, 39). Uppsala, Sweden: Department of Education, Uppsala University.

Lindblad, S., & Popkewitz, T.S. (Eds). (2001). Education Governance and Social Integration and Exclusion: Studies in the Powers of Reason and the Reasons of Power. Uppsala Reports on Education, 39.

Lindblad, S., Lundahl, L., & Zackari, G. (2001). Sweden: Increased inequalities—Increased stress on individual agency. In S. Lindblad & T. Popkewitz (Eds.), *Education governance and social integration and exclusion: Studies in the powers of reason and reasons of power (A report from the EGSIE Project)* (Vol. Uppsala Reports on Education, 39, pp. 261–298). Uppsala, Sweden: Department of Education, Uppsala University.

Meyer, J., Boli, J., Thomas, G., & Ramirez, F. (1997). World society and the nation-state. *American Journal of Sociology 103*(1), 144–181.

Novóa, A. (2002). Ways of thinking about education in Europe. In A. Novóa & M. Lawn (Eds.), *Fabricating Europe; The formation of an education space(pp. 131–156).* Dordrecht: Kluwer Academic Publishers.

Nóvoa, A., Alves, N., & Canário, R. (2001). Portugal: School and social exclusion—From promises to uncertainties. In S. Lindblad & T. Popkewitz (Eds.), *Education governance and social integration and exclusion: Studies in the powers of reason and reasons of power (A report from the EGSIE Project)* (Vol. Uppsala Reports on Education 39). Uppsala, Sweden: Department of Education, Uppsala University.

Pereyra, M., Luzón, A., Torres, M., González Faraco, J. C., & Sevilla, D. (2001). Social inclusion and exclusion in Spain: The blurring images of a reformed schooling. In S. Lindblad & T. Popkewitz (Eds.), *Education governance and social integration and exclusion: Studies in the powers of reason and reasons of power (A report from the EGSIE Project)* (Vol. Uppsala Reports on Education, 39). Uppsala, Sweden: Department of Education, Uppsala University.

Popkewitz, T.S., & Lindblad, S. (2000). Educational Governance and Social Inclusion and Exclusion: A Conceptual Review of Equity and Post-Modern Traditions. *Discourse, 21*(1), 1B44.

Rose, N. (1999). *Powers of freedom: Reframing political thought.* Cambridge, MA: Cambridge University Press.

Simola, H., Rinne, R., & Kivirauma, J. (2001). Shifting responsibilities, insolvent clients and double-bound teachers—The appearance of a new system of reason in constructing educational governance and social exclusion/inclusion in Finland? In S. Lindblad & T. Popkewitz (Eds.), *Education governance and social integration and exclusion: Studies in the powers of reason and reasons of power (A report from the EGSIE Project)* (Uppsala Reports on Education, 39). Uppsala, Sweden: Department of Education, Uppsala University.

The Swedish Way Towards a Learning Society. A Report to the OECD. (1992). Stockholm: Ministry of Education and Science.

part II

EDUCATION RESTRUCTURING
IN DIFFERENT CONTEXTS

CHAPTER 5

GOVERNANCE BY SPIN

The Case of New Labour and Education Action Zones in England

Sharon Gewirtz, Marny Dickson, Sally Power

INTRODUCTION

The chapter draws on a three-year study[1] of the English Education Action Zones (EAZs) policy. This policy was one of a number of area-based initiatives introduced in England by the New Labour[2] Government in their first term of office (1997–2001). The initial Government publicity suggested that EAZs would be "standard bearers in a new crusade uniting business, schools, local education authorities[3] and parents to modernize education in areas of social disadvantage" (DfEE, 1998). Allocated via a process of competitive bidding, twenty-five "first-round" EAZs were introduced between September 1998 and January 1999, followed by a further forty-eight "second-round" EAZs in the period September 1999 to April 2000. The zones, resourced by a combination of state and private funding, were established in a mixture of urban and rural locations. The policy was short-lived, however, and has since been eclipsed by other initiatives. The purpose of this chapter is not to provide an analysis or evaluation of the EAZ

Educational Restructuring: International Perspectives on Traveling Policies, pages 97–120

policy. Rather, we intend to use the case of EAZs to explore issues around the role of impression management in educational governance. In particular, the chapter is concerned with processes of governance which attempt to manage, contain or render invisible potential controversies that relate to policy development and implementation by impression management, or what has become known as "spin."

In the collection and analysis of the data from our study of the EAZ initiative, spin has arisen as an unexpectedly prominent theme. For example, spin was often raised explicitly by those we interviewed as an activity that they needed to be reflexive about and engaged in. It was described as shaping the fortunes of the policy or in some cases as constituting the policy. We were often aware that we were being spun a line about the "successes" of the policy and frequently overt attempts were made by those we were researching to try to "persuade" us of a particular spin, which we should put on our own research questions and/or reports. The following examples from the data illustrate some of the diverse articulations of the theme of spin that emerged in the course of our fieldwork. Crudely, some of these are spin, some are about spin and one is an example of the study itself being caught up in spin:

> [Y]ou always have to have a headline for the press when you publish a bill and we decided that Education Action Zones should be the headline because a lot of the other content of the Bill was detailed stuff about the GM [grant-maintained[4]] sector becoming Foundation Schools and so on which is not very interesting at all. So ... we decided to highlight them and that went really—that worked perfectly, it was a model of policy development, press announcement, got good attention, and plenty of column inches, air time, message was right ... (Civil Servant A)[5]

> "...[T]he whole EAZ experience has been a fun time. All Year 6 pupils in the zone went to the Dome as a learning day out. We were covering the day as journalists and interviewing people about what they thought of the trip and taking photographs ... I think the EAZ is a brilliant way to boost educational standards and help all the children get a brighter future for themselves." (Ben Borthwick, Year 7, Kingswood High School, Bransholme, Kingston Upon Hull EAZ, "quoted" in Department for Education and Employment's [DfEE][6] EAZ newsletter, Issue 1, Summer 2000)

> It was very much the style of the early days of the government, early initiatives of the government, establishing a certain position vis-à-vis [the] public, the readership of the Daily Mail.[7] They were not going to be seen as going into a kind of social partnership with trades unions, teachers ... they were going to be seen as sorting out, and quickly, long-standing problems, which through a mixture of action and spin, you know, would be rapidly alleviated. Even

though there were long-standing problems in our education system. (Teacher union official)

I was worried that it [joining an EAZ] could be perceived as something that a school in crisis got involved in rather than a successful school ... So I was worried that that's how people within our community who we are trying to attract to the school might perceive it. It doesn't seem to have happened that way, largely because it's not been, because, as I said before, it's been presented to parents as "we're part of an Education Action Zone—it's dynamic and we get lots of money from it!" (Teacher, Greenbrook EAZ)

The results have gone up, you know, quite dramatically ... I think the zones contributed to it. I mean, it would be totally false for me to say it's exclusively due to the zone, because obviously the schools have, you know, greatly played a part in that and I think the schools would have a few misgivings if we presented [the improved results] as totally the impact of the zone, you know. In a sense, we were required to send the zone figures in that way to the DfEE, so it was a bit of a sort of, um, shall I say, a bit of a game.(Seaham EAZ director)

Both schools have done lots to improve and they certainly let you know about it. I'm getting a bit suspicious with Secondary A—maybe overkill on telling us how good things are as there are still lots of problems there. (Nairnton parent survey, 2001)

...We all know that when they work well, partnerships with businesses are empowering for young people, staff, schools, businesses and members of the local community ... One thing remains certain—the significant role that EAZs play in raising achievement and improving the life chances of young people. (Jackie Turner, Department for Education and Skills (DfES) EAZ Education Advisor, quoted in DfES's EAZ newsletter Issue 4 Autumn, 2001)

Dear Marny,
I would like to thank you on behalf of the [EAZ group] for attending the meeting on .... I hope the points raised at the meeting prove useful in your continuing research into EAZs. In particular, I hope [you are] able to take on board concerns expressed by [group] members at the meeting that it appeared research findings were being compared unfavourably with claims made by ministers at the time EAZs were launched. Members believed it would be particularly unfair to draw this comparison as those working within EAZs are trying to implement the policy they were presented with, not claims made by ministers and the media ... (Extract from letter to Marny Dickson from an EAZ grouping)

There is other data in correspondence and field notes, which show attempts to bring influence to bear on how we represent the policy in our own research reports, but because of possible sensitivities we are not able to use it here.

Attempting to deconstruct the various manifestations, rationales, instances, processes and effects of spin that have emerged in the course of our research and reconstruct them into a coherent analytic account has been no easy task. However, despite this complexity, it can be argued that spin has played a crucial role in the trajectory of the EAZ policy. Various articulations of spin have appeared across our project database, which includes press coverage of EAZs, EAZ publicity materials, interviews with DfES, LEA and union officials, EAZ directors, head teachers, teachers and EAZ partners as well as surveys of teachers and parents.

The overarching purpose of the chapter is to illustrate the complex relationship between spin and policy. In the first section we define spin and place the concept in historical context. We then go on to outline the contours of our emerging analytic framework—in particular, the double-coded nature of much spin and its dynamic, endemic and constitutive characteristics. Finally, in the conclusion, we draw out the implications for policy analysis of this complex conceptualization of the spin/policy relationship.

IMPRESSION MANAGEMENT AND THE GROWTH OF POLITICAL SPIN

> [Politicians] … like to be thought well of and want to control the message and the messengers as far as possible. There is nothing new or even disreputable about this: it comes with the job. What is new though, is the systematic and professional way in which it is now undertaken. The wearisome gibes about spinners and sound bites do capture the modern enterprise of news management that is central to contemporary politics. The practitioners of these black arts are increasingly the key figures in the political world. (Wright, 1999, p. 20)

Contemporary usage of the term spin derives from the United States. A Guardian columnist, first imported the concept of "spin doctors" into Britain in 1988, but it was not until the general election campaign of 1997 that the expression had become widely used within the British media. Esser et al. (2000, p. 210) argue that the spin phenomenon is associated with a new political landscape which was forged in the United States: "The rules of the political game have changed: parties bring in management consultants for a more efficient party organization, advertising experts for better dealing with the mass media, and brainpower—gathered together in policy units and think tanks—for the ideological content."

Whilst "news management is an inescapable part of politics" (Cockerill et al., 1984, p. 233) and not unique to New Labour, New Labour is constantly presented—by the media and political opponents - as being obsessively concerned with impression management to the detriment of both transparency and substantive policy-making. As the British political commentator, Andrew Rawnsley (2002), put it: "Spin has come to be the shorthand which sums up New Labour's reputation for over promising and under-achieving." Consequently, spin has become a central plank of Conservative Party attacks on the Labour Government:

> [T]he Tories has become the greatest devotees of spin. Virtually everything they say about the Government or about themselves revolves around spin... It's not by winning policy arguments that they calculate that they will best the Government. Rather, they hope to depict New Labour as a bunch of morally bankrupt twisters who can never be expected to tell the truth about anything. (Rawnsley, 2002)

Thus, it could be argued that spin itself is a spun concept. The negative connotations associated with spin—dishonesty, manipulative and/or inappropriate behavior—mean that those supposedly doing the "spinning" very rarely use the term publicly. Instead, those who are hostile to the Labour Government typically use allegations of spin to challenge and undermine the authority of the "official line." Accusations of spin have proved to be a useful tool with which to discredit political opponents in the battle over public perceptions and public trust. Spin is clearly not an "innocent" concept. Nonetheless, we argue that the growth of spin is not merely a political invention, and that the concept and practice of spinning reflect both qualitative and quantitative changes in the nature of media-political relations, evident particularly in the following trends:

- The growing significance, influence and capacity of the media. Politics has become increasingly dominated by mass media communicated messages as television, in particular, has become the public's principal source of political information (Jones, 1995). Unsurprisingly, as the role of the media has become more important, politicians have become increasingly aware of the links between media performance, policy presentation and public perceptions. As a consequence, "Politicians and their media advisors have become skilled at conveying their messages in ways appealing to the broadcasters" (Riddell, 1999, p.13). The media assumes particular importance at the time of a general election. As Barendt (1999, p. 108) puts it, "Everyone knows now that elections are won by the press." Accordingly, recent elections have become primarily media rather than party affairs and the significance of party members has declined as the role of political consultants has expanded (Esser et al., 2000).

- An increased politicization of the news media. Cockerill et al. (1984) describe a close association of particular government ministers and certain members of the press as dating back at least one hundred years in Britain. However, many commentators have claimed that these relations underwent a qualitative shift in the 1970s under Prime Minister Harold Wilson at the time of the Rhodesia crisis when his press secretary, Joe Haines, is said to have established a so-called "white commonwealth" group of favored correspondents who could be relied on to give positive coverage to the government over this issue. This tradition is said to have continued during Margaret Thatcher's government under press secretary Bernard Ingram through to the Governments of John Major and Tony Blair (Cockerill et al., 1984). The creation of an "in-group" clearly presupposes the existence of an "out-group" of journalists who find their access to exclusives, interviews and breaking stories denied if they fail to accept the government line. However, although complaints about media coverage, bullying and intimidation have been "part of the media scene for a long time," under the current Labour government, it has been argued that what is new is "how consistently, aggressively and fast they complain" (Esser et al., 2000).

- The professionalisation of news management within political parties. Campaign management within modern political parties is now characterized by centralized planning and controlling of communications as part of an integrated strategy that follows the pattern of commercial PR (Esser et al., 2000). Political parties now place professional experts in PR, marketing, advertising and polling at the center of their campaign teams. In Britain, this process is said to have begun in earnest under the Conservative government of Margaret Thatcher (Cockerill et al., 1984) and accelerated under New Labour (Esser et al., 2000). In addition, New Labour have been credited with creating a particularly efficient news management regime which involves the close monitoring of all media outlets and the collation of data about the inner structure of media organizations, journalists and the electorate. The creation of detailed databases made it possible for the party to release advantageous information effectively and allow for the "rapid rebuttal" of critics' claims. Perhaps most importantly, effective impression management requires some level of control over the messages, which the media receive. In the run up to the 1997 election, Labour campaign headquarters centralized all communications to ensure that all party members stayed "on message" in their dealings with the media—a model of news management that the party has retained in Government.

In order to understand why New Labour chose to adopt such a proactive model of impression management, it is important to understand the context in which their fear of "bad press" developed. Pre-1997 much of the British press exhibited a longstanding antipathy towards the Labour party. Perhaps unsurprisingly, given this history of Conservative bias prior to the 1997 election, Labour spin doctors embarked on a concerted effort to win over the newspapers owned by News International, eventually winning front page endorsement by the Sun, Britain's highest selling—and traditionally Conservative Party-supporting—daily paper. Subsequently political commentators have repeatedly argued that it was the superiority of the Labour media operation that secured Labour's election victory (Esser et al., 2000).

RETHINKING SPIN

So although New Labour is clearly not the first government to try and manipulate information by attempting to control journalists, suppress dissent from within the government's own ranks and control the "information" that the government sends out, it appears to have taken impression management to new extremes. As Norman Fairclough (2000) has argued, specifically in relation to New Labour's attempts to "calculatively manipulate" language, it is "the scale and intensity" which is new. There also now appears to be a greater degree of reflexivity about the process. Spin is not something the government is ashamed of. Rather it is paraded as both a virtue and a necessity. Indeed, as Franklin has pointed out, New Labour is the first government explicitly and "genuinely committed to the belief that the presentation of policy is as important as the policy itself" (1998, p. 5).

This quote from Franklin is fairly typical of the way in which the relationship between spin and policy is constructed in the public domain and in academic analyses. That is, spin is conventionally understood as something separate from policy, as something that is "done to" policy in order to make it attractive to particular constituencies. Those constituencies range from the whole of the "business world," to the archetypal Daily Mail reader (see footnote 7) and middle Englander[8] and, in terms of conventional party politics, its polar opposite—the resident of Old Labour's heartlands.[9]

In this chapter we want to argue for a more complex understanding of the relationship between "spin" and "policy." We want to suggest that spin needs to be understood as operating on two levels, often simultaneously. At one level it operates as a strategy of impression management, where a range of tactics are used to attempt to control the impression that "the public" gets of New Labour policies. However, those policies and the spin that represents them to "the public" cannot be understood as distinct and separate entities because the policies cannot be neatly abstracted from the spin. Thus, at another level, we also need to focus on the constitutive role that "spins" plays. We are using the term constitutive here to highlight the way in which spin is not simply "done to" a policy but is also something, which "makes up" a policy. In other words, spin is simultaneously a process of managing the presentation of policies and a process that contributes to their construction. A key example here is that certain policies require the demonstration of progress and success and that this in itself becomes an intrinsic feature of the policies rather than something outside of them. This idea is developed more fully later in the chapter.

Another characteristic emphasis in the current debate around spin has been the almost exclusive focus on Downing Street and the central government civil service based in Whitehall as the key sites within which spin is produced and struggled over. In this chapter, we suggest that spin is more endemic to the policy process and the culture of policy making than is suggested by this focus on central government. Thus we look more broadly at a range of sites into which the culture and practices of spin have penetrated (e.g., local authorities, zones, schools, teacher unions, private companies as well as the DfES). In doing so, we attempt to trace the ambiguous and conflicting rationales and interests that are played out in struggles over the production of spin/policy in and across these different sites.

NOT ONLY BUT ALSO

How we understand the underlying rationale for New Labour's commitment to impression management depends on which of New Labour's spins on the policy of spin we believe—as it would seem that the Government's finely tuned art of spin has also subtly been applied to the strategy of spin itself. Thus those on "the left" are encouraged to believe that spin is necessary to render traditional Labour policies underpinned by commitments to redistribution and social justice palatable to "middle England" by dressing them up as being business-friendly. In contrast, the rationale for spin constructed to appeal to those on the right is that business-friendly policies need to be cloaked in a language of social justice in order to secure the support of "the left." New Labour's extensive use of the strategy of "double coding"—the "not-only-but-also" discursive repertoire (Fairclough, 2000), which is particularly reflected in the discourse of the "third way" (Gewirtz, 1999)—enables these two mutually exclusive readings of its rationale for spin to co-exist side by side.

The EAZ policy was presented at its launch as emblematic of New Labour's third way. The policy was a New Labour "flagship" which would raise standards in disadvantaged areas—areas subject to nearly two decades of Conservative neglect—whilst at the same time allowing business to get more involved in the running of schools. Civil Servant A, in the quote reproduced in the introduction to this chapter, described the launch as a model of policy development in that it got "good attention … plenty of column inches [and] air time" and the "message was right." There are a number of senses in which this civil servant thinks that the message was "right." As he goes on to explain, first, the policy was emblematic of New Labour's policy agenda and, second, the focus on EAZs meant that attention could be deflected away from other potentially more troublesome aspects of the Bill:

> They were a symbol of New Labour because they were about innovation addressing disadvantage. They've got the sort of core Labour values of addressing disadvantage and the New Labour angle on it which is new ways of doing it, so they were a very good symbol for the reform and put the focus on achievement whereas a lot of the Bill's actually about the technical details of governing bodies and some of which is very boring, and in any case we didn't particularly want to debate it in public at length cause it would all be about—if you had a big debate about that it would be about abolishing the grant maintained sector, which would not be a very constructive debate. (Civil Servant A)

The message conveyed by the announcement of the policy was also "right" in the sense that it complied with the message the Downing Street press office was insisting at that time that all department's convey (i.e., that New Labour was a "modernizing government," "for all the people," "delivering on its promises," with "mainstream policies" providing new directions for Britain (memo quoted in Franklin 1998, p. 12)). And the double-coded nature of the message—that EAZs were simultaneously promoting social justice and enterprise—enabled the policy to be received enthusiastically across the political spectrum of the mainstream media. Thus, for example, Martin Bright and Patrick Wintour (1998) of The Observer[10] could write of Britain's "whirlwind of reform" that it was designed not only to make "our state schools safe for Middle England" but also "to prove that the system can deliver on its early egalitarian promise." Whilst at the same time an article in The Times (O'Leary, 1998) could welcome the opportunity the policy gave for allowing businesses a greater role in the provision of education, whilst acknowledging that it had not been taken up in practice.

However, whilst the policy was *presented* as central not only to New Labour's education agenda but to its social policy agenda more widely, Civil Servant A claims that the initiative was not necessarily "really" viewed as particularly central at the time. On his account, there was a core agenda which was "the basic approach to dealing with school standards, like putting data in a system, giving schools responsibilities, disseminating better practice, intervening where schools aren't working, the literacy strategy, the numeracy strategy" and it was this core agenda that was central. The EAZ policy, on the other hand, was simply one of a number of initiatives the Government was trying out:

> I couldn't have said in 1997 which of our policies would become the central planks and which weren't. I would always have known that the National Literacy Strategy was, and the National Numeracy Strategy were the top priority so I could have predicted that, but the others you're doing a range of things … you're trying things out and some of them will be big successes and some of them will become things you tried out but didn't work quite as you expected. (Civil Servant A)

SPIN AS DYNAMIC

The spin that has been put on the policy by the DfEE/S has not been static. Whilst the double coding has been present throughout, the mix in the "message" has shifted to some extent as the policy has developed. For example, the earlier press releases and ministerial announcements emphasized the radical nature of the policy and its potential for creating innovative approaches to tackling disadvantage, holding it up as a "flagship" and a test-bed for the "future of public service delivery." In the initial bidding guidance particular care was taken to ensure that the role of business was made to seem paramount. Indeed, according to one of the civil servants who drafted the guidance (Civil Servant B), one of the changes that the Secretary of State for Education's special advisor, Conor Ryan, made to the EAZ documentation was to change the order of the partners (schools, local education authorities (LEAs), parents and business) so that business came first. As we shall see when we discuss the later development of the policy, in retrospect it seems that the spin-doctors may have got the balance wrong and the prominence given to business back fired.

Later press releases and comments tended to be more muted, and increasingly the EAZ policy was eclipsed by another policy for improving education provision in disadvantaged areas—Excellence in Cities (EIC)—which seemed to take over as the flagship initiative.

As the EAZ policy progressed, there was also a shift in the spin away from emphasis on business leadership. For example, the press notice announcing the establishment of second round zones was headlined "Schools leading second round of Education Action Zones" and in the text businesses were mentioned alongside (and after) parents as partners whom the initiators—head teachers and schools—had sought to involve. Thus here head teachers and schools were constructed as the active agents, and parents and businesses were cast in a more passive role in the sense that they were presented as having become involved as a consequence of head teacher initiative.

Later press releases also focused more on the policy's "successes." The key discourses here were EAZs "making a difference" and the "celebration of success." Thus, for instance, the press release accompanying the announcement of the second round zones provided some examples of EAZs "making a difference both in terms of performance and securing sponsorship." These included Wigan's "companies in classrooms" initiative which the press notice claims had led to improvements in pupils' work. "Parents as Educators" was identified as "one of the key successes within the [Blackburn with Darwen] EAZ—with over 160 parents having completed the course by the end of last term—smashing the target of 60 originally set...." The press release also claims that Newham's "competency based staff development model ... has resulted in the number of teachers leaving EAZ schools this summer down 28% on a year ago, compared with a 1% fall for the whole of Newham!" The language of "smashing targets," "making a difference" and the liberal use of exclamation marks has strong echoes of commercial styles of promotion.

In autumn 2000 figures were released which purported to show that the EAZ policy was directly contributing to rising SATs[11] scores, particularly in primary schools in the zones. Issue 2 of the DfEE's newsletter for zones announced that:

> Across the country zone schools have been celebrating some encouraging GCSE[12] and KS results. These show a positive trend, with year-on-year improvements in zone schools above—and sometimes well above—the national average ... On this page we pick out some of the zones where results have been particularly creditable and encouraging. If your zone has achieved similar or better results but is not featured this time—congratulations anyway!

The claims made by the DfEE about improved performance were at some variance with our own analysis of the performance data for EAZ schools, which show a more mixed picture (Power et al., 2003). Doubts also need to be raised about the validity of making claims about the impact of EAZs a) over such a short timescale (the first EAZs had been up and running for less than two years when the initial claims about improving performance were made; and b) when so many other changes were being implemented at the same time. Indeed many of the head teachers we spoke to were themselves acutely aware of the impossibility of isolating out the effects of zone status when so many other government initiatives were simultaneously having an impact on schools.

Part of the explanation for the shifts in emphasis in the spin was the negative reporting of the policy following a speech by Michael Barber (then head of the DfEE's Standards and Effectiveness Unit) to the North of England Education Conference where the bidding guidance was launched. The civil servants and teacher association officials we interviewed all saw this event as a key turning point in the policy's fortunes. In the speech Barber had mentioned that the DfEE expected one of the first round Zones to be "led and run" by business. In response to a question from one of the delegates, Barber stated that zones could be run for profit and he provided the names of some companies which might be interested in such a possibility. The press reporting of the event that evening and the next day focused on the zones as a privatisation story. According to the civil servants we interviewed, this was seen to be and thus was very damaging to the policy. Indeed, this "negative" press reporting was held in large part to be responsible for the policy's demise. More specifically, these civil servants were arguing that the privatisation spin that the press put on Barber's speech fuelled teacher opposition to the policy which in turn hampered the activities of local EAZ partnerships, and that the speech was, therefore, a major miscalculation. As Civil Servant A commented, the DfEE had not anticipated that this was a big news story. If it had been, a Minister would have made the announcement. Furthermore, under the Government's strict press management regime all major print and broadcast media appearances, the policy content of major speeches, press releases, new policy initiatives and the timing of announcements must be cleared by Downing Street (the Prime Minister's office) (Mountfield, 1997). The launching of the bidding guidance was not considered to be a major news story as Barber was not announcing anything that was not already in the public domain. It was thought to be "a purely technical matter" (Civil Servant A) and so it was not felt to be necessary to clear it with Downing Street. This was, according to Civil Servant A amongst others, a mistake which was presented to us as having "dire consequences for the policy" because:

> everybody thought it was a privatisation story, which is how it got written. Whereas it was never a privatisation story, it was never a privatisation policy but that's how it got written in the press, so then the unions and the local authorities and everybody out there thinks that's what it is even though it wasn't that. (Civil Servant A)

> the problem with the speech was that it over-hyped the expectations for the policy.... I think after that, you know, the education correspondents, having all written up this great sort of privatisation story, were determined that unless there was a radical, huge privatisation that the policy was going to be dumped ... after that the media were totally setting the agenda on Education Action Zones. And, you know, it happens with some policies. People seem to think that we are able to greatly manipulate the agenda on these things. I would say, after January 1998 the media had total control of the agenda and I

think there was almost an inevitability that they were going to damn Education Action Zones from then on in. (Civil Servant D)

The role of the private sector, on Civil Servant A's account, was "a kind
of small bit of the policy that had a huge consequence."

One possible reading of this version of the policy's demise—as emanating from the media reporting of the North of England speech—is that it
represents part of a sophisticated strategy of spin designed to deflect attention from what might be viewed as fundamental flaws in the policy by blaming "mischievous" journalists, local government officials and trade union
activists—or a failure of spin—for the policy's demise. Such flaws include
the decision to establish EAZs as separate legal entities, which resulted in
enormous administrative costs; and the short time scale allowed for the
establishment of the first round zones. The latter meant that many zones
were established without consultation with teachers and parents, and,
according to one source (Civil Servant C), in some cases applications for
zone status were submitted without even head teachers knowing their
schools were included in a bid. Rather than focusing on these flaws, it is
more convenient for those responsible for promoting New Labour policies
to focus on the spin:

> So we made a mistake in the actual drafting of the policy documents. We
> obviously made a mistake in thinking it was a technical thing, not a press
> story, and we were then on the defensive and it's actually the consequence of
> that for the policy. You know a lot of the very shallow policy comments you
> get on the Today program[13] and so on and you get this comment about New
> Labour especially that it's spin not substance, and this story's the perfect
> example of how you can't separate the two. They're actually—they're inte-
> grally related. If you get the story wrong it actually affects the policy, whereas
> if you get the story right then it gives it a really good. (Civil Servant A)

This failure of spin seems to have had knock on effects for how the policy was subsequently spun. Thus, as we pointed out above, there was less of
an emphasis on business leadership and more on the role of schools in initiating bids; there was an increased emphasis on celebrating success; and
mention of EAZs became rarer as the EIC program, as the new flagship
policy, eclipsed them.

At one point the Secretary of State for Education at the time, David
Blunkett, explicitly "admitted" to the press that some of the difficulties the
EAZ policy had faced stemmed from the fact that it had been "over-hyped"
at the outset. This "admission" in itself should perhaps not simply be read
as an "innocent" expression of Blunkett's candid views on the policy. It is
possible, for example—and, of course, we are speculating here—that Blunkett's "admission" was contrived as part of the new strategy of spin which

had been designed to limit the damage caused by the fact that the policy was about to be dropped by the DfEE. Certainly, the strict regime of press management emanating from Downing Street (Franklin, 1998) means that we have to be skeptical about the possible existence of any innocent announcements.

SPIN AS ENDEMIC—THE CASCADING CULTURE OF SPIN AND ITS DISCIPLINARY EFFECTS

The DfEE/S civil servants, based in Sanctuary Buildings, used a variety of strategies to ensure that "appropriate" messages about the EAZ policy got out. For example, all press releases and policy documents were shown to Blunkett's special advisor, Conor Ryan, so that he could check that the "right" message was being conveyed. However, it was not just via the press that the civil servants were aiming to impress the public. The DfEE's EAZ newsletter, from which we have quoted above, was produced presumably both to raise morale in EAZs and schools at a local level and to convey the key messages about the policy that schools in turn were meant to convey to their local "communities."

Academic researchers were viewed as another vehicle for spin. One of the civil servants we had contact with (Civil Servant E) appeared to have as one of his briefs keeping an eye on academic researchers and trying to persuade them to tell the "right" story. Thus, for example, in our meetings with this civil servant we were asked for information as to which academics were researching EAZs and who was funding them. In one meeting one of us presented him (and the three colleagues he brought with him) with one of our interim reports. The civil servants' response to our report was that we were asking the wrong questions, and one of our research questions—which was concerned with the relationship between the state and civil society—was rather mockingly described as resembling a secondary school essay question. In a critical analysis of New Labour's approach to news management, Franklin (1998) has written of the government's attempts to directly control journalists through a system of punishment and reward. Friendly journalists who produce pro-New Labour copy are rewarded with "exclusives." Those who write critical stories are ignored, harangued or publicly humiliated (Viner, 1997, cited in Franklin, 1998, p. 7). One of the best publicized examples of New Labour's bullying news management tactics is the leaked letter sent to the BBC by New Labour's director of communications, Dave Hill. The letter was sent following an interview on the Today program (see footnote 13) by the radio journalist John Humphrys with the then Social Security Secretary, Harriet Harman, in which Harman was pressed about the Government's decision to cut benefit for lone-parent families. The letter threatened a Government withdrawal of cooperation with the program—i.e., not allowing Ministers to appear. More sinisterly, Andrew Neil, former editor of the News International-owned Sunday Times, has suggested that prior to the 1997 General Election, Tony Blair made a pact with the proprietor of News International, Rupert Murdoch, in which Blair effectively promised favorable treatment of Murdoch's media interests in return for favorable treatment of the Labour Party both in the run up to the election and once the Party was in government (Franklin, 1998).

Although the tactics used with us were not as strong armed as this, it would seem that similar tactics might be being employed with academic researchers in order to control research. This kind of approach can encourage self-censorship when access is seen to be dependent on saying the "right" things about policies.

So far we have focused on Sanctuary Buildings as the key site of spin production and "news management." However spin has been produced in a variety of sites. At a local level, EAZs and schools were themselves involved in developing strategies of spin. In our experience, most head teachers, whether working within an EAZ or not, are highly skilled spinners. Interviews with head teachers are frequently characterized by their attempts to present themselves and their schools in glowing terms, and this has long been the case. Indeed, it is head teachers' skills of impression management that presumably have played a key role in securing their appointment to headships in the first place. However, the EAZ policy has produced a range of additional incentives for spin. The DfEE/S explicitly conveyed to EAZs the importance of celebrating the successes of the policy. As Civil Servant C explains, extreme pressure was put on EAZs to demonstrate that they were "making a difference" and this pressure was seen to have emanated from the fact that the press had initially "savaged the policy":

> The biggest disappointment was, having launched the initiative, to see how the press just savaged it and, because the press savaged it, the politicians then wanted information to sort of defend it, so we were in a bizarre situation where the people from above on floor 7 of Sanctuary Buildings [were] demanding facts—what has the zone achieved? And this was in the … end of September [1998]. Well sorry, they've achieved, they've got a forum together. Yes, but you know, how [much] better are the results? … I then had to go back to the project directors and they were concerned because I was asking them questions they couldn't answer, and as much as I tried to wrap it up and work with them to find creative ways to answer that question, it was unrealistic so time scale demands were huge. (Civil Servant C)

The EAZ directors in turn conveyed the vital importance of celebrating success to head teachers who in turn impressed it upon teachers involved in aspects of local EAZ programmes.

The incentive for spin was rooted not only in direct pressure from the DfEE/S conveyed via its EAZ "advisors," but also emanated from another form of pressure—the short term nature of EAZ funding. EAZs were initially funded for a three-year period, potentially renewable to five. In order to secure the extension of their funding, EAZs needed to "demonstrate" success.

Again at this local level, academic researchers were seen to have a key role to play. Most of the initial bids for EAZ status included reference to proposed university evaluations of the zone presumably because of the signal this gave that evaluation was being taken seriously by the zone. And on several occasions zone directors and/or other forum members took us to task on comments we had made in our interim reports that might have been construed in negative terms either by the DfEE/S or other readers. The letter cited in the introduction to this chapter by one EAZ grouping exemplifies the kinds of attempts that were made to influence our output. One zone director went as far as to tell us that our report was inappropriate because it was not "celebrating success."

Other institutions, which were key sites of spin production, included the teacher associations and private companies. In some cases there was also a significant merging of such sites. For example, the National Union of Teachers (NUT)[14] commissioned a report by the private consultancy firm PriceWaterhouse Coopers (PWC) on the EAZ policy. Whilst the Union has a longstanding relationship with PWC, the choice of a private company to conduct EAZ research can also be seen as part of a strategy of spin being developed by the Union—a strategy perhaps designed to convince the government specifically that the research has a particular kind of credibility and more generally that the NUT is not fundamentally hostile to the private sector and therefore should perhaps be more trusted/listened to. The resultant document tells a story about the EAZs with its own distinctive double-coded spin which appears to bring together the interests of the NUT and the interests of PWC—a company which has a growing financial interest in the education sector. Thus on the one hand the PWC/NUT report identifies professional development "as one of the programme's most successful achievements":

Both the NUT survey [of teachers in EAZs] and our fieldwork, indicate that [professional development] opportunities have increased significantly, that in the main these are of reasonably high quality, and that there is an increasing trend for these opportunities to be appropriately based on the needs of teachers themselves. Investment in the professional development of staff is likely to produce sustainable improvement in a way in which, for example, additional support staff does not, in that there will be a benefit after additional funding has been withdrawn. (PWC 2000, para 29)

In terms of lessons for the profession emerging from our evaluation, the main finding is that involvement in programmes such as EAZs offers many advantages, both in terms of creating better opportunities for the pupils they teach, and in terms of their own professional development. These advantages included an increased level of collegiality, the opportunity to exercise greater creativity and the chance to see welcome additional funding directed towards the pupils. (para 43)

These comments clearly relate closely to the NUT's agenda of persuading the government to invest more in schools and in professional development. The language of celebrating success in which they are couched can be seen as, at least in part, a strategic device to persuade the government both of the legitimacy of the NUT and its specific arguments in the report. There is also an emphasis in the report on encouraging the Government to "trust teachers and others to deliver" (para 41) and on success being dependent on "an appropriate level of professional involvement and consultation ... a large degree of local autonomy" (para 46). The "making a difference in the classroom" discourse is also present:

Our own impression is that teachers have been willing to accommodate change where they have seen a link to improving opportunities for pupils. (para 45)

At the same time, the report identifies as another of the research's "wider messages for government" the value of business involvement:

In terms of learning points that go more widely than the EAZ program, DfEE appears to have moved on from the model of separate statutory EAZs in terms of future area based improvement programmes. New programs will be either within Excellence in Cities, or in the form of Excellence Clusters, which will work within the LEA framework ... however, we note that business involvement is not a requirement of the Clusters. We would ask the DfEE to consider whether there is merit in ensuring that wider partnerships with business and the community can be created and, if so, how to achieve this. (paras 38 and 39)

The Conclusion elides the two codes in the double coding, that is the two sets of concerns about the value of teacher involvement and professional development on the one hand and the value of business involvement on the other within an overall discourse of success:

> The EAZ program itself appears to have been largely successful both in involving teachers and in many of the subsequent achievement [sic]. It has shown there is merit in providing funds for locally managed initiatives, and that teachers, heads, businesses and pupils can benefit as a result. (para 47)

These are just some examples of the endemic nature of spin, of how it is produced in a variety of settings in addition to Whitehall. The rationales for the spin are diverse. The rationale is often simultaneously personal and institutional—i.e., individual's jobs or opportunities for promotion depend, or are seen to depend, on the perceived success of the policy. This applies as much to civil servants in Sanctuary Buildings as it does to EAZ project directors, teachers, learning mentors and support assistants. For some within the DfEE, the rationale was possibly as much about furthering the reputation of the DfEE within government, as it was about promoting the policy to "the people." The "flagship" spin that was initially put on the policy enabled the DfEE to be viewed in turn as a flagship, can-do, archly loyal New Labour department, thus enhancing its image within government. This was an impression also promoted by the fact that the Department was the first to produce a bill—within 4 months of New Labour coming to power.

However, whilst the rationales for spin were diverse, some of the similarities in the content of the spin are striking. Thus, for example, the discourses of "celebrating success" and "making a difference" were just as evident in the PWC/NUT report as they were in the DfEE press releases as they were in the way in which some head teachers presented the initiative to us. In Foucauldian terms, spin can be seen to operate simultaneously as a form of both sovereign and disciplinary power. We have clear evidence of direct pressure on EAZs to promote their successes by DfEE officials. But it is also the knowledge that DfEE officials can potentially observe large swathes of EAZ activity, the knowledge of the existence of a DfEE "gaze"—for example, DfEE officials are included on EAZ director appointment panels and the fora that are meant to run EAZs—which may function to "prompt" individuals to ensure that the "right" message is conveyed.

Those involved in implementing EAZ policy are not of course passive agents in all of this—unwittingly speaking and playing out the discourses that the DfEE has made available to them. There are varying degrees of reflexivity and cynicism about the process. Some of those we interviewed spoke the New Labour discourse as if it had been wholly internalised and as if it was wholeheartedly believed in. Members of this group appeared to lack any consciousness that they were even speaking a specifically New Labour discourse in the first place. However, others were clearly aware of the strategic importance of language and were able to consciously, and sometimes cynically, move across a range of discursive repertoires for strategic purposes.

SPIN AS CONSTITUTIVE

So far we have discussed the way in which spin is used as a strategy of impression management. We have emphasised that spin is both dynamic and endemic. In the previous section we also suggested that spin acts in a disciplinary fashion. A key way in which the disciplinary ends of spin are achieved can be seen in its constitutive nature. That is the spin plays a role in creating reality at the same time as representing it. For in order to produce the relevant spin, social and educational practices need to be transformed in particular ways.

We have numerous examples, for instance, of the way in which school practices have been re-orientated to enable EAZs to demonstrate success in the narrow performance indicators that they are expected to meet and celebrate:

> I am not convinced that some of the results being publicized by some Zone schools are true reflections of true achievement. I think there has been so much pressure to push up results that I think we've had schools making the decision that Year 2 and Year 6 are SAT years so we have deprived children of what I call [a] rich balanced curriculum, and I know that because my Year 6 teacher talks to other Year 6 teachers and knows what's going on. (Head teacher, Primary School, Nairnton)

> I do feel very cynical about it ... I really thought the money was going to support inequalities, but it wasn't, it was going to improve results. Now ultimately yes of course, children learning to read will support their life chances, but I mean current research is showing that a lot of these improvements and results are actually quite false ... (Head teacher, Primary School, Wellford)

Frequently in interviews, those involved in implementing the policy at a local level complained about how the emphasis on the production of short term results had diverted attention from activities which are viewed either as intrinsically worthwhile but not relevant to SATs performance or as having a longer term benefit to those who participated.

Within the DfEE also there is evidence of the way in which spin may have played a constitutive role in the drafting of legislation. Comments made to us by Civil Servant A, quoted on p. 105, above, suggest that the highlighting of the EAZ policy in the press announcement of the Schools Standards and Framework Bill was prompted in part by concerns to deflect media and public attention away from the provisions to abolish grant-maintained schools which were included in the same Bill. The abolition of the grant-maintained sector was a sensitive issue and potentially a source of discontent with those sections of the electorate New Labour was particularly concerned to woo—i.e., "middle England" (see footnote 8). However, the decision to include EAZs in the legislation in the first place may itself have been driven by concerns to deflect attention from this potentially unpopular policy. According to Civil Servant B, the civil servants working on the legislation had counselled against having primary legislation for the EAZ policy because it was viewed as simply unnecessary. Everything that ministers wanted EAZs to be able to do could, they argued, already be done under existing legislation. However, according to this version of events, Stephen Byers, the Schools Standards minister at the time, insisted there had to be some primary legislation, and so the decision was made to set EAZs up as separate statutory bodies.

Now there are a number of possible explanations for why Byers insisted on primary legislation. One interpretation given to us by one of the civil servants responsible for drafting the legislation was that this was simply an instance of macho politicking. Byers, according to this interpretation, had legislation drawn up for the reason that other men purchase large and powerful cars. A second possible explanation is that for Byers the primary purpose of EAZs was to erode the taken-for-granted assumption that LEAs should automatically be viewed as the sole provider of state schooling. On this explanation, by establishing EAZs as separate statutory bodies, the Government was paving the way for private companies to take over the running of clusters of schools from LEAs. However, as later developments showed, it was quite possible for private companies to be given a major role in the provision of schooling and to take over the running of schools from LEAs without the creation of separate statutory bodies. A third possible explanation, which is not incompatible with the first two, is that by enshrining EAZs in legislation, the Government was creating a big "good news" story that could eclipse the bad news of the loss of resources for grant-maintained schools.

If it is the case that the EAZs were incorporated into the Bill partly for image management purposes—whether the image that was being managed was that of Byers himself or of New Labour's education reforms—then this turned out to be a costly public relations exercise. The separate statutory status of EAZs generated much red tape and was largely responsible for the high proportion of EAZ funds which were diverted to administration; and it is these excessive administration costs which appear to have contributed, at least in part, to the policy's quiet demise.

CONCLUSION

In this chapter we have drawn attention to the dynamic and endemic characteristics of spin. Clearly spin cannot explain everything about the development of a policy. Indeed we have suggested in this chapter that some of the policy makers we have interviewed may have been using spin and the failure of spin as a convenient excuse for the failure of the policy—convenient because it acts as a means of deflecting attention from some of the flaws in the EAZ policy. In other words, the failure of the policy has been explained as a failure of spin rather than as a consequence of a policy that was flawed in other ways. However, whilst key policy players might at times have exaggerated the constitutive nature of spin in some respects, there are other ways (not acknowledged by policy makers) in which spin is constitutive which are important. In particular the emphasis on "celebrating success" and "making a difference" has contributed to a refocusing of EAZ resources on activities that can make an immediately measurable (yet perhaps superficial) difference in the classroom. And we have suggested that the decision to give EAZs a distinct statutory status, a decision that has incurred significant administration costs, may in part have been generated by concerns of spin.

Criticism of New Labour's preoccupation with spin and what has been called its control freakery has centred on its adverse implications for democracy. First, there is a concern about the politicisation of the civil service and the fact that its traditional "neutrality" is being even more heavily compromised than ever before so that there is an increasing blurring of the boundaries between party political interests and the interests of "effective" government. Second, there is a concern about the impact of centralised control and government spin on the nature of public discourse. The concern here is that the colonisation by government of large swathes of the media means that critical public debate has, to a significant extent, been stifled. Franklin has argued that in the process of colluding with the government "the media obfuscate rather than clarify policy choices" (1998, p. 16). This in turn has, he suggests, contributed to the production of a passive and de-politicised political culture, where "politics, like football, has been transformed ... into a largely spectator sport with viewers inclined to watch the match from the comfort of their favorite armchair rather than becoming embroiled in the game" (Franklin, 1998, p. 17).

Fairclough (2000) argues that the predominant mode of communication between the New Labour government and the public tends to be promotional rather than dialogical. For Fairclough, essential characteristics of genuine dialogue are that people are free to disagree, their differences are recognized, there is equality of opportunity for people to participate in it and there is space for consensus but consensus cannot be guaranteed. Yet in their communications with "the public," for example, in green papers, the government exudes certainty—"readers are hardly ever asked, they are told. And although in the nature of things there is a great deal of uncertainty, readers are told things as if they are certain—there are no "maybes" or "perhaps." Neither questions nor "maybes" sit easily within promotion. The Government's green papers may be "reader friendly" but they are also "reader directive" (Fairclough, 2000, pp. 13, 136–137; see also CPPR, 2002).

However, our research suggests that spin has implications not only for the relationship between the government and "the public" but also for the policy process. In evaluating policies it is important not only to analyze their main "planks" and see spin as something that interferes with, distorts or obscures the analysis. In addition, we need to see spin as an important object of analysis in its own right and an object, which has real effects on educational and social practices.

NOTES

1. We are grateful to the UK Economic and Social Research Council for funding the study (no. R000238046), to our co-researchers, David Halpin and Geoff Whitty, for their contributions to the collection of the data we are using here and to Alan Cribb for very helpful conversations which have fed into the writing of the chapter. An earlier version of this chapter was included in a Special Issue of the *Journal of Education Policy* (Vol. 19, No. 3, May, 2004), and we would like to thank the journal editors for allowing us to present the material here.

2. The British Labour party repackaged itself as "New Labour" in the run up to the 1997 General Election, signifying a shift away from traditional Labour connotations of working-class representation, nationalisation and overtly re-distributive policies. This process of repackaging, of which the expression "New Labour" is just one part, is characteristic of the current Government's preoccupation with impression management, which is the subject of this paper.

3. These are the statutory authorities traditionally responsible for the organisation of educational provision at a local level. As a result of a series of reforms since 1988 many of their powers have been eroded through being devolved to schools or taken over by central government. In addition, the role of the private sector in the provision of educational services has increased.

4. Grant-maintained schools were state-funded schools, which received their funds directly from central government and operated independently of LEAs. They had been introduced by a Conservative government in 1988 as part of a wider attempt to introduce more market "diversity" into the education system. The Labour Government abolished the grant-maintained sector under the same legislation, which established EAZs. The coming together of provisions to abolish the grant-maintained sector and to estab-

lish EAZs in the same Act of Parliament is potentially significant for understanding the spin-policy relationship, as we discuss below.

5.   This chapter makes use of several quotes from Civil Servant A. This reflects the fact that Civil Servant A was a key informant who was centrally involved in the development and implementation of the EAZ policy.

6.   The DfEE is the government department with responsibility for education policy. It was renamed the Department for Education and Skills (DfES) in 2001.

7.   Right-wing tabloid newspaper whose readership is typically viewed as emblematic of conservative-minded lower middle-class voters, whose support the Labour Party needs if the Party is to be successful in elections.

8.   Middle England is a term popularized by media political analysis and used to capture conservative-minded middle-class voters often associated with non-metropolitan areas and rural living.

9.   Classically, urban centers of the old "heavy" industries.

10. A centre-left Sunday broadsheet.

11. SATs (Standard Assessment Tasks) are national tests in English, Maths and Science taken by students at the end of three "Key Stages." Key Stage 1 covers school years 1–2, Key Stage 2, years 3–6 and Key Stage 3, years 7–9. Schools have to set targets for the percentage of students in a given year reaching the "expected level" in the SATs for each Key Stage and the results are published, providing a "key indicator" used to judge the performance of schools.

12. General Certificate of Secondary Education examinations are national examinations usually taken by students at the end of Key Stage 4 (school years 10 and 11). The results are published. The percentage of students getting at least 5 A-C grades at GCSE is used by the government and the press as the key indicator for comparing the performance of secondary schools.

13. BBC Radio 4's "flagship" current affairs program.

14. The largest teacher union in England

REFERENCES

Bright, M., & Wintour, P. (1998). Revolution in Schools. *The Observer*, 29 Nov.

CPPR (Centre for Public Policy Research). (2002). Achieving Success? Discursive strategies and policy tensions in New Labour's White Paper for schools. *Education and Social Justice*, 4(1), 15–25.

Cockerill, M., Hennessy, P., & Walker, D. (1984). *Sources close to the Prime Minister: Inside the hidden world of the news manipulators*. London: Macmillan.

DfEE (Department for Education and Employment). (1998). £75 million boosts radical education action zones to raise standards. DfEE Press Release, 23 June.

Esser, E., Reinemann, C., & Fan, D. (2000). Spin doctoring in British and German election campaigns. *Journal of Communication*, 15(2), 209–239.

Fairclough, N. (2000). *New labour, new language*. London: Routledge.

Franklin, B. (1998). *Tough on soundbites, tough on the causes of soundbites: New Labour and news management* (Catalyst Paper 3). London: The Catalyst Trust.

Gaber, I. (2000). Government by spin: an analysis of the process. *Media, Culture and Society, 22,* 507–518.

Gewirtz, S. (1999). Education Action Zones: emblems of the "third way." In H. Dean & R. Woods (Eds.), *Social policy review 11.* Luton: Social Policy Association.

Jones, N. (1995). *Soundbites and spin doctors.* London: Cassell.

Mountfield, R. (1997). *Report on the Working Group on the Government Information Service.* London: Cabinet Office/HMSO.

O'Leary, J. (1998). State and the obvious: private business can do it. *The Times,* 11 September.

Power, S., Gerwitz, S., Halpin, D., & Whitty, G. (2003). *Paving a third way? A policy trajectory analysis of Education Action Zones,* ESRC end-of-award report. Available at: http://www.regard.ac.uk/research_findings/R000238046/report.pdf

Rawnsley, A. (2002). It's the Tories who are addicted to spin. *The Observer,* Sunday July 11.

Riddell, P. (1998). Members and millbank: The media and Parliament. In J. Seaton (Ed.), *Politics and the media: Harlots and prerogatives at the turn of the millenium.* Oxford: Blackwell.

Viner, K. (1997). The ministry of truth. *Guardian,* 9 August: 3.

Wright, T (1998). Inside the whale: The media from Parliament. In J Seaton (Ed.), *Politics and the media: Harlots and prerogatives at the turn of the millennium.* Oxford: Blackwell.

CHAPTER 6

THE MODERN TEACHER

A Textual Analysis
of Educational Restructuration

Meg Maguire
Centre for Public Policy Research,
Department of Education and Professional Studies
Kings College, London

INTRODUCTION

For some time, research in the UK and elsewhere has charted the way that teacher education and what it means to be a teacher has been susceptible to reforms and restructuring in the light of market disciplines and new managerialism (Lawn, 1995; Lingard, 1995; NCTAF, 1996; Gewirtz, 1997; Darling-Hammond & Sykes, 1999; Ball, 1999; Apple, 2001). As Furlong et al. (2000, p 163) have argued, "Systemic change in education, including teacher education, is... a transnational phenomenon and not just a peculiarity of the English." "New policy frameworks have been *done* to teachers who have been perceived as implementers of policies framed elsewhere and by other people" (Lingard, 1995, p 1). In England, as elsewhere, educational reforms have been tied in with marketisation and standards and

Educational Restructuring: International Perspectives on Traveling Policies, pages 121–141
Copyright © 2004 by Information Age Publishing

consequently, the need to reform teachers has been part of this movement. In this paper, I intend to examine how these reforms are discursively brought off in the English setting. In what follows I want to concentrate on one dominant motif in what Hartley (2001) has called the social policy lexicon of New Labour; that is, the move to modernisation.

Some time ago, Black and Coward (1981) highlighted the way in which a desire to move beyond a reductive account of the social formation generated discussions about the role of ideology and language. Discursive formations, they argued, were involved in the shaping of social practices and had outcomes in materiality. They suggested that an analysis of discursive activity could illustrate how ideas and beliefs functioned as systems of power and control. An engagement with language and meanings could assist in the uncovering of a complex and parallel process. It could reveal the naturalness through which policies are authenticated but also disclose the contradictions, oppositions, gaps and taken for granted assumptions which are also involved. As Clarke and Newman (1998, p 4) have argued more recently, " for a discourse to achieve the hegemonic position of being the accepted or taken for granted truth, the competing alternatives must have been overcome."

In this paper my intention is to undertake a textual review of modernisation in relation to the project of reforming the teacher. Modernisation is a key motif in the glossary of New Labour and has been carefully and repeatedly deployed in speeches, documents, Green and White papers[1] as well as in formal legislation in the UK. My purpose in this focus on text—and one specific discursive move—is to illustrate the way in which discursive practices play a powerful, if sometimes un-remarked, role in shaping social policy. The skilful deployment of particular discourses works to control, set and manage policy agendas. So, there is a need to identify and examine these powerful discursive attempts to establish common sense reforms and sideline any policy alternatives. In starting this review it is necessary to outline the way in which New Labour has deployed and continues to deploy modernisation more widely.

MODERNIZATION AND NEW LABOUR

"The Prime Minister has made the modernisation of Britain a key theme of the new Labour administration" (Kelly, 1999, foreword). Indeed, modernisation has been a key tool in the restructuring of the British Labour Party. Kenny and Smith (2001) argue that the British Labour Party has always utilised a version of modernisation. However, since the early 1980s, and particularly under the leadership of Neil Kinnock, the UK Labour Party has actively worked to seek re-election as a modernising and modern movement. In the long years of opposition (1979–1997), the Labour Party positioned itself as new and as modern both in an attempt to separate itself off from its immediate past as well as from traditionalist moral-majority (but not the economics of) aspects of Conservatism. Kenny and Smith see modernization as a contested rhetorical device which contains a range of narratives and which is consequently characterised by a large degree of ambiguity. This ambiguity has been seized on and worked and reworked by New Labour in its policy statements. In so many ways, modernization has an almost unassailable appeal. Who cannot be in favour of being modern? This appeal is used to drive forward the policies of New Labour. "Politicians… are skilled in neutralizing the social movements that have brought them to power," Bourdieu, (1998, p. 93) and modernization is one of these neutralising devices.

> In many usages the term modernization has become infused with a sense of ineluctable progress, and is strongly teleological. In the political realm, modernization is frequently used to signal the need to bring the political world into line with changes conceived to have occurred in other domains, principally society, economics and culture. (Kenny & Smith, 2001, pp. 238–239)

In trying to unravel the ways in which New Labour has utilized modernization, it has been difficult to elicit exactly what is intended in the policy documents themselves. In all these documents, modern is used without any qualification. This itself is a regulating device. For example, New Labour has published documents such as *The Way Forward—A Modernised Framework for School Governance* (DfEE, 2001). Strikingly, while modernisation appears in the title and as a heading towards the end (p. 27) it is never explained. Instead, terms like "flexible," "delivering the freedoms" and "fresh approach" are used synonymously with modern. There are however some contradictions, such as: "keeping the best of the current arrangements, while modernising the approach to provide for a forward looking framework" (p. 28). Traditions have a part to play in the modernisation thesis of New Labour. The modern can involve the old where the old is the best—so a sleight of hand can transform the old into the new—an Aladdin-like strategy.[2]

Perhaps modernisation is best understood through the work of Giddens, one of the architects of New Labours politics. It is worth citing Giddens at some length in respect of the modernisation thesis. Giddens recognises the way in which modernization has been utilised and in what follows, shows how an Aladdin-like discursive tactic is deployed. Note too, in what follows, the critical placement of "obviously" used to underscore the rightness of the approach:

> The issue of modernization is a basic one for the new politics.... Tony Blairs speeches, for example, are peppered with talk of modernization. But what should modernization be taken to mean? One thing it means, obviously, is the modernization of social democracy itself—the breaking away from classical democratic positions... Modernization... is conscious of the problems and limitations of modernizing processes. It is alive to the need to re-establish continuity and develop social cohesion in a world of erratic transformation... (Giddens, 1998, p. 67)

In the extract, which follows, it is interesting to see the way in which Giddens has explained continuities with the past but has rejected any connections with the immediate political past by moving beyond tradition into a new reflexive social context (see Beck et al., 1994). What is striking is the way in which bits of the old can be incorporated if it is pragmatically useful in forging the new and managing change. What is also striking is what is left out (Hammersley & Atkinson, 1983, p. 143); that is, who decides which aspects of the past are to be respected and whose view (here of science and technology) is to lead?

The theme of philosophic conservatism is central. Modernization and conservatism, of course, are normally treated as opposites. However, we must use the tools of modernity to cope with living in a world beyond tradition and on the other side of nature where risk and responsibility have a new mix.

> Conservatism in this sense has only a loose affinity with the way it has been understood on the political right. It suggests a pragmatic attitude towards coping with change; a nuanced view of science and technology, in recognition of their ambiguous consequences for us; a respect for the past and for history; and in the environmental arena, an adoption of the precautionary principle where feasible. These goals are not only incompatible with a modernizing agenda; they presuppose it. (Giddens, 1998, pp. 67–68)

Modernisation can be attached to any policy development, which is put forward by a modernising government—anything can be modern or new if it is so labelled.

In reading New Labour policy, Kenny and Smith (2001) believe that competing understandings of modernisation can be identified. They suggest that one take on modernization relates to its inevitability in a globalising world. Another view of modernisation is related to the developments in information technology, which require a national/economic response. Kenny and Smith suggest that modernisation has been utilized to distinguish New Labours devolution policies and to stand as a contrast with Conservative national and European strategies; New Labour—the modern party. Kenny and Smith argue that modernisation has been worked with other concepts to reinforce and underpin policy moves. As they say:

The point, in analytic terms, is to decode usages of modernization rhetoric and to probe their meanings in combination with other concepts (Kenny & Smith, 2001, p. 240)

This paper has only time to engage briefly with the contemporary way in which New Labour has taken up modernisation (see Clarke et al., 2000); the intention now is to examine how modernisation has impacted Education, Education, Education.[3]

MODERNIZING EDUCATION

New Labour came to power elected on a strong wave of anti-conservatism as much as on the basis of their much-vaunted policies of modernization; a point they frequently seem to overlook. However, their election manifesto was premised on their commitment towards establishing and maintaining economic stability and then improving public services such as health and education which had been denigrated, demonized and financially cauterized under a series of Conservative governments (1979–1997). As David Blunkett, Secretary of State for Education in the first New Labour government said; "We set out our strategy for achieving our (educational) ambitions in the White paper, Excellence in Schools, published just 67 days after the election" (Blunkett, 1999, p. 5). By any standard, for a new government to be able to publish a White paper on a key area of public service delivery so quickly, testifies to its determination to make changes.

The UK Conservative education legacy, which was inherited by New Labour, is well known and has been well documented (Ball, 1990; Whitty et al., 1993; Gewirtz et al., 1995; Whitty et al., 1998; Gewirtz, 2001). Essentially, education had been subjected to a plethora of discourses of derision(Ball, 1990) in order to mobilise support for the marketised reforms which were put into place, notably through one key piece of legislation; the Education Reform Act of 1988 (ERA). These reforms were extended to incorporate teacher education. Teacher Education, now referred to as Teacher Training in the UK, was restructured in the period of Conservative Government (1979–1997) through a welter of legislation based on a demonisation of teachers and their pre-service preparation. Teachers were blamed for low standards in schools and, it was claimed, they needed to be disciplined and controlled. This process had to start with their professional preparation. Far-reaching and centralising changes in the content and management of courses, more school-based training (to get rid of irksome and irrelevant theory) as well as competence-based assessments (now standards) were introduced in this period. At the same time, various strategies to deregulate training, moving it away from the institutes of higher education and into the work place, were also put into place. All this has also been well documented (Hill, 1990; Maguire et al., 1998; Moore & Atkinson, 1998; Furlong et al., 2000; Furlong, 2002). The Conservative legacy to New Labour in respect of teacher education already contained the contradictions apparent in modernisation; that is, something old and new as well as something pragmatic—Giddens' social cohesion in a world of erratic transformation (Giddens, 1998, p. 67).

The Conservatives located the need for restructuring in discourses of blaming teacher education for in-school failure. As Furlong has argued (Furlong, 2002, p. 23) the deregulators of teacher education brought off change in a particularist way; "their influence was mainly achieved through a complex web of interlocking political networks that took them close to the seat of power. In these circumstances public debate was not necessary." The Conservative deregulators published a series of glossy pamphlets, which were distributed to key individuals (OHear, 1988; Lawlor, 1990). In this way, a small group of ideologues were able to assert that state education was in crisis and standards were unacceptably low. It was argued in these pamphlets that it was essential to wrest control for teacher education away from higher education institutions in order to systematically control the production of teachers and, thus, raise standards.

In 1997, when New Labour came to power, it was clear that the project of restructuring the teacher was to continue—only now the project was located in a new discursive formation—the need to modernize the teaching profession. Blame was still utilized to a degree, but the talk now was of world-class education, and taking up the standards crusade (Blunkett, 1999, p. 5). The extracts, which follow, illustrate the shift into the modernization discourse—the inevitability of modernization and its location in a marketized and managerialist discourse of performance management. As Newman (2000, p. 46) has demonstrated, the modernization project sought to "distance itself from the outright assault on public services" which had been the key feature of Conservative public-welfare policy. The New Labour modernization project was to be a dynamic response to international change:

> The status quo is not an option. After decades of drift, decisive action is required to raise teaching to the front rank of professions. Only by modernisation can we equip our nation for the new century. (Blair, 1998, foreword to DfEE, 1998, p. 5).

> Success in the 21st century will depend crucially on having an ambitious, forward-looking, outward-facing teaching profession in which success is recognised and rewarded. This means a profession, which is well led and properly supported, with teachers who have time to teach and keep their skills up to date. We need a profession, which is perceived by society as leading us into

the learning society and in which ambitious graduates see opportunities for rapid career advancement. Our educators need to have the same confidence in themselves, the same ambition, the same relish for change, that we find in our best businesses. (Blunkett, 1999, p. 10)

Since coming to government in 1997, New Labour has produced swathes of documentation (Tomlinson, 2001), which have the modernising of teachers at their centre. There have also been a vast number of circulars which have attended to details in the training and assessment procedures as well as in the setting up of new routes into teaching in order to meet the acute labour shortages in English schools. I do not want to suggest that these policies are all of a piece; certainly there are contradictions and internal inconsistencies, as well as other policies in circulation which pose conflicts and dilemmas in practice (Elmore, 1996). For example, the almost non-stop pressure on ratcheting up the demands made of trainee-teachers and teachers in schools at a time when recruitment and retention is a problem might be precipitating some unwanted secondary effects; excessive demands on teachers might be contributing to some of them leaving the job (Maguire, 2002). Nevertheless, there are some continuities and patterns, which can be traced in the key policy documentation of the Green and White papers. In what follows I want to concentrate on sections of some significant documents in order to explore the ways in which modernisation has been deployed in New Labours work on the teacher. These key documents are *Excellence in Schools* (DfEE, 1997); *teachers meeting the challenge of change* (DfEE, 1998); *Schools: Building on Success* (DfEE, 2001a) and *Schools: Achieving Success* (DfEE, 2001b).

EXCELLENCE IN SCHOOLS (DFEE 1997) (WHITE PAPER)

Excellence in Schools was published in July 1997. In the foreword, David Blunkett introduced the paper by saying that it was "as much about equipping the people of this country for the challenge of the future as it is about the Government's core commitment to equality of opportunity and high standards for all" (DfEE, 1997, p. 3). And while the modernization theme permeates the document in phrases like "challenge of the future," it is only directly deployed once. Significantly, this is in the title of Chapter Four, *Modernising the comprehensive principle.*

As a textual example of the newness of New Labour, the documents dissemination incorporated a very modern approach. The document was widely circulated (and was available at super-market checkouts). The summary document was available in six world languages. The document was accompanied by a video (copyright restrictions lifted) and was published

on the departments' website—called, interestingly enough, open.gov.uk/
dfee. The paper is carefully color coded; each chapter has its own color
(blue for the chapter on teachers); each chapter contains colored summary boxes; snappy summaries of the key questions for consultation are
highlighted in the chapters color-code; lively color photographs taken in
schools are interspersed throughout; mini-case studies of good practice are
contained in color-coded bordered boxes. In its wide-ranging sweep (from
pre-school to secondary provision, including the role of the local education authority and the professional development of teachers, heads of
schools and new community partnerships) this is a broad agenda for raising standards; "our top priority." Again, in the foreword, Blunkett sets the
tone for what is to follow:

> To succeed we need the commitment, imagination and drive of all those
> working in our schools and colleges, if we are to set aside the doubts of the
> cynics and the corrosion of the perpetual sceptics. We must replace the cul-
> ture of complacency with commitment to success (p. 3).

Excellence in Schools made only one major attempt to revise and reverse
Conservative educational policy when it stated that it would shift resources
from the Assisted Places Scheme (a policy which paid for clever but poor
children—who mainly turned out to be middle-class—to go to private
schools) into early years provision (p.11). What has never been followed up
is the fact that the APS was not cut-off but is still being phased out at time
of writing (2002). *Excellence in Schools* displays continuity with many of the
major planks in the Conservative education policy agenda. The accelera-
tion of testing, targeting and national guidelines on best practice [for
example; "we make a presumption that setting should be the norm in secondary schools" (p. 37) and "in some cases it is worth considering in primary schools" (p. 38)] illustrate that New Labour's modern approach was
alive to the need to re-establish continuity (Giddens) with Conservative
reforms and with a Conservative agenda. The difference is that this would
be justified along the lines of being beyond tradition and pragmatically
based on what works in New Labour's view.

Excellence in Schools devotes chapter five to "Teaching: High Status,
High Standards." The chapter starts very much in the way it goes on:

> We promise teachers a new deal: there will be pressure to succeed, but it will
> be matched by support to do their job well and recognition and appreciation
> of their achievements (p. 45).

The new deal outlined refers to more regulation of pre-service provision
and training for headship, a new grade of teacher (the advanced skills
teacher), a new General Teaching Council set up by New Labour to speak

for the professionals (p. 52) as well as steps to improve appraisal. Very much a business as usual approach to teachers and certainly to the regulation of teacher training and centralisation of professional development. However, it is in *teachers* (DfEE, 1998) where this work is fleshed out more directly. (Note the modern approach towards policy production—the document is entitled in lower case to match what was currently fashionable in typography and design—perhaps the major modern intervention!)

TEACHERS MEETING THE CHALLENGE OF CHANGE (DFEE 1998) (GREEN PAPER)

Of all the documents being considered in this paper, *teachers* is the one which is most directly and unambiguously concerned with the modernization of the teacher. Here modernization concentrates on and is synonymous with changes to teachers pay and conditions—attempts to reward the good teacher and specify their working conditions. For this reason, this Green paper has received a great deal of attention from teacher unions as well as educational researchers in the UK (see for example, NUT, 1999; ATL, 1999; Mahony & Hextall, 1999; Ironside & Seifert, 1999; Tomlinson, 2000). While the rhetoric of teachers is of needing to meet the challenge of change, the detail of the paper concentrates on performance management:

> It is important to emphasize that the roots of performance management lie deep in the private sector and that it was moved into the public sector as a key element in the managerialist restructuring of the public services during the 1980s and 1990s (Mahony & Hextall, 1999, p. 2).

This aspect—performance management through differential payments—underpins the modern teacher. Mahony and Hextall support this argument by citing an earlier White paper Modernizing Government (Cabinet Office, 1999), which had positioned modernization and performance management against being outdated (used twice in the following short phrase):

> Pay must be flexible and put service needs first. This means reforming outdated systems by tackling aspects, which make insufficient contribution to performance. It means challenging outdated assumptions, for example the idea that fair pay means that everybody should get the same increase (Cabinet Office, 1999, para. 28, p. 8 cited in Mahony & Hextall, 1999, p. 2).

Unlike the Conservatives who were hostile to teachers and frequently located their reforming moves in discourses which demonised them, New Labour has taken a somewhat different approach. In Blunketts "Having taught for seven years in a further education college, I know what it is like. Sheer hard work. Sometimes frustrating, but always rewarding" (DfEE. 1998, p. 5) and inclusive statements under the heading Modernising the teaching profession why it is necessary such as "Teachers themselves would readily acknowledge that the present reality does not acknowledge this ambitious vision" (DfEE, 1998, para. 14, p. 14), Labour has sought to present their version of modernisation (a business/performance management model) as one which common-sense shows is the only alternative and is the right way forward. The modern is essential and the private sector model is the only way to move forwards. After all, who wants to be outdated?

At the same time that *teachers* has attempted to bring teachers on side, by praising good teachers—ambitious, flexible teachers—there is still criticism of other sorts of teachers (Merson, 2000). Some teachers are still " afraid of change and therefore.... resist it" (DfEE, 1998, para. 23, p. 16). "Many seem to believe they are unique victims of constant change"... who hold a "fatalistic view"..."that nothing can be done to change things" (DfEE, 1998, para. 24, p. 16). *teachers* divides teachers into two types—the old style teacher with "the shabby staffroom and the battered electric kettle" (p.13) and the modern teacher taking "on the challenge of improvement" (p. 16) with a sense of "energy and purpose"(p. 16). The modern teacher knows that there are outstanding performers in the classroom whose excellence needs to be rewarded—like them for example. *teachers* divides teachers into good/bad practitioners and then uses a well-established discursive tactic whereby this is justified on common-sense grounds—all teachers know this to be the case anyway! (Cochran-Smith & Fries, 2001). In what follows, tradition is pitted against modernisation—although in other contexts, tradition is modern.

The tradition in teaching is to treat all teachers as if their performance was similar, even though in every staffroom teachers themselves know this is not true (DfEE, 1998, para. 20, p. 15). *Teachers* (DfEE, 1998) are divided into six chapters whose titles make clear the goals of New Labour. The first chapter is called The imperative of modernisation and is followed by; Better leadership; pay, performance and development; Better rewards for teaching; Better training; better support and new possibilities followed by a conclusion. The message is straightforward; "teachers in a modern teaching profession" (DfEE, 1998, p. 14) will need to raise their expectations and "accept accountability." They will need to be responsible for their professional development and work with others in school and outside school. They will need to be able to "welcome the contribution that parents, business and others can make." They will need to be able to "base decisions on evidence of what works in schools in this country and internationally" (p. 14) and will have to be able to "anticipate change and promote innovation" (p.14). Following this is a bolded heading Modernising the teaching profession: why it is necessary under which appears a statement which seeks to legitimate its claim through the discursive device of appealing to the common-sense and experience of teachers and other readers—an incorporatist tactic which can be hard to disengage from. Where the text-reader is a teacher for example, the response might be well, I suppose so. Where the text-reader is a parent or school governor, the engagement may be even stronger. Well , if teachers think this, then it must be so.

> Teachers themselves would readily acknowledge that the present reality does not match this ambitious vision. The challenge of modernisation is immense. There are fundamental issues to tackle. (p. 14)

Discursive tactics like this seek to justify the policy prescriptions being floated on the basis of an appeal which shows familiarity with the context (the scruffy staffroom, the old kettle and the worn out photocopier are all mentioned early on to establish the credentials of the writer(s)—who always write in a plural voice we although they never say who they are) and through linguistic tags such as, teachers would readily acknowledge, teachers themselves know this is not true (p. 14).[4] All this begs the question of who the reader is and which audience is being targeted by the document in question?

Teachers are concerned to reward "our leading professionals. To recruit, retain and motivate high quality classroom teachers by paying them more" (p. 6) through performance related pay systems. The document recognizes that there is a shortfall in recruitment and that there are "high wastage rates in the early years of teaching," *teachers* claims that this dilemma is mainly due to the lack of incentives for good performance, lack of professional development and the poor image of teaching—note that there is no recognition of excessive work—loads in this document or unrelenting government sponsored initiatives which have to be implemented as well as high housing costs in certain parts of the country. *teachers* only responds by claiming that the key to raising standards is to modernize teaching and the insertion of private sector pay mechanisms is the way to achieve this.

Rather than working through the details of *teachers* what I want to highlight is the way in which a particular version of the modern is presented in the document. As Merson says (1999, p. 162):

> Although the paper seeks to present itself as about the modernisation of the profession, there is very little truly modern in the proposals. The claims to be modern are pivoted on three areas, the adoption of new management regimes, new conditions and structures of work and the promotion of IT.

teachers draws on an out of date and somewhat discredited management regime in order to discipline teachers who are "redolent of the fordist workers of the public sector, reluctant to change and develop" (Merson, 1999, p. 164). The modern teacher, in contrast, is flexible, ambitious (words used repeatedly in the paper) and driven by competitive individualism. Utilizing their ICT skills and their leadership training, and speeding ever forwards to meet targets, setting ever higher targets and enhancing their performance, the modern teacher stands at the centre of this Green Paper as an isolated, uncollegial, competitive individual who is motivated by financial gains and nothing else. Their tasks have become narrowed—a concern with raising standards (measured by targets and testing) in order to deliver a "world-class education system where every school is excellent or improving or both" (para. 3, DfEE, 1998, p. 6)—another key phrase in the New Labour education lexicon.

In the Green paper, the modern teacher is not very modern at all. Payment by results has been tried and seen to fail in the past. As the NUT put it under the heading, New Labour, Old Ideas. (para. 56) "in its desire to be modern and new, the Government has resurrected an old beast, a scourge that bedeviled teaching and learning for some 25 years" (NUT, 1999, p. 7)—Giddens continuity with the past perhaps?

Hammersley and Atkinson (1983, pp. 142–143) suggest that textual analyses need to ask the following questions:

> How are documents written? How are they read? Who writes them? Who reads them? What is recorded? What is omitted? What is taken for granted?

teachers has been written by a group/team of unnamed civil servants led by unnamed and thus, unaccountable policy- makers and is heavily characterized by New Labour discourse (see Hextall & Mahony, 2000 for a discussion of under-reporting of disagreement or opposition in government consultation exercises). This discourse justifies and legitimates a particular set of policies, which are constructed as common sense, which simultaneously work to "undermine competing policies" (Cochran-Smith & Fries, 2001, p. 2). One of the cleverest and more transparent rhetorical devices in the paper is contained in the following extract. The extract picks up and repeats (repetition is a common vehicle for strengthening the political message and here the words of Tony Blairs foreword are woven into the fabric of the paper—incidentally signaling his ownership of the project) a motif but couches it in a negative-positive "we plead guilty—guilty to wanting modern teachers"—and who wouldn't!. It is worth citing this paragraph, which is alone in the document through being completely bolded, in full:

We will be accused of being visionary and excessively ambitious. We plead guilty. After the years of drift, vision and ambition are surely what is needed. Creating a world-class education service was never going to be easy but that is what the economy and society of the future require. A modern teaching profession is central to this process. If teachers rise to the challenge of modernisation in the next few months they themselves, along with pupils and parents, will undoubtedly be major beneficiaries. We urge all those with an interest in the future of our education system to give this Green paper the most careful consideration and to grasp the historic opportunity that now presents itself (para 35, p. 19).

An alternative version of the modern teacher as a team member, as a member of an ethical group of workers who have a degree of professional integrity and who sometimes need to resist the tyranny of central imposition in the longer term interests of those they work with and for—is rendered mute and silenced in the discourse of flexibility and competitive individualism. What is omitted and what is taken for granted in this Green Paper shores up a specific vision of the modern teacher, which can then be used to control and set further policy agendas.[5]

The move from this paper to the following Success papers is itself a skilful discursive move. What has been proposed and sent out for consultation has somehow been achieved and is part of the success story of New Labours education program.

SCHOOLS: BUILDING ON SUCCESS (DFEE 2001A) (GREEN PAPER) AND SCHOOLS: ACHIEVING SUCCESS (DFEE 2001B) (WHITE PAPER)

In these Papers, (which have reverted back to using upper case), New Labour has continued its presentation of "the way things are" and the inevitable and common sense way forward (CPPR, 2002, p. 15). *Building on Success* is mainly, but not exclusively, concerned with "seizing this opportunity to modernize our secondary system" (p. 7) and transforming education. Chapter Five deals specifically with "Teaching—a 21st Century Profession." Much of the rhetoric from *teachers* is simply cut and pasted into *Building on Success*.

Paragraph 13 (DfEE, 1998, p. 14), which outlines what is meant by new professionalism, appears again on page 65 of *Building on Success*. "The vision of the 1998 Green Paper may not yet be realized but progress towards it is remarkable"(DfEE, 2001a, p. 66).

Building on Success works discursively to legitimate the proposals made in *teachers* as well as providing a summary of a range of other policy developments in relation to the job of teaching. Chapter Five discusses further reforms to teacher training, further steps to enhance professional development including a range of new initiatives such as sabbaticals and time to undertake research at local universities. It claims that recruitment problems are now being resolved. Chapter Five also discusses the differentiation, which has been inserted into teaching as well as moves to cut bureaucracy—enabling teachers to teach"(p. 73). The chapter summarizes its teacher modernization thrust;

> We promised to reward good teachers and to offer good teachers better pay progression. The new pay structure has now been put in place, with higher salaries and better prospects.... To modernise the teaching profession (DfEE, 2001a, para. 5.56, p. 77).

One of the more striking discursive features of these success papers, is the way in which they follow on from earlier papers, which argue for change and outline proposals, which are then seen, as succeeding in the subsequent papers. It is important to remember that these papers have been published at key points in the UK election cycle. The first White paper must have been prepared before the election victory and was rushed into circulation almost immediately. The Green Paper (1998)—probably of less interest to the general public—was a mid-government publication. The *Success* documents straddle the second term in government for New Labour. *Building on Success* sets out the achievements and *Achieving Success*—led by a new Secretary of State for Education, Estelle Morris—is about "significant further achievements" (DfES, 2001, p. 7).

It is worth considering the foreword in *Achieving Success*. Here the new Secretary of State legitimates the document by drawing immediately on her own well-known biography;

> I know from my own years of teaching and from visiting literally hundreds of schools over the last nine years that there is a real desire to bring life and meaning to the phrase, raising standards for every child (first sentence of the White paper, p. 3).

She continues that "No one can deny the progress we have made" (p. 3). Even more strongly, the introduction concludes with a challenge for the future—the new educational regime led by a teacher of 17 years experience and a new group of policy advisors, new ministers and (probably) new document writers:

> We will not rest until we have a truly world class education system that meets the needs of every child. Whatever it takes (DfES, 2001, para.1.10, p. 7).

While the main thrust of this document is concerned with transforming secondary education provision, many other reforms are envisaged in this document (see CPPR, 2001). And, interestingly for this paper, the word modernization has slipped back into usage. The document talks of modernizing the profession (although "there still remains a great deal to do to implement in full the vision set out in the 1998 Green Paper" para. 7.3. p. 53); modernizing (which here means deregulating) education law and teachers pay and employment provisions; school buildings (and PFI is signaled in para. 8.22, p. 68); the revenue funding system; modernizing LEAs to deliver centrally determined targets and policies "removing any legislative barriers that exist to any of the innovative ideas now coming forward" (p. 67).

> Chapter 7, Valuing and supporting teachers in school, seeks to continue the modernization project." The key themes… leadership, rewards, training, support… will remain at the centre of our thinking" (p. 53).

> This White Paper is about achieving success in schools. At its heart are proposals for improving teaching and learning. And at the heart of teaching and learning are those who work in schools—heads, teachers, classroom support staff, technicians, administrators and all who shape a school. They have been central to what has been achieved so far in raising standards—we recognise and are grateful for the huge contribution they have made. And as we strive to raise standards still further it is essential that we support them all as they educate our children (p. 53).

> We are clear that teaching must be, and feel, a manageable job as well as a valued and important profession (p. 55)

To paraphrase a recent critique of the White Paper, (CPPR, 2001) , these extracts do a particular discursive job; they appropriate the oppositional space of critics and position the government as honest and responsive in accepting that "some major issues remain so far unresolved, and that some of these loom larger than they did in 1998" (p.55). There is some recognition that the government needs to win the support of teachers. However, only a partial story of progress and modernisation is contained in the White paper:

> The first eight paragraphs of Chapter Seven outline the considerable progress , which has been made by the Labour government—not the teachers (pp. 53–55). The White Paper cites effective training (which the government mandated), performance-related pay awards (which organised teachers resisted), the General Teaching Council (which many teachers have refused to join) and a range of strategies designed to tackle under-recruitment and retention (which do not seem to have made much difference at all). Indeed, if teachers had spent all this money and time on such poor

returns, they would have been castigated in a way, which the TTA and central government never have been! (CPPR, 2001, p. 21).

Achieving Success positions teachers as deliverers of policies, mainly concerned to raise standards—as if teachers would want to lower standards—in a climate of linear constructions of success. However, "woven into this chapter is a move away from the idea that those who can teach towards the idea that everyone can teach" (CPPR, 2001, p. 22).

Achieving Success accepts the need to support teachers in their work and the Government recognises that workloads are high and that there are teacher shortages. It is suggested that greater flexibility is needed and that teachers can delegate some of their responsibilities to others in school. This White Paper promises that New Labour will provide 10,000 more teachers and 20,000 more support staff. Flexibility, a key strand of modernisation, will be useful in opening up "alternative routes to qualification"(p. 54) (deregulation). The paper also reveals its view that modern individual teachers are motivated by opportunities to enhance their own pay through meeting increased performance targets. And while there is recognition that high workload, continuing development and concerns about challenging behaviour in schools can deter teachers from staying in the job, the response towards this is largely (but not only) couched in terms of flexibility and performance related pay; "We will make sure that head teachers can assess teachers performance for pay purposes..."(p. 74) and even more worrying, the government will give itself powers to over-ride the School Teachers Review Body (the independent group that advises on teachers salaries etc). Modern teachers and modern teaching need to be flexible, de-regulated (where it suits government purposes) and highly regulated where it does not (pre-service provision in HE institutions).

In *Achieving Success*, the modern teacher is hewn out of a marketised discourse; any other version is just not compatible with the laptop-carrying manager of learning, a target-hitting performance enhancer. Consider an alternative view of a modern teacher who needs to be creative and imaginative, who needs to be able to provide "an education in courage and questioning, not merely competence and compliance" (Seddon, 1994, p. 12 in Lingard, 1995, p. 21)—and who is edited out of New Labours construction of the modern teacher.

SUMMARY AND CONCLUSIONS

Some time ago, Toulmin (1990, p. 170) argued that modernity rested on three attributes; certainty, systematicity and the clean slate. Certainty involves believing that progress can be made and that scientific-rationality can steer this process. Systematicity involves the application of rules, which will move the process forward. The clean slate approach means that, "We can set aside history and culture and cast ourselves anew" (Hartley, 2000, p. 120). In the process of modernising the teacher, which is envisaged in the key New Labour policy documents, Toulmins attributes are embedded in the tone, language and approach being taken. Teacher reform is seen as susceptible to the rational and systematic application of (outmoded and rejected) business systems. A tone of certainly, of knowing best, of rightness and righteousness permeates these documents. Fascinatingly, the clean slate approach is applied when it is convenient, and marginalised when it is not—re-establishing continuity in a politically and pragmatic style (Giddens, 1998). As Merson (2000, p. 159) puts it, "like many apparent modernisation proposals, their (New Labours) justification lies in an interpretation of past practices being dismissed as part of a cultural aberration". Toulmin (1990, p. 208) suggested that in the future the name of the game will be *influence*, not *force*: thus, winning legitimacy becomes a critical element in the struggle for power. And here it is important to note, as Newman (2000, p. 60) points out:

> The discourse of modernisation is still emergent and unstable: it is the focus of continued social and political agency in the struggle to shape a new settlement.

Newman (2000, p. 45) suggests that "studying discourse through documentary analysis is an imperfect technique for at least two reasons." She argues that there is a danger that this approach might valorise language and sideline practice. Her point is that language is utilized to legitimate change as well as signal its direction. Her second concern is one, which applies to the work undertaken in this paper; the concern that "insufficient attention is paid to differences between documents... and to the subtle shifts of emphasis over time" (p. 46). The documents considered in this paper are important, for the work they do is powerful in marking out, setting and justifying new policy agendas. Where one document asserts a need and suggests an intervention, a successive document asserts its success and bolsters up the policy work. Thus, a cycle of problem, solution, success and new problems is articulated across the documents which have been examined in this paper. This cycle is closed and there is no space for dissent or positing different sorts of dilemmas although there are shifts across the documents, notably in relation to teacher recruitment and retention issues.

Centrally however, "As always, it is a matter not just of what is said but of who is entitled to speak" (Ball, 1994, p. 50) and who, by inference, is not entitled to speak. The problem of teacher education and teachers is there out datedness; the solution lies in a version of modernisation. Certainty and conviction characterise the tone of these documents. Thus, a particular version of the New Labour policy world is legitimated, any opposition to its rightness is discredited even before it is presented, and the common-sense of its solution is used to set the policy agenda not an agenda for dialogue (Cochran-Smith & Fries, 2001)—an agenda which New Labour will not shrink from tackling, however hard the task!

And the price of all this, the price of the modern teacher? If the modern, ambitious, teacher, driven by performance indicators is to be seen to succeed, then this success will have to be predicated on someone else's failure—and this visibility of performance indicates more surveillance and stress on measurable outcomes. What of the outmoded teacher or the teacher who is not modern enough? What too, of the schools the modern teacher will choose to teach in and the children they will need to teach in order to demonstrate their excellence? More importantly, what of the schools who cannot attract modern teachers or modern students? And most importantly, what will the modern teacher mean in terms of the sort of society which they will be educating to achieve? If values of competitive individualism are valorised above all else, what then will happen to the ethics of collaborative, collegial working practices which have sustained many schools, many teachers and many children? What sort of world will the modern teacher be teaching for?

NOTES

1. Green Papers are documents issued by the UK central government in order to consult on policy and practice. White Papers are statements of policy intent, which then become Bills and are put before Parliament where they are confirmed (or rejected) as Acts of Parliament and then become enacted as Law.

2. In a folk tale, Aladdin, a magician into selling his old, but unknown to himself, magic lamp for a new lamp deceives a poor youth. The magician's cry was Old lamps for New—an offer too good to miss and one with an enduring history.

3. "Tony Blair famously describes his three main priorities in government as education, education, education." (Giddens, 1998, p. 109).

4. Silverman (1993) notes that the visual images of texts need analysis. The work these do—beyond words—in setting and framing policy perspectives is important but has not been attempted in this paper. The documents considered in this paper are professionally produced and contain vignettes of schools and teachers, colour photographs, sometimes highly distinctive, full-page, black and white photographs of teachers. Symbolic of New labours inclusiveness, these images portray a multi- racial group of children and their teachers, frequently looking full face and confidently into the

camera—portraits of the modern teacher, however atypical they may be in reality.

5. One of the demands in the Green paper is for teachers who will be able to base decisions on evidence (p. 14) yet the paper itself is based on common-sense claims which are not themselves backed up by any empirical evidence whatsoever but which are sometimes contradicted by evidence (e.g., performance related pay as a motivator)

REFERENCES

Apple, M. (2001). Markets, standards, teaching and teacher education. *Journal of Teacher Education*, 50(2), 229–254.

Association of Teachers and Lecturers. (1999). *The Governments Green paper and Technical Consultation Document*, March 1999. London: Association of Teachers and Lectureres.

Ball, S. J. (1995). Intellectuals or Technicians? The urgent role of theory in educational studies. *British Journal of Educational Studies*, 33(3), 255–271.

Ball, S.J. (1999). *Educational Reform and the struggle for the soul of the teacher!* Lecture delivered by Prof. S.J.Ball on 27 November 1998 as Wei Lun Visiting Professor to The Chinese University, Hong Kong. Hong Kong: The Chinese University of Hong Kong.

Beck, U., Giddens, A., & Lash, S. (1994). Reflexive modernization. *Politics, Tradition and Aesthetics in the Modern Social order.* Cambridge: Polity Press.

Black, M., & Coward, R. (1981). Linguistic, social and sexual relations: a review of Dale Spenders Man Made Language. *Screen Education*, 39(Summer), 69–86.

Blunkett, D. (1999). World class education for all. In G. Kelly (Ed.), *Is new labour working?* (pp. 5–11). London: The Fabian Society.

Bourdieu, P. (1998). Acts of Resistance. *Against the New Myths of OurTime.* Cambridge: Polity Press.

Cabinet Office. (1999). *Modernising Government.* London: Cabinet Office

Campbell, J. (1999). Recruitment, retention and reward; issues in the modernisation of primary teachers. *Education, 3–13, 27(3), 24–31.*

Clarke, J., Gewirtz, S., & McLaughlin, E. (Eds.). (2000). *New managerialism New Welfare?* London, Thousand Oaks, New Delhi: Sage Publications.

Cochran-Smith, M., & Fries, M.K. (2001). Sticks, Stones and Ideology: The Discourse of Reform. *Teacher Education, in Educational Researcher,* 30(8), 3–15.

CPPR. (2002). Achieving Success? Discursive strategies and policy tensions. *New Labours White Paper for schools in Education and Social Justice,* 4(1).

Darling-Hammond, L., & Sykes, G. (1999). (Eds.) *Teaching as the learning profession: Handbook of policy and practice.* San-Francisco, CA: Jossey Bass.

DfEE. (1997). *Excellence in schools.* London: HMSO.

DfEE.(1998). *Teachers meeting the challenge of change.* London: HMSO.

DfEE. (2001a). *Schools* building on success.* London: HMSO.

DfEE. (2001b). *Schools: Achieving Success.* London: HMSO

Elmore, R.(1996). School reform, teaching and learning. *Journal of Education Policy,* 11(4), 499–505.

Furlong, J., Barton, L., Miles, S., Whiting, C., & Whitty, G. (2000). Teacher education in transition. *Reforming professionalism?* Buckingham, Philadelphia: Open University Press.

Furlong, J. (2002). Ideology and reform. Teacher education in England; Some reflections on Cochran-Smith and Fries. *Educational Researcher, 31*(6), 23–25.

Giddens, A. (1998). The third way. *The renewal of social democracy.* Cambridge: Polity Press.

Hammersley, M., & Atkinson, P. (1983). *Ethnography: Principles in practice,* London: Tavistock.

Hartley, D. (2000). Shoring up the pillars of modernity: Teacher education and the quest for certainty. *International Studies in Sociology of Education, 10*(2), 36–43.

Hextall, I., & Mahony, P. (2000). Consultation and the management of consent: Standards for qualified teacher status. *British Educational Research Journal, 26*(3), 323–342.

Hill, D. (1990). *Something old, something new, something borrowed, something blue: Schooling and the radical right.* Britain: Tufnell Press.

Hood, C. (1999). *The art of the state.* Oxford: Oxford University Press.

Ironside, M., & Seiffert, R. (1999). A critical comment on the Governments Green Paper; Teachers meeting the challenge of change. *Education and Social Justice, 1*(2), 17.

Kelly, G. (1999). (Ed.). *Is new labour working?* London: The Fabian Society.

Kenny, M., & Smith, M.J. (2001). Interpreting new labour. In S. Ludlam & M.J. Smith (Eds.), *New labour in Government.* London and New York: Macmillan Press.

Lawn, M. (1995). Restructuring teaching in the USA and England; moving towards the differentiated, flexible teacher. *Journal of Education Policy, 10*(4), 347–360.

Lawlor, S. (1990). *Teachers mistaught: Training in theories or education in subjects?* London: Centre for Policy Studies.

Lingard, B. (1995). Rearticulating relevant voices. *Reconstructing teacher education.* The annual Harry Penny Lecture, University of South Australia, Underdale Campus, Friday 12 May.

McCaig, C. (2001). New labour and education, education, education. In S. Ludlam & M.J. Smith (Eds.), *New labour in Government.* London and New York: Macmillan Press.

Maguire, M. (2002). Globalisation, education policy and the teacher. *International Studies in Sociology of Education.*

Mahony, P., & Hextall, I. (1999). *Modernising the teacher* (pp. 1–24). Paper given at ECER, Lahti: Finland. (http://www.leeds.ac.uk/educol/documents/000001341 .htm).

Mahony, P., & Hextall, I. (2000). *Reconstructing teaching: Standards, performance and accountability.* London: Routledge.

Merson, M. (2000). Teachers and the myth of modernization. *British Journal of Education Studies, 48*(2), 155–169.

Moore, A., & Atkinson, D. (1998). Charisma, competence and teacher education. *Discourse; studies in the cultural politics of education,* 19(2), 171–182.

National Commission on Teaching and Americas Future. (1996). (NCTAF). *Doing what matters most: Investing in quality teaching.* New York, NY: National Commission on Teaching and Americas Future.

National Union of Teachers. (1999). *Teaching at the Threshold. The NUT response to Meeting the Challenge of Change.* London: National Union of Teachers

Newman, J. (2000). Beyond the New Public management? Modernizing public services. In J. Clarke, S. Gewirtz, & E. McLaughlin (Eds.), *New managerialism New Welfare?* London, Thousand Oaks, New Delhi: Sage Publications.

OHear, A. (1998). *Who teaches the teachers?* London: Social Affairs Unit.

Sachs, J. (2001). Teacher professional identity: Competing discourses, competing outcomes. *Journal of Education Policy,* 16(2), 149–162.

Seddon, T. (1994). Decentralisation and Democracy. *National Industry Education Forum* (pp. 1–15). Decentralisation and Teachers: Report of a Seminar. Melbourne: NIEF.

Silverman, D. (1993). *Interpreting qualitative data: Methods for analysing talk, text and interaction.* London, Thousand Oaks, New Delhi: Sage Publications.

Silverman, D. (2000). Analyzing talk and text. In N. Denzin & Y. Lincoln (Eds.), *Handbook of qualitative research.* Thousand Oaks, CA:Sage Publications.

Tomlinson, H. (2000). Proposals for performance related pay for teachers in english schools. *School Leadership & Management,* 20(3), 281–298.

Tomlinson, S. (2001). *Education in a post-welfare society.* Buckingham: Open University Press.

Toulmin, S. (1990). *The Cosmopolis: The hidden agenda of modernity.* New York, Free Press.

CHAPTER 7

RESPONSIVENESS AND INNOVATION IN HIGHER EDUCATION RESTRUCTUTING

The South African Case

Johan Muller
University of Cape Town

INTRODUCTION

This paper is about the social institutions of higher education in South Africa, and their complex relation to the problematic of restructuring. Even with so bald a statement, possibilities of confusion and misrepresentation arise. Global policy terms travel through various iterations of policy borrowing and become translated, recontextualised and transformed. As Latour (1999, p. 298) has said: ...transfers of *information* never occur except through subtle and multiple *trans*formations (see also Callon, 1995). Restructuring is just such a term. In South African higher education policy discourse, restructuring refers specifically to the policy of institutional mergers, gazetted on 24 June 2002 (see The South African Universities Vice-Chancellors Association or SAUVCA, 2002), which aims in the

Educational Restructuring: International Perspectives on Traveling Policies, pages 143–165
Copyright © 2004 by Information Age Publishing
All rights of reproduction in any form reserved.

interests of quality and efficiency to reduce the number of higher education institutions in the country from 35 to 21. In contemporary South African policy-speak, restructuring and mergers are synonymous.

If however we ask what it is that discursive clusters like restructuring are doing, it is soon clear that they form part of the macro-cluster of what Lindblad and Popkewitz (2002) call the problematic of the new governance. The master term for this in South Africa is transformation, and it is being pursued at a central policy level at a hectic pace. The SAUVCA calculates that there are at present 30 change initiatives, which in 2002 demanded higher education management time and resources (see Appendix A). Diverse as these transformation policies are, they all face in one of two directions: they are directed towards equity and access (social inclusion/exclusion) on the one hand; or innovation and economic development on the other. To put that in different terms, the redemptive longings driving higher education transformation in South Africa are salvation from the dead hand of apartheid on the one hand, and progress towards global economic competitiveness on the other. These two longings anchor the political theology of restructuring in South Africa. The logics of these two redemptive longings are, unfortunately, contradictory—the logic of equalization (Lindblad and Popkewitz "problematic of equity") is in strict contradiction to the logic of differentiation (their "problematic of knowledge")—but this contradiction rarely if ever becomes visible in the policy discourse itself, and the contradictory ensemble constructs a discursive alibi for the overall transformation agenda that placates but can never resolve the salvation anxiety driving the new governance (ibid).

The focus of this chapter is not to analyze the lineaments of the new governance, which have been adequately dissected elsewhere in this book, but rather to examine the response of higher education institutions to this double-edged exhortation, which comes exogenously from either the policy prescriptions of the national government, or from the multiform facets of global markets, or often from both together. In governance terms, this exhortation generates a complex generic pressure on higher education institutions to be more responsive or more relevant. But to what or to whom should they be responsive and relevant? The answer recapitulates the contradictory couplet: to society (the logic of equalization) and to the market (the logic of differentiation). This contradictory imperative forces institutions to make strategic choices. This chapter is about how they arrive at their choice. In particular, it is about the constraints placed on choice or responsiveness by their sedimented histories, by their inherited institutional forms, which project particular dispositions for action. For the purposes of this paper, I shall discuss two dimensions of institutionality, the institution of organisation and management on the one hand, and the institution of knowledge on the other. Because the policy exhortations I shall be concentrating on here are targeted at the knowledge core business of higher education—academic programs and forms of research—I shall concentrate mainly but not exclusively on the institution of knowledge. The specific question I wish to investigate is: how does the knowledge structure of a program and the strength of its historical presence in a particular university affect the way it responds to the political theology of restructuring? Consequently, I want to investigate if and how knowledge structure strength and capacity construct social limits to the possibility of restructuring and transformation.

The chapter proceeds by looking at recent research in South Africa which assesses the degree to which the universities have changed their curricula from discipline-based programs to interdisciplinary–based programs in response to national policy imperatives; and the degree to which they have changed their research profiles from basic to applied research in response to market imperatives. In each case, the response is neither direct nor simple. The chapter will argue that universities make largely rhetorical accommodations to interdisciplinary curricula, especially where the discipline and the disciplinary tradition is strong, except where universities are in search of students or a market niche. It will also suggest that universities respond to the new market demand for relevant academic research neither by changing their cognitive or epistemic structures, but more often than is recognized by shoring up their basic research programs within research contracts awarded for relevant research; that is, by clothing their usual research practice in the lineaments of the new relevance.

The paper will conclude by suggesting that universities respond to exogenous pressures for restructuring—from government policy, society or the market—in large part on the basis of features internal to the science system (the structure of disciplines, their state of innovation) and internal to university institutions (their intellectual and managerial capacity or capital). The post-modern froth about the end of universities, of disciplines and of epistemology as we know it notwithstanding, the paper will attempt to make the case that science as an innovation system, and universities as its primary carrier, are far more durable and resistant to external pressures to change than either policy analysts or market pessimists usually give them credit for. They respond, or not, in ways that have far more to do with their internal organisation as institutions than is normally recognized. Changing science and universities can thus best be done via steering, rather than by plans or money. Both may be important, but the institution of science also keeps its own council, a fact the social engineers of central policy are all too prone to forget.

INTERNAL AND EXTERNAL EXPLANATIONS
OF CHANGES IN KNOWLEDGE

The generic discourse of higher education restructuring embeds the assumption that universities in general, including their knowledge activities of academic programs and research, are amenable to exogenous propulsion; that is, that they can be pushed by policy and pulled by the market. In traditional academic accounts of knowledge change, by contrast, far more attention is paid to internal dimensions of knowledge and its environment than it is in the policy literature concerning restructuring. In science studies, for example, there are currently two main approaches to explaining change in the science system endogenously. First, there is the *institutionalist* (or neo-institutionalist) approach, which deals with changes in the institutional settings of research, including science policy (e.g., Mayntz & Schimank, 1998; Weingart, 1998). This approach focuses on the structural conditions and mechanisms created to direct science, and on the institutional responses of science. Secondly, there is the *cognitivist* approach, which deals with changes internal to the knowledge structure of science as the driver of change, focusing on changes in the mode of knowledge production. The two main contending theories here have been the Starnberg group's finalization theory, and the mode 1/2 account of Gibbons, Scott, Nowotny and others (Gibbons et al., 1994). There are other contenders, like the triple helix approach of Etzkowitz & Leydesdorff (1995) and Rip's socio-cognitive approach (Rip, 1997), which I will return to later.[1]

Accounts of change in the South Africa science system, generally speaking, employ neither a cognitive nor an institutionalist approach. Rather, the standard form of account is heavily policy-based. Such accounts start with invoking a change in policy, and then enquire as to whether university change has followed in accordance with the policy (Cloete & Bunting, 2000). The explanatory line for curriculum and research restructuring thus leads from policy suggestion (the National Commission on Higher Education, 1996), to policy proper (the White Paper, Department of Education, 1997), to funding levers, thereby to changes in research or curriculum patterns. To put it another way, most of the literature on restructuring in South African higher education locates itself in a typical rationalist policy paradigm, in accord with global restructuring policy literature, a position that typically underestimates the effect of endogenous factors on knowledge configuration and change.

I begin by suggesting then that basic research disciplinary traditions respond to responsiveness pressure—that is, exogenous pressure towards applications and relevance—in different ways. Some disciplines or disciplinary fields show a marked convergence between basic and applied research (e.g., molecular biology, biomedicine), while in others, the two are as far apart as ever (most of the humanities, cosmology; Glaser, 2001). In those knowledge fields where basic and applications driven research is drawing closer together, basic research can either lead to successful applications or it can pass itself off as relevant. But here lies a potential danger, since to accede to relevance may require not following the knowledge-driven path of growth, hence running the risk of curbing the growth of knowledge in the interests of demonstrating its utility. This need not be life threatening to this kind of discipline. Imagine though the costs of this strategy of piggybacking basic on applied research in knowledge fields where basic and applied are much further apart in the developmental cycle of the discipline, where it is consequently far more difficult to pass normal innovation off as strategically relevant. The result must be the crowding-out of basic research. Policy-driven or market pressure for applied research—under apartheid, in the state socialist societies, and now with the new political correctness of responsiveness runs the risk of creating the opposite effect it intends to: "Thus, in most cases, science policy does not redirect research on the micro-level. Instead, old research trails are cut off and new ones started" (Glaser, 2000, p. 462). This is if we are lucky. Whole trains of promising research may die out simply "because new lines of basic inquiry do not emerge, and the old ones face a constant fall in resources" (ibid, p. 463). From this it is plausible to presume that the dynamism of science can be *leveraged* from without, but must be *propelled* from within. Without good research scientists, good graduate programmes, or cutting edge research programmes—some of the institutional preconditions for the internal propulsion of knowledge growth—all the external propulsion and good intentions in the world may produce but a withered vine.

There are then basically two strategies for explaining changes in knowledge: endogenous and exogenous. The argument so far has been that exogenous strategies (market or policy-driven), and hence explanations based solely on them, are limited by the state of play of the endogenous factors. What then are these endogenous factors? There are two kinds of explanation. The first accounts for knowledge change by looking at changes in the internal dynamics of knowledge-based activity and knowledge growth in the system. The conclusion suggested above is that unilateral change to the funding regime from basic to applied could have exactly the opposite result intended, because the roots of the vine may become inadvertently starved by this strategy, or the strategy may only be productively accommodated by some disciplines in the system, and not by others.

The second explanation, neo-institutionalism, has so far received less attention in this chapter. The institutionalist strategy for accounting for science change begins by looking at institutions as adaptive systems, and at the university system as a series of institutions that can be placed on a graded continuum of stability and adaptability (see Bunting, 2002; Gourni-tzka & Maassen, 2000). However, unlike the exogenous view of change, which in its policy restructuring manifestation imagines that change is produced by articulating politically desirable good intentions, the institutionalist approach takes change, or transformation, as the exception rather than the norm:

> The chief problems an organisation encounters in developing a new structural pose are, 1) recursiveness, and 2) the capacity for learning. These factors are inter-connected, they appreciate that an organisation possesses a repertoire, which is durable and robust over time. The corollary is that organizational transformation is more difficult than is generally supposed; ... (Clark & Carter, 1999, p.7).

Before globalization sped up the transformation agenda of higher education, higher education institutions were able to get away with endogenously paced change. This has become much more difficult globally. The pressure is compounded in South Africa's political climate. Lack of transformation in a time of virtuous social change, such as that which South Africa has recently passed and is still passing through, is a heresy, and usually attributed to political recalcitrance. The institutionalist position sketched below would suggest, on the contrary, that some institutions may not change, not because of bad faith, but rather because the supposedly desirable change cuts across their niche strength and would undermine it; others simply do not have the capacity to adapt. On the other hand, some institutions may change in the desired direction not for reasons of policy adherence but rather as part of their niche or market-searching strategy, from weakness so to speak. The truth of the matter is, university systems *as systems*, when they have relatively stable systemic capacity, change slowly; the USA big four (Harvard, Yale, Princeton, and Stanford) and the British top rank have hardly changed place over the last century. It is not hard to see why; they possess the physical and social capital, and therefore the cultural capital to steer their own path—the top academics, who will naturally nurture the basic intellectual roots and who will then also naturally attract good colleagues from elsewhere, and last but by no means least, they therefore tend to attract the best students. This Bourdieuian reproductive dictum is well-nigh universally observed, superficial signs of turbulence sometimes notwithstanding (Bourdieu, 1988).

Institutions are, at any given point, quite differently disposed regarding intellectual and administrative capacity, and therefore responsive capacity, usually for clear historical reasons. To step back briefly in time for a moment, it is useful to recall the three distinct phases of development of the university system in South Africa (see Muller, 1991). The first saw the evolution of the small handful of elite institutions that, up until 1948 at least, pursued a classical, basic disciplinary agenda. The then Prime Minister Field-Marshall Jan Christian Smuts could himself still write the annual report of national scientific progress for the London-based Royal Society each year. Next, a group of Afrikaans institutions were established to train the upper reaches of the civil service and private sector, including the teachers and lawyers. It was in this phase that the new Nationalist government began the drive to applied research, spearheaded by the national research councils, and later the other research parastatals, a move tailor-made for the niche-seeking Afrikaner universities as we shall see below. The final phase was the establishment of the black institutions in the so-called homelands to train personnel for the civil service for the "homelands." The correlative research expectation for the three sets of institutions, underwritten by resourcing, was: the elite universities would do basic research, the second phase Afrikaans institutions would do applied research, and the black institutions were not expected to do research at all, at least initially. This is now imprinted into the institutional histories of these institutions. We may of course expect individual institutions to break their mould, as has of course happened, but it would be unusual indeed for an entire category to jump over its historical shadow. If this is so, the question that then arises is: what kind of responsiveness capacity predisposes institutions to change, and how?

ON ATTRIBUTING IMPACT TO POLICY

Policy impact is a difficult concept to nail down once one has abandoned any hope that policy proceeds in a linear way through to practice (Ball, 1993). It simply never does. This difficulty is compounded by new indirect forms of governance that seek to precipitate beneficial effects rather than to bring them into being by decree (see Lindblad & Popkewitz, 2002). The most effective policies, it can be surmised, leverage a balance of forces that bring into virtuous structural alignment various aspects of the demand/supply environment with the institutionalised strengths of an institution. This of course makes it much more difficult to design an investigation to filter out the contending variables so as to assess what contribution the policy itself makes to determinate empirical outcomes. Nevertheless, to forsake linearity in policy analysis does not spare us from the task of assessing policy impact; quite the contrary.

Research on higher education is sometimes considered an under-developed stepchild of theoretically and empirically more sophisticated school-based research. Supporting this view, we sometimes find in higher education policy research the kinds of misattributions that are usually criticized and avoided in school-based research. One such misattribution is that of the effects of policy on practice. The error consists in generalizing from policy intent (what school-based studies call the *intended* policy) to practice effects (the *learnt* policy) without taking into account the crucial intervening variable, the mediating context that translates the policy into practice (namely, the *enacted* policy).

Recent studies on university curriculum change in South Africa are instructive in this regard (see Ensor, 2000, 2001). Both the White Paper (1997) and the Higher Education Act (1997) exhort universities to programmatise their curricula, a measure seen by policy planners as necessary to break the grip of disciplinary majors on curricula and to promote greater interdisciplinarity and thereby greater relevance. Instead of uniform compliance, the result was a spectrum of institutional accommodations to program policy, from high accommodation to low, from enthusiastic to reluctant. Insofar as the institutions had to make at least a token response to programmatisation because their statutory funding depended upon it, we could have expected some change in each institution. But the range and unevenness of change is noteworthy. More importantly, it is unclear whether the changes that were made were because of the policy, or because the universities were reading the need for change off some other market-based script. Indeed, the very varieties of change, and in one case, change in advance of the policy, makes it plausible that the proximate cause was something else over and above the policy (see Muller & Ogude, 2002).

So what can we conclude about institutional responses to the policy of curriculum program restructuring? First of all, we cannot conclude, on the evidence, that the policy caused the change: and secondly, we don't know whether the national policy as represented by the policy documents influenced the new programs of the various institutions (the enacted curriculum proper, i.e., whether it was actually taught like that in the lecture rooms), let alone whether the students actually learnt anything significantly different because of the policy. What we can conclude from the evidence (see Ensor, 2002) is that changing the curriculum in that particular way (towards interdisciplinary programs), was resisted by the institutions, such that attempts to break down disciplinary boundaries, especially with subjects that have robust disciplinary identities, from physics to history, resulted in internal disciplinary enclaves within the programs, rather than in integrated programs. In other words, the form of accommodation was observed, but not its substance.

Whereas curriculum restructuring towards relevance was mandated by national policy documents, though relatively weakly policed, university research towards greater relevance, though advocated in the White Paper of 1997, was more indirectly steered by changing the allocatory conditions for research awards to favor relevance and applied research. The results are ostensibly more positive. There is a dramatic shift away from basic to applied research, a shift from 75% to 50% denoting a 25% shift over a five-year period (Bawa & Mouton, 2002, p. 315). The question is how we interpret this shift. Bawa & Mouton are inclined to see this as a response to both urgings on the part of government as well as a response to global pressures for more applied research (Gibbons et al., 1994). The intended policy is read as having an effect on research, here conceived not as research practice (enacted) but as published research (learnt). They infer that a global research shift towards applications-driven research is translated into policy (the White Paper, 1997), which is then read by researchers and acted upon effectively, yielding the change in the desired research direction in completed/published research. The evidence is simply not there to make this conclusion with confidence, as the authors admit. The intervening variable of changed research practice has only begun to be studied, and since this has not been the focus of study here, the researchers could not assess whether the changed research practice (if indeed it has changed, which is debatable) has changed because of the policy, or because of something else: say, lucrative consultancies with government, or the private sector, or bilateral and multilateral donor funding, a global shift that is increasingly evident. What we can say is that there is more published applied research in South Africa than there used to be, relative to published basic research, and that this is consonant with the policy. But why the two are consonant, or even if there is any relationship between them, is unclear. In fact, this may well be an artifact of something else altogether—like Internet publishing of basic research, a form of research not counted by the research referred to earlier.

To summarize so far: the research on curriculum restructuring concludes that the knowledge structure of a discipline shapes the form of accommodation to market and policy fashions; the research on research type restructuring concludes that knowledge production may very well follow policy. What are we to make of this?

It may be useful to reflect briefly on knowledge morphology and morphological change. First of all, the forms (that is, the formal units) of knowledge are, like the desert, always in motion, in response to innovation and knowledge growth at the apex of the discipline. The traditional knowledge form is the discipline (both for research as well as for teaching purposes), and disciplines often grow towards each other in response to converging research programs. At a given point, although not yet fixed together, disciplinary singulars form a loose regional association and they become regionalized. When the regionalizing amalgamation process is sufficiently advanced, the region morphs, or integrates, into a new stable singular again at a higher level of conceptual integration and abstraction (Bernstein, 2000).

A plausible explanation for the policy of programmatisation then is that the program-policy advocates read the signs that we are, globally, in a period of rapid knowledge growth, hence of generalized rationalization (growing together of disciplines). Since the traditional disciplines naturally hold onto their turf, a way must be found to circumvent this reaction in order to teach the new transitional regions to a new cadre of students; hence the need for interdisciplinary programs.

There are two arguments against this explanation for programmatisation. The first is that, in the Humanities, where the drive to programs has been the most avid, we are unlikely to get a successful transition from singulars, through a process of growing together or rationalization, to a new higher-order singular, because the Humanities, nearly all having a relatively horizontal knowledge structure with a weak internal grammar, simply proliferate new languages of description. That is, horizontal knowledge structures exhibit movement laterally, into the formation of sub-disciplines with low explanatory power, like cultural studies, or critical legal studies for example, rather than vertically into a higher order regional integration. They don't easily morph into higher-order singulars (there are exceptions—usually in response to changes in a knowledge field adjacent to science, i.e., to a more vertical knowledge structure, like archaeology and urban studies). Under such circumstances, programmatisation looks suspiciously like trying to force rationalization on the terrain of production (research) from the terrain of reproduction (curriculum), which can't easily be done. Knowledge forms can only stably be changed at the sharp end of innovation and genuine knowledge growth, not by trying to teach a premature integration of disciplines.

The second argument against the plausible explanation is that it assumes that in order to acquire applied or interdisciplinary skills (or whatever else in the programs it is assumed is lacking in the traditional disciplinary curriculum) it is necessary to teach them directly, often in place of the disciplines. Here the old debate about *learning transfer* rears its head. A broad church of curricularists, including the social Darwinist Herbert Spencer (of the original useful knowledge argument), the behaviorist Thorndike, vocationalists of every stripe, and the protagonists of outcomes-based education (by no means an exhaustive list) believed and believe that knowledge cannot be generalized across contexts, and that each knowledge or skill for each context must be explicitly taught, (see Supovitz, 2001). This is the low-transfer school of curriculum thought, intellectually compatible with the mode 2 research form change theorists Gibbons and Scott mentioned above. The high-transfer school, on the other hand, including an equally broad church of congregants that would include certain curriculum traditionalists (after all, Latin was retained for so long in both the university and the school curriculum because it was assumed that

Latin conveyed a mental discipline that was transferable to all other contexts), but also Durkheim, Gramsci and the situative cognitivists who hold that learning is a combination of context-specific knowledge and general problem-solving abilities. Here, generalisable conceptual tools are learnt only in the course of acquiring a domain-specific knowledge base. But not all domain-specific knowledge bases have generalisable conceptual tools (or, as I said in cognate terms above, they do not all have a vertical knowledge structure with a strong internal grammar). Many low-transferists, ignoring such relative differences in knowledge structure, imagine that any subject is equivalent to any other in teaching higher-order thinking. John Dewey once notoriously said in a public lecture that children would learn as much from laundry as they might from zoology (Ravitch, 1999, p. 59), a misconception widely-held amongst curriculum engineers seeking to promote equivalence via schemes like programs, unit standards, and other forms essaying to replace the continually-evolving morphological structure of the conventional discipline.

In the South African higher education policy debate, I have advanced a form of the high-transfer view against that of Gibbons and Scott, and against current government program policy (see Ensor, 2002), who favor teaching an integrated interdisciplinary curriculum to undergraduates the more quickly to induct them into useful, applied, and interdisciplinary creative work. My argument (Muller, 2000) was that integrated interdisciplinary cognitive skills could only be acquired once one had already acquired a base of disciplinary skills, (that is, domain-specific knowledge with vertical extension and generalisable conceptual tools). Teaching interdisciplinary knowledge (that is applied skills), before giving students the conceptual tools with which to situate that knowledge in its larger coherent pattern, I argued, was to leave the students in a procedural "how to" mode, without tools of extension and innovation, precisely the skills that the interdisciplinary advocates wish the students to learn.

At the beginning of this section on assessing policy impact, I asked what weight could be attached to the conclusion that program policy was confuted by the dialectic between knowledge forms and academic identities, or that policy had changed the social formats of knowledge production and the habitual practices of an entire research community. Unfortunately the answer must be—not very much. The evidence simply does not demonstrate policy impact, conventionally understood. Without the evidence, there's not a lot we can say about the impact of policy on either university curricula restructuring or on the domain of academic research practice.

RESPONSIVENESS VERSUS INNOVATION

In *The Constant Gardener*, his recent novel, John le Carré all but accuses the pharmaceutical companies of insidious, methodical corruption of scientific opinion, by buying favors, targeting grants to universities, to centers and to favored researchers on a scale that makes normal governmental corruption look almost quaint. So saturated is medical research by doing company quid pro quos, insinuates le Carré, that the suppression of inconvenient conclusions is commonplace, of inconvenient researchers too. The impartial medical journals, that premier indicator of research excellence, become mouthpieces of corporate propaganda under professorial imprimatur. Why does the press not expose this? Well, reporters are even more easily bought than professors: and besides, the issues are complex, and the companies can, with laughable ease, buy politically correct public opinion. This is the general substance of le Carré's charge.

In a world where academic merit is measured in part by the amount of research funding garnered, and in a world where, by the end of the 1990s, the statutory funding bodies of central government couldn't begin to compete with private money, then defining responsiveness as responsive to societal needs was less a faded dream than a bad joke. As Jansen (2001, p. 6) says: The single most important mistake made by the former CSD (Centre for Science Development) and the former FRD (Foundation for Research Development; the names of the state run statutory funding councils) was to think that a small amount of money could be spread so thinly within research—weak institutions and make any difference at all. Researchers like Subotzky (1999) like to draw a distinction between noble private money (usually from global donors) for noble social ends, and other private money for other more market-related ends. But what really is the difference? Organizations, once committed to an externally funded project of whatever kind, become socially locked in for financial rather than intellectual reasons. The truth is, once you're in the market, once you're chasing money for the sake of it, or rather, once private money pushes out public money, then these things blur, and market logic blots out social responsibility niceties. Countries, South Africa included, that pursue third-way center-left political policies that attempt to steer a path between rampant free market ideology and state collectivism, are thus likely to have higher education restructuring strategy statements that attempt to "reflect both the 'marketization' as well as the 'equity' strands of the 'third way' political frameworks" (Naidoo, 2000, p. 26)[2] as we saw in the Introduction. Does this mean that third way policies manage the balancing act? Unfortunately, no. Because the trade-off is not forthrightly faced, they end up managing to widen stratification and widen exclusion.

The reason though is not because the market trumps policy. Rather, the unintended consequences arise directly from the exogenous pressures (the market or policy) trying to direct endogenous intellectual activity, (the growth of science and the kind of research the universities, and other institutions, do). In a classic paper, Michael Polanyi (1962) points out the similarities between market dynamics and science dynamics. The dynamics of both are created by the accretion of multiple independent initiatives mutually adjusting themselves at every successive stage stepwise towards a joint achievement. Such self-coordination—by means of an invisible hand—is what is common (see also Lindblom & Cohen, 1979). But the differences are also important. Mutual adjustment in the market is on the basis of prices motivating agents to exercise economy in terms of money. Scientists, by contrast, are motivated by professional standards—plausibility, accuracy, importance, intrinsic interest, and above all, originality (see Polanyi, 1962, pp. 56–59). The net result is coordinated action in general, but also subversion in particulars. Scientific growth depends on principled subversion, on the precise enunciation of the unknown. This is what the economists call innovation.

Polanyi goes on to explore attempts to direct science either for ethical (serving social needs) or practical (relevant) ends, and concludes that it is only possible to stop scientific trends, not create or direct them: "You can kill or mutilate the advance of science, you cannot shape it. For it can advance only by essentially unpredictable steps, pursuing problems of its own, and the practical benefit of these advances will be...doubly unpredictable" (Polanyi, 1962, p. 62). As far as unpredictability goes, Polanyi goes on to give the example of a BBC Brains Trust program in January 1945 where he and Bertrand Russell had both denied any practical value to Einstein's theory of special relativity: a few months later in August 1945 the atom bomb was dropped on Hiroshima.

It has become customary, in these postmodern times, to say that the "republic of science" turns into the entrepreneurial university (Slaughter & Leslie, 1997) because it has lost the autonomy on which it was built (see Rip & van der Meulen, 1996; Delanty, 2001). While this captures a part of the story, it misses the contemporary relevance of Polanyi's analysis, which aimed to provide a political and economic theory of scientific innovation, and which anticipates central insights of current economics of innovation. In this body of work we find the conundrum, already alluded to above, that normal novelty (first order learning) is relatively easily predictable and directable, but real or reconstructive novelty (learning to learn) is in its essence uncertain: "it is unpredictable and therefore cannot be selected by rational choice" (Nooteboom, 1999, p. 128). In other words, real research novelty—true innovation—cannot be rationally directed by policy on the supply side, or by users on the demand side. This is the classical picture, and it means that, classically, the core conditions for the production of innovation operate optimally at a relative necessary distance both from supply-side control (the states control model which van Vught (1991) shows is inimical to innovation) and from the demand-side tyranny of short term utility.

We do not live in classical, but globalising, times. The key entailed feature for higher education, technology aside, is the circumscribed role of the state, shifting it inexorably from the role of main provider (predominant source of funding) to that of regulator (Delanty, 2001, p. 121). Universities worldwide get less and less of their funding from government. The University of Wisconsin-Madison now receives 23% from the state, down from 33%: the state University of California is similarly down to 30%. In South Africa the average is still a relatively high 60%. For all universities world wide, the balance must come from the private sector, pushing universities inexorably into academic capitalism (Slaughter & Leslie, 1997) and multiple stakeholder contracts, and away from the singular influence of the state.

The optimal condition for innovation above can therefore be re-stated as: preserving necessary distance especially from the user interface, when reputational advantage, professional standing, even survival, depend on an ever greater dependence on multiple sources of funding. The danger from this interface lies in the possibility of stunted research agendas, in the unintended consequence of crowding out basic research as we saw above (Glaser, 2000), but it lies also in the danger of premature utilization. All the user interface terms currently used to designate research applicability—relevance, responsiveness, context-of-application research—embed the idea that the commissioning interface is necessarily the one the research results will be most applicable to. The economics of learning recognizes that this is rarely so: Its early use may occur where its fit with the prevailing architecture is feasible with a minimum of systemic changes rather than where it is most productive (Nooteboom, 1999, p. 138). Many of sciences most dramatic applications occur in a different time and space to that of the original discovery itself. The case of special relativity and nuclear fission is just one example. The peril of premature relevance is that eager commissioners at the user interface, anxious to show spending efficiency to their financial bosses, tend to go off half-cocked. The systemic consequence is a flaccid and malfunctioning innovation system.

The user interface is thus potentially now a greater danger to innovation than during the time of greater autonomy. What is to be done? The IDRC Report (1993) believes that the thirty-year old idea of a "republic of science" (that is, scientific autonomy), in its simplest formulation, is still, in fact a guide to the operation of South Africas long-term S&T policy (IDRC, 1993, p. 24), but this states the requirement—for greater distance—rather than the means for achieving it. Certainly the clock is not going to be turned back to full state provision, the classical condition for full autonomy. What then is the contemporary condition for necessary distance in research? In some quarters, the answer is seen as lying in the deployment of the idea of strategic research.

The National Commission on Higher Education Report (1996) had mentioned strategic research as one of four research types, the others being traditional, applications-driven, and participation-based (see Mouton, 2001, p. 6). Mouton goes on to trace the provenance of the idea of strategic research, showing that it is sometimes placed closer to applied, sometimes closer to basic research (basic research with a long term perspective). Rip (1997, 2001) extends this idea of what he calls the *emerging regime of strategic science.* In his view, scientists have begun to internalize the global pressure towards relevance and accountability, while holding on to the basic longer-term trajectory of knowledge growth. In other words, scientists increasingly attend to global scientific horizons by means of framing them in terms of local issues (think local, act global): "Strategic research combines relevance (to specific contexts, possibly local) and excellence (the advancement of science as such), and may therefore bridge the eternal tension between the regional and global" (Rip, 2001, p. 4). But because this is not directly and narrowly applications-driven, "(a) distance is created between the research and its eventual uptake..." (ibid). Strategic research is thus a strategic synthesis of basic research with the new press to relevance specifically to avoid the "dominance of short-term considerations" (Rip, 2001, p. 5)—to tap into the money available for social problem solving while preserving a distance from the user interface. Or as Mouton (2001, p. 26) puts it, "to address the seemingly conflicting demands from internal and external stakeholders."

There are two questions that arise here. The first one is whether the strategic regime is a genuinely new mode of knowledge production, superseding basic and applied modes, or whether it is merely a resource mobilizing strategy, a rhetorical device to get to the money while holding on to autonomy and necessary distance. Rip and Mouton both consider that it is a real, rather than just rhetorical, phenomenon. Rip particularly sees it as a natural correlative to the emergence of regional development and innovation centers (see Castells, 2001) in the global economy, where the growth of the economy and the growth of knowledge are equally nurtured. Maybe, but we will have to wait and see: perhaps it is a bit of both. Certainly South African researchers increasingly embrace the term, and it is a distinct organizing category in the national data set (see Mouton, 2001). The second question is whether strategic research is not just a beguiling term adopted by newer and less established institutions who are systemically marginal, in other words weak, used to bid for a more central position, in money and status terms, in the reputational field. Rip acknowledges the possibility, but denies that it impairs the theory. After all, that is what the Afrikaans universities did in the 1960s, and this facility with strategicality, initiated under apartheid and refined over the last decade, probably accounts for the unexpected and uncontested ease with which Pretoria University, once the ideological home of apartheid, has laid claim to the statutory Centre for Scientific and Industrial Research (the most potent of the former statutory research agencies). Strategic research, with a foot in both basic and applied, is tough-minded research, bringing in the money and advancing knowledge growth. The currently marginal institutions will not easily improve their position by embracing participation-based or action research alone, as some have suggested (for example, EPU, 2001).

CONCLUSION

This paper has been concerned to elucidate two key features of restructuring and the new governance in South African higher education. The first is the restructuring of the governing principles that relate the individual (here the individual higher education institution) and the state (Lindblad & Popkewitz, 2002). We have seen that this complex dynamic has driven universities into a new strategicality in relation to their increasingly diverse environmental network of pacts and partners. One facet of this dynamic is certainly that the state loses a certain influence over universities, but more important still, the university must deploy a multidirectional strategic cunning in order to survive. The second feature is that the "problematic of knowledge" (ibid), one of the two redemptive longings anchoring restructuring, drives a logic of differentiation, both within the institution between departments and faculties, and between institutions, that makes a one size fits all state-driven policy increasingly unworkable. The "problematic of equity," the other redemptive longing and one that necessarily looms large in the South African political imaginary, currently blinds policy makers to this insight. The paper has tried to demonstrate these points in relation to the two domains of knowledge work of universities, curriculum programme organisation, and research policy and practice.

What can we then conclude about the impact of educational restructuring on research and curriculum practices in universities in South Africa? First, we should accept the argument of Delanty (2001) above that the state, under globalisation, recedes as a financial provider and hence too as the most singular source of influence over public higher education. Universities are increasingly embedded in a cross-meshed network of public-private partnerships that include government, industry, and the professions, an environment of multiple markets that cannot easily be reduced to a single source of influence. It comes as no surprise then that we have no hard evidence that state policies in either research or curriculum have had any fundamental influence on what academics actually do. It would be tempting to conclude that this was so simply because of the weakness of the state, but that too would be inaccurate. Not only are multiple markets more influential, but—and this has been a central argument of the paper—the institutions themselves also contribute powerfully to this effect. Institutional theory shows that organisations are easier to influence from without only when the outside signals correspond to their internal criteria of, and learnt capacities for, relevance. When the external signals go against these, they become highly resistant: they are able to ignore control signals, to forego incentives, and to absorb sanctions, without changing their ways in the direction desired by government policy makers (Scharpf, 1987/1988, p. 105). Scharpf goes on to say that many institutions will collapse rather than change their internal value system. In similar vein, van Vught (1991), in a wide-ranging discussion of why university curricular reforms invariably fail, concludes, like Scharpf, that fundamental reforms will fail because the institutions cannot absorb their complexity:

> When complexity is defined as the combination of the degree to which an innovation is a departure from existing values and practices with the number of functional areas aimed at by the innovation, the level of complexity of an innovation process in higher education may be expected to be negatively related to the rate of adoption of the innovation. The more complex an innovation, the less successful that innovation will be in getting adopted (van Vught, 1991, p.34).

It is highly likely that the sheer complexity of curriculum programmatic change was entirely underestimated by the state policy makers in South Africa. Programmatic curriculum restructuring thus partly failed because of its ambitiousness, and partly too because policy makers underestimated the diversity of institutional capacity in the system.

The same holds in the realm of research. One may be inclined to conclude that the balance of power has, in the case of research, swung from the state to the multiple markets commissioning and funding a veritable flood of new research, but that would be to underestimate the power of the endogenous features of the higher education institutions. The swing to the user interface, conventional fastidiousness about the instrumentalisation of knowledge aside, does not present the same kind of structural threat to knowledge-based practice as that presented by programmatisation, which after all in its maximal form would have entailed the end of conventional departments as well as conventional disciplines.

If suppositions about strategic research, advanced by Rip and Mouton above, hold up, then it is quite likely that the imperatives of knowledge growth and relevance will both be served by the new if seemingly contradictory impulsions behind strategic research. But as was said above, not all disciplines can present an equally effective strategic face to the world, and it will take a discerning policy to nurture those disciplines with a great gap between their basic and applied activities, while those with a narrower one prosper by the strategic route.

A main conclusion arises from considering the impact of exogenous factors on universities. First, consider *government policy impact* on universities (alternatively, institutional responsiveness to policy). Here, as in other domains of education, South African commentary dwells over-much on the intended policy, investing it with an importance that is rarely borne out empirically. We tend naturally to expect that the policy can and should have its intended impact, and are invariably surprised when it doesn't. Secondly, the same goes for multiple market impact, which, all too often reduced to a singular force, is either wholeheartedly welcomed as the private solution to public inefficiency, or treated as the evil eye. One consequence of this simplification and its consequent distortion, the analysis above suggests, is that we do not take the institutions and *institutional responsive capacity* sufficiently seriously. Were we to do so, we would have different and differentiated expectations about institutional response possibilities. Furthermore, were the policy makers to take institutional responsive capacity more seriously, together with the differential impacts of markets on different kinds of institution, they may very well frame their policy levers in more differentiated ways.

South African universities, like their peers elsewhere, are thus beholden to their exogenous partners, but not fatally so, with the specific exception of a small group of institutions in the country that are historically poor in social and cultural capital. It is only from their perspective that state support in the form of input-based subsidies makes the difference between financial survival and ruin. For all other kinds of institutions, state and markets are both exogenous forces with variable possibilities, to be treated with variable degrees of caution and strategic guile. *Endogenous self-propulsion* is probably still the mode best suited to the long-term health of the science and innovation system, as the IDRC Report (1993) affirmed. Under these circumstances, a globally repositioned state like South Africa should adopt a more nuanced, more differentiated, and principally reward-based approach, if it is to get the best from its higher education system.

APPENDIX
CHANGE INITIATIVES IN HIGHER EDUCATION

Over 30 change initiatives from various government departments currently demand higher education management time and financial resources.

Policy Issues Requiring Integration

Restructuring
- National Working Group proposals
- Minister of Educations proposals for restructuring
- Merger discussions, with array of attendant issues
- Regional aspects of restructuring
- Formation of new types of institutions—e.g. Institutes of Technology, National Institutes of Higher Education, comprehensive institutions

Research
- Programmes for capacity building
- Emphasis on innovation
- Ratings for researchers in Humanities

Academic Planning
- Provisions of National Plan for Higher Education (NPHE)
- Mission and niche documentation
- Programme and Qualification Mix (PQM)
- Regional discussions/proposals on identified programmes
- Three-year rolling plans
- Changing admissions requirements
- Implementing National Higher Education Information and Application Service (NHEIAS)

Quality Assurance
- Institutional audit framework proposals
- Programme accreditation framework proposals
- Research framework being prepared
- Teaching and Learning support framework in progress
- Institutional visits by Higher Education Quality Committee (HEQC) now under way

National Qualifications Framework: Programmes & Qualifications
- New academic policy
- Revision of South African Qualifications Authority (SAQA) under way
- Outcomes-based formats for programmes/qualifications
- Procedures for registration/approving funding of new programmes
- Regional clearing of new programmes

Governance
- Council on Higher Education (CHE) Policy Report: Promoting Good Governance in South African Higher Education

Policy Issues Requiring Integration (Cont.)

Equity & Labour Issues

- Implementation of labour legislation
- Employment Equity Act
- Institutions formulating equity policies, plans and reports
- Skills Development Act
- Transformation processes within institutions

Data Collection & Reporting

- Changeover from SAPSE (South African Post-Secondary Education system) to HEMIS (Higher Education Management Information System)
- Production of institutional annual reports
- Issues of reporting vis-à-vis governance, with reference to King Report II
- Responding to requests for information from government departments

Funding

- New funding formula awaited—will impact on academic planning and PQM
- Funding for mergers, for redress, for deficits

NOTES

1. None of these approaches ignores the social dimension, but they understand it in a more analytical sense than the policy literature generally does, and they are always concerned to understand how the social dimension interacts with the cognitive dimension.

2. A cruel contemporary jest: what is the difference between Margaret Thatcher and Tony Blair? Answer: Thatcher believed in privatisation; Blair just likes rich people. What the joke insinuates is that entrepreneurialism has become a new age aesthetic.

REFERENCES

Ball, S. (1993). What is policy? Texts, trajectories and toolboxes. *Discourse, 13*(2), 10–17.

Bawa, A., & Mouton, J. (2002). Research. In N. Cloete et. al. (Eds.), *Transformation in higher education: Global pressures and local realities in South Africa.* Lansdowne: Juta.

Bernstein, B. (1996, 2000). *Pedagogy, symbolic control, and identity.* Oxford: Rowman & Littlefield Publishers.

Bourdieu, P. (1988). *Homo academicus.* Cambridge: Polity Press.

Bunting, L. (2002). *Measuring institutional change: the application of two theoretical models to tw South African higher education institutions.* Unpublished Masters Dissertation, University of Cape Town.

Callon, M. (1995). Four models for the dynamics of science. In S. Jasanoff et al. (Eds.), *Handbook of science and technology studies.* London: Sage Publications.

Castells, M. (2001). Think local, act global. In J. Muller et al. (Eds.), *Challenges of globalization.* Cape Town: Maskew Miller Longman.

Clark, P., & Carter, C. (1999). *Academic capitalism and explacit knowledge* (mimeo). University of Birmingham.

Cloete, N., & Bunting, I. (2000). *Higher education transformation: Assessing performance in South Africa.* Pretoria: Centre for Higher Education Transformation.

Cloete, N., Fehnel, R., Gibbon, T., Maassen, P., & Moja, T. (Eds.). *Transformation in higher education: Global pressures and local realities in South Africa.* Lansdowne: Juta

Delanty, G. (2001). *Challenging knowledge: The university in the knowledge society.* Buckingham: SRHE/OUP.

Department of Culture, Science, and Technology (DACST). (2002). *South Africa's national research and development strategy.* Pretoria.

Ensor, P. (2001). Education programme planning in South Africa: Three institutional case studies. In M. Breier (Ed.), *Curriculum restructuring in higher education in post-apartheid South Africa.* Pretoria: Centre for Science Development.

Ensor, P. (2002). Curriculum. In N. Cloete et al. (Eds.), *Transformation in higher education: Global pressures and local realities in South Africa.* Lansdowne: Juta.

Education Policy Unit (EPU). (2001). *Case study: The integrated nutrition programme.* Public Health Programme, University of the Western Cape.

Etzkowitz, H., & Leydesdorff, L. (1995). The triple helix: University-industry-government relations. A laboratory for knowledge based economic development. *European Society for the Study of Science and Technology Review, 14,* 14–19.

Glaser, J. (2000). Limits of change: Cognitive constraints on "postmodernization" and the political redirection of science. *Social Science Information, 39*(3), 439–465.

Gibbons, M., Nowotny, H., Limoges, C., Trow, M., Schwartzman, S., & Scott, P. (1994). *The new production of knowledge: The dynamics of science and research in contemporary societies.* London, Sage.

Gournitzka, A., & Maassen, P. (2000). Hybrid steering approaches with respect to European higher education. *Higher Education Policy, 13,* 267–285.

International Development Research Centre (IDRC). (1993). *Towards a science and technology policy for a democratic South Africa.* Montreal: IDRC.

Jansen, J. (2000). Mode 2 knowledge and institutional life. In A. Kraak (Ed.), *Changing modes.* Pretoria: HSRC.

Jansen, J. (2001). *Changing institutional research cultures* (mimeo). University of Pretoria.

Kraak, A. (2001). Changing modes: A brief overview of the mode 2 knowledge debate and its impact on South African policy formulation. In A. Kraak (Ed.), *Changing modes.* Pretoria: HSRC.

Latour, B. (1999). *Pandora's hope: Essays on the reality of science studies.* Cambridge, MA: Harvard University Press.

Lindblad, S., & Popkewitz, T. (2002). *Education governance in transition: Stories of progress and denials and dissolutions of policy conflicts.* Paper presented to EERA (September). Lisbon.

Lindblom, C., & Cohen, D. (1979). *Usable knowledge: Social science and social problem solving.* New Haven: Yale University Press.

Mayntz, R., & Schimank, U. (1998). Linking theory and practice. *Research Policy, 27,* 747–755.

Mouton, J. (2001). *Between adversaries and allies: the call for strategic science in post-apartheid South Africa.* Stellenbosch: Centre for Interdisciplinary Studies, Stellenbosch University.

Meyer, J-B., Kaplan, D., & Charum, J. (2001). Scientific nomadism and the new geopolitics of knowledge. *International Social Science Journal, 168.*

Muller, J. (2000). *Reclaiming knowledge.* London: Routledgefalmer.

Muller, J. (2001). Connectivity, capacity and knowledge. In J. Muller et al. (Eds.), *Challenges of globalisation.* Cape Town: Maskew Miller Longman.

Muller, J. (1991). South Africa. In P. Altbach (Ed.), *International higher education: An encyclopaedia.* New York: Garland Publishing.

Muller, J., & Ogude, N. (2002). Curriculum reform in higher education in South Africa: How academics respond. In E. F. Beckman (Ed.), *Global collaborations: The role of higher education in diverse democracies.* Washington, DC: Association of American Colleges and Universities.

Muller, J., & Subotzky, G. (2001). What knowledge is needed in the new millennium? *Organisation, 8(2),* 163–182.

Naidoo, R. (2000). The "Third Way" to widening participation and maintaining quality in higher education: lessons from the United Kingdom. *Journal of Educational Enquiry, 1/2,* 24–38.

Nooteboom, B. (1999). Innovation, learning, and industrial organization. *Cambridge Journal of Economics, 23,* 127–150.

Polanyi, M. (1962). The republic of science. *Minerva, 1(1),* 54–73.

Ravitch, D. (1999). *Left back: A century of failed school reform.* New Jersey: Simon & Schuster.

Rhoades, G. (2000). Who's doing it right? Strategic activity in public research universities. *The Review of Higher Education, 24(1),* 41–66.

Rip, A. (2001). Regional innovation systems and the advent of strategic science, *Journal of Technology Transfer.*

Rip, A. (1997). A cognitive approach to relevance of science. *Social Science Information, 36(4),* 615–640.

Rip, A., & Van Der Meulen, B. J. R. (1996). The post-modern research system. *Science & Public Policy, 23,* 342–352.

Scharpf, F. W. (1987/1988). The limits of institutional reforms. In T. Ellwein, J. J. Hesse, R. Mayntz, & F. W. Sharpf (Eds.), *Yearbook on government and public administration, 1987/1988.* Baden-Baden: Nomos.

Shinn, T. (1999). Change or mutation? Reflections on the foundations of contemporary science. *Social Science Information, 38,* 293–309.

Slaughter, S., & Leslie, L. (1997). *Academic capitalism: Politics, policies, and the entrepreneurial university.* Baltimore: Johns Hopkins University Press.

South African Universities Vice-Chancellors Association (SAUVCA). (2002). *A vision for South African higher education: Transformation, restructuring, and policy integration* (Position Paper, November). Pretoria: SAUVCA.

Subotzky, G. (1999). Alternatives to the entrepreneurial university: New models of knowledge production in community service programmes. *Higher Education, 38*(4), 401–440.

Supovitz, J. A. (2001). Translating teaching practice into improved student achievement. In S. Furhrman (Ed.), *From the capitol to the classroom: Standards-based reform in the states.* Chicago: Chicago University Press.

Taylor, N. (2001). *Outcomes, effort, and values in schooling* (mimeo). Johannesburg: Joint Education Trust.

Van Vught, F. A. (1991). *Autonomy and accountability in government/university relationships* (mimeo). World Bank.

Weingart, P. (1998). Science and the media. *Research Policy, 27,* 869–870.

Weingart, P. (1997). From "finalisation" to mode 2": Old wine in new bottles? *Social Science Information, 36,* 591–613.

CHAPTER 8

EDUCATION RESTRUCTURING IN FRANCE

Middle-Class Parents and Educational Policy in Metropolitan Contexts

Agnès van Zanten
Observatoire Sociologique du Changement
Centre National de la Recherche Scientifique
Paris, France

INTRODUCTION

Education restructuring is concerned with the transition from government to governance; that is, with changes in the role of the State, with decentralization and participation of a larger set of actors in the formation, the enactment and the evaluation of policy in different ways in different contexts. Nevertheless, analyses still tend to conceptualize it as a top-down process. Changes that have led in many countries around the world to an increased marketization of education are for instance usually studied as the consequence of reform of national legislation concerning parental choice and school autonomy. This perspective is to a large extent relevant, espe-

Educational Restructuring: International Perspectives on Traveling Policies, pages 167–189
Copyright © 2004 by Information Age Publishing
167

cially concerning countries such as England where an impressive amount of new policies have been formulated both by Conservative and New Labour governments in the last twenty years (see Gewirtz et al. and Maguire chapters). However, even in these cases, this perspective may overplay the impact of political decisions at the central level and underplay that of cultural and social shifts visible at the local level (Kenway et al., 1993). It is my contention in this paper that, at least in the French case, it is necessary to adopt a complementary bottom-up perspective and to analyze the policy process as a complex interaction between grass root influences and national decisions (Ball, 1994, van Zanten & Ball, 2000). Whether this should be seen as a reduction of State power leading to the emergence of a Hollow State (Peters, 1980) or as a subtle way for the State to steer the system at a distance (Weiler, 1990) remains an open question.

Education restructuring can be described as a profound reshaping of State and civil society distinctions (Popkewitz, 2000; Lindblad & Popkewitz, this book). In the French case, two converging processes have fostered this. On the one hand, there is a growing gap between central national policy, enforcing an abstract ideal of equality and relying on bureaucratic rules to regulate public action, and local dynamics, especially in metropolitan contexts. These are characterized by growing inequalities between social groups and between schools that are reinforced by the individual and collective practices of local actors. On the other hand, the Central State itself has introduced official reforms leading to a considerable extension of the autonomy of local political bodies—regions, departments and municipalities—and local educational authorities—Rectorats, Inspections Académiques—and to changes in the power relations between different groups (head teachers, teachers, parents) in the educational arena. Both movements are leading to an increasing fragmentation of the educational process that is eroding the traditional distinctions between policy and practice, between makers and recipients of policy and between center and periphery. The Central State still keeps the official power of formulating and legitimating main policy directions but it leaves the increasingly complex burden of connecting principles and goals to social environments to individuals, schools and locales (van Zanten, 2002a).

One of the main consequences of this social—that is, not just legal or technical—process of decentralization has been the increasing power acquired by parents in the educational system. The formal system of decision-making at the national level still relies on a strong alliance between the State and Teacher Unions typical of European centralized systems that largely excludes parents (Barroso, 2000). However, the informal process of practice-as-policy at the local level is strongly informed by parent's micro-decisions and actions concerning choice of school and direct and indirect intervention in school affairs. A significant example of this is the fact that although school choice in the public sector is officially forbidden except for a limited number of cases, research has documented situations in the Parisian periphery where more than 25% of pupils are not enrolled in the school of their catchments area (Broccolichi & van Zanten, 2000). Middle-class parents, whose professional situation, lifestyles and values have historically entertained a more privileged relationship with school capital than those of other social classes are the main actors in this process (Bourdieu, 1979; Ball, 2002). Their role as policy-makers is however a very problematic one for at least two reasons. The first is that the diverse and frequently contradictory positions and interests of various middle-class fractions leads them to develop different lines of justification and action, creating controversies that prevent unity and coherence. The second is that, although not all middle-class parents position themselves exclusively as individual consumers of education, the orientations and modes of organization of present public policy leads them to give a much greater importance to their private interests than to the search for the public good.

MIDDLE-CLASS PARENTAL ESPECTATIONS AND PREFERENCES AND THE REDINITION OF THE PUBLIC SCHOOL

In the current debates about the importance of class in postindustrial societies (Westergaard, 1995, Pakulski & Waters, 1996), the position adopted here is that class still matters. The analysis of more than a hundred interviews with middle-class parents and the comparison with other interviews with lower-class parents shows the maintenance of different expectations towards schooling between different classes.[1] These differences result both from early socialization into still distinct family, local and school environments and from anticipation of future work and life conditions. This does not mean that there are no transformations in the dynamic relationship between class and schooling. As concerns the middle-class, which is the focus of our analysis in this chapter, three different changes must be underlined. The first has to do with the impact of the restructuring of capitalist economy and the educational system on the relationship between the middle-class and other classes. The globalization of capitalist national economies and the growing importance of credentials has led to an increase in the competition between traditional managers and professionals on the one side and a new generation of top managers, what Adonis and Pollard (1997) call the super-class on the other side which concentrates on access to elite higher-education institutions (Collins, 1979). At the same time, the democratization of entry to secondary and some types of higher education and the development of new policies of positive discrimination have increased the anxiety of middle-class parents, especially of its lower fractions (Ball & Vincent, 2001). This leads them to adapt their exclusionary educational strategies to close off opportunities to the increasing proportion of members of the lower-classes that are having access threatening their position (Parkin, 1979; Murphy, 1988).

The second change has to do with the reinforcement of divisions between different middle-class fractions that these transformations have produced. In France, the official code of classification of professions and social categories distinguishes between managers and professionals, between lower and upper fractions of these categories, and between those who work in the private and in the public sector (Desrosières & Thévenot, 1982). I have found these distinctions relevant as concerns schooling. A third change has to do with middle-class parents' participation in schooling. Although it is possible to show that educational reform has for the last two centuries been oriented toward the expansion of the middle-class and to the satisfaction of its expectations, politicians, administrators and teachers mainly made decisions. From the beginning of the 1980s, however, educational restructuring has contributed to the increase of middle-class parents direct influence on schooling. It is my contention here that the expression of their changing preferences as concerns the instrumental, expressive and social role of schools is a main factor in the redefinition of the public school in France, especially at the secondary level (van Zanten, 2002b).

ADAPTING THE PUBLIC SCHOOL?

Although the public secondary school has undergone profound transformations in the last fifty years as concerns pupils numbers and social make up, its curriculum has not changed in significant ways. The only exception concerns a major transition from the dominance of the classics to that of mathematics, which has become the main instrument of selection to move up into prestigious higher education institutions (Cherkaoui, 1982). Now, however, in anticipation of their children's professional and social futures in the new global economy, middle-class parents are becoming more demanding as concerns the teaching of subjects such as modern languages or new technologies. These expectations have not yet had a direct impact on secondary school curricula as middle class parents still rely on private forms of education in these areas including language lessons at home or in commercial agencies, travels and summer camps in other countries or domestic and outside school use of computers and internet. Nevertheless, new forms of competition are emerging between international schools offering bilingual classes and traditional elite schools and the latter are trying to improve the teaching of modern languages by hiring native-language helpers and increasing the number of linguistic exchanges with other schools. Similar changes are observed in the introduction of new technologies.

Economic and social changes have also had an impact on parental preferences concerning the form of schooling. In order to adapt to the flexible economy, many of the parents we interviewed insisted on the importance of learning work methods in schools. By this is meant autonomous work and work in small groups, as well as good communication skills. At the same time, middle-class parents have also become more demanding concerning results and are asking for more evaluations and controls. They want their children to be ahead, from an early age, in the race for credentials and to acquire a competitive character through confrontation with others with similar or higher educational capital. This leads them to be particularly anxious about the level of other children who are considered in terms of their instrumental value in the classroom:

> The teacher isn't the only one in the class. There are the other children too. Their verbal level is either a benefit or a disadvantage for your child. Depending on whether they make grammatical errors when they speak or use the right words and have a rich vocabulary, your child will either benefit from good language skills or hear rudimentary language. (Parents both psychologists)

Many of these parents do not believe that teachers are able to provide a good education for children of superior ability in comprehensive schools and classrooms either because there are important and insurmountable differences between children or because educational reforms have failed to create appropriate learning contexts or both.

Parental instrumental demands should lead them to choose schools according mainly to school results. This however is not always the case as instrumental demands are frequently combined with more expressive expectations on schools and teachers. The importance given in France to the rational and intellectual dimension of schooling has traditionally implied much less emphasis on the affective dimension, even in primary schools. Nevertheless, schools have not remained impervious to the individual hedonist tendencies, the cult of personal development and of children as a private form of re-enchantment that characterize post-industrial societies (Bernstein, 1967; Beck, 2001). Student-centered education is part of this movement in many countries around the world (see Chen's chapter). Parental expectations in this area translate themselves into demands for attending the whole personality of children and adolescents, for protection against academic pressure and for children's happiness in schools. Although these demands are partially contradictory with the instrumental focus on results, they can also be seen as efforts to limit excessive ambition and its destructive potential and as not necessarily incompatible with new forms of disguised control in the job market (Lipovetsky, 1983).

There are however differences in the instrumental and expressive preferences of different middle-class fractions, especially between managers working in the private sector and public sector professionals. These differences can be related to the fact that while the first group tends to rely on financial and organizational assets, the second gives priority to cultural assets (Savage et al., 1992). Managers appear more modernist and more demanding as concerns results. They are, for instance, more likely to focus on school quality than on any other factor when choosing a school. Professionals, especially those working in the public sector, appear more attached to traditional cultural contents, less demanding with respect to the school level and more attentive to the expressive desires of children. These reasons partially explain why they are more likely to leave their children at local schools at least until they enter the lycée but also why some of them choose non-selective private school:

> I had a choice between S. and N., and in conducting my own little inquiry I realized that parents who sent their children to S. were very concerned that they succeed and get good results. It's a school that gives children a great deal at the intellectual level. That wasn't at all what I was looking for, I wanted my child to blossom as a person. Of course I want him to reach a high level, but he should get something else, in addition. (Father public accountant, mother private school teacher)

More important to our purpose in this paper is the role that parents attribute to schools as agents of social integration. The majority of the parents interviewed in the study declared that schools were important to learn to live with others and to internalize societal rules. Nevertheless, most of their discourse was centered on the schools as agents for creating local forms of sociability among children and among parents. In areas where school mix reflects a more or less important degree of urban mix, these forms of sociability may be the basis for the construction of positive attitudes towards others in society. However, even in these cases, it is important to note that children and their parents tend to choose school friends, whether consciously or unconsciously, who match their social background and that open friendships are more and more discouraged as children grow older. In areas characterized by strong social and ethnic homogeneity, interactions between schoolchildren in and out of school naturally create and reinforce class-based sociability patterns, that are viewed, by the most strategic parents, as specific forms of social capital (Bourdieu, 1979):

> In the district we live in, most people are renters, like us; they have the same lifestyle. They often have large families, and the children all go to the same

schools. To give you an idea, in the three-story building we live in, there are three boys the same age as my son, they go to the same school, do almost the same scholastic and sports activities—it makes for a very convivial neighborhood atmosphere. In neighborhoods where the people are owners, it's different. Here most of the people are senior managers or civil servants, in transit for their career, or back from working abroad—they don't stay long. It is very enriching. (Father financial consultant, mother director of local branch of national employment agency)

Parental views on local forms of school sociability are strongly related to their view of society and of schools as mirrors of society. Parents working in the private sector, especially managers, tend to view society as composed of sets of highly compartmentalized social groups and the role of the school as that of fostering social integration by integrating each individual into its own group. The key word for these parents is identification with their own kind:

At the end of the year, there was a party at the school at T, and I saw that there was nobody like us. There were a lot of…. Self-managed rap groups with the principal on drums—that's fine, but it wasn't us… She felt good there for first grade, but as time would have gone on, there would have been fewer and fewer little girls like her, wearing dresses with puffy sleeves and rounded collars. I know it's a stereotype, but you don't want everyone to be like you, but you don't want to be completely isolated either—that's no favor to your children. Its good to be open, but you've still got to identify with something. (Father bank manager, mother at home)

There is a tension however between this kind of social insulation and the competitiveness and adaptation that these parents think are required by the modern job market and especially by the type of professional activity that they want theirs sons and daughters to exert. This explains why some of them view contact with social diversity in schools as a positive element in character formation. For these parents, social and ethnic mix might help children become accustomed to "real life," that is to a certain level of misunderstanding and aggressiveness from others, and more able to manage the work of lower-class employees. It is however important to underline that the degree of confrontation with real life remains fairly limited in these predominantly middle-class schools environments.

Parents working in the public sector, especially professional, are more likely to have a cosmopolitan vision of modern society. Society is conceived as a mosaic of groups—social, ethnic, religious, geographical—who should be able to interact in public spaces without being bounded by their origins (Bidou, 1984; Robson & Butler, 2001). The key word for these parents in terms of social integration in schools is tolerance towards others:

I think that a certain degree of mixing is good for everyone. Choosing highly elitist schools with children who all come from the same background—I don't think that's doing the children any favor. After all, they're in real life! And the whole business of learning tolerance and difference that gets compromised. So I think a certain mixing of origins, behaviors, and traditions ... but also with respect. (Mother and father both pharmacists)

A closer analysis of this attitude reveals however its utopian character. It is easier for these parents to hold this discourse to refer in an abstract way to their social environment than to talk in concrete ways about interactions with others. It is significant in that sense that while many parents view social and ethnic mix as a positive element in primary education where it could help the child catch a glimpse of the diversity of stratified, multi-ethnic urban French society, their discourse changes significantly as children become adolescents. Here the need for a more restricted form of class socialization appears necessary to most middle-class parents for instrumental, expressive and social reasons. In their view, adolescents placed in mixed schools may suffer both from the lower academic and cultural level of their classmates, from their disruptive or violent behaviour and from their lack of manners and social capital.

These attitudes reveal parents' anxiety about their incapacity to control the socialization of their children and thus their construction of their social identities in mixed, metropolitan environments. However, they are also related to a pervading lack of trust in the public schools present capacity to build a civic culture (see Dussel's chapter). Most parents are not convinced that the schools can play a central role in social integration because of the individualist, pluralist and laissez-faire orientation of school curriculum and of educational professionals' ideology. They feel that as concerns socialization—and not just instruction—there is little value added by public schools and that interaction inside these schools merely reflects interactions in urban society. When these schools are located in heterogeneous environments, many parents are afraid that the deficit of common values and of common ways of dealing with problems of authority and discipline will reinforce the dangers of social and ethnic mix. They fear that their children will at best unlearn the good habits learned at home and, at worst, will develop deviant behaviors or be bullied by violent classmates.

A PRIVATE VIEW ON PUBLIC SCHOOLING?

The diverse expectations that parents from different fractions of the middle classes hold for schools is a leading force for differentiating and hierarchizing them, especially at the secondary level. However, French parents tend to operate discriminations between public schools according mainly, and frequently exclusively, to pupil intake and to location. Good schools, both from an instrumental and a social point of view, are those located in residential areas and bad schools those located in mixed or lower class areas. Many parents consider that only the information on social, ethnic and academic mix that they can gather, mostly from other parents, is objective and valuable. On the contrary, information on school programs and activities is considered subjective and of little value. This is so because of the official ideology of equality through standardization, which has translated into little pedagogical autonomy for public schools but also because of parents lack of trust in public school professionals capacity to deal with the effects of school mix on learning and social integration. In fact, public schools are considered as providing a framework for the actualization of social relationships in society much more than a pedagogical and political model to transform them. The reproduction paradigm once denounced by Bourdieu and Passeron (1971) has in fact diffused in a very powerful way among middle-class parents (van Zanten, 2003):

> On the whole, differences are a matter of the population attending the school. It's mathematical, scientific; it's not even a matter of philosophy or political opinion—its scientific. If you're in a place where the population is, for example, poorer than a place where the populations richer or the parents are all high-level professionals, lets say, I know I'm taking extremes, but it's obvious that the quality of the schools won't be the same. That's just how it is, you can't do anything about it. (Father army engineer, mother at home)

To the devalued image of public schools parents oppose an enhanced image of private schools. Enjoying considerable autonomy as concerns pupil intake and the development of specific projects, schools from the private sector, operating with public funds and officially recognized as serving the public interest, were able from 1960 on to develop the image of the adaptable sector as opposed to the rigidity of the public sector (Prost, 1981; Ballion, 1982). Almost all of the parents interviewed—including those who had no personal experience of the private sector and who declared themselves in principle against its existence—saw it as offering much more interesting possibilities for a patterned education for their children or at least as a last resort in case of problems in the public sector. Private schools in fact correspond strongly to the flexible, caring and class-socializing institution that many middle-class parents would like public schools to be, although not all middle-class fractions support this model to the same extent.

Many private schools in urban areas select pupils in terms of ability and put very high demands on pupils as concern results. Although these strategic orientations make them very attractive to parents who are looking for a competitive learning environment, they do not prevent criticism from other parents who worry about the potential destructive dimension of this model of educational excellence:

> The atmosphere is lousy, all the children are stuck up. In my opinion, those children are vectors for what their parents put on their shoulders. There's terrible pressure... They always have to be the best. They're the elite. From seventh grade on, they're constantly being told they're the elite. (Father and mother both doctors)

However, other private schools are more interested in attracting parents who are not looking for instructional excellence but who want their children to acquire good work habits and learn in peaceful environments. Still some others specialize on pupils with learning difficulties. Because of this large spectrum of learning environments, which are publicly promoted as such in school brochures and interviews with parents, middle-class parents tend to see the private sector as the flexible sector, although some of them question the merit of private school professionals given the importance of selection and the educational investment demanded of parents in and out of school.

Parents who choose private schools are looking as much for care as they are looking for results and flexibility. The attractiveness of private schools lies as well on the quality of the global supervision of children and youngsters made possible by the combined effect of social segregation, of a more docile teaching body recruited by the head teacher, and of the stronger support of parents. Public schools are criticized for the anonymity of relationships between educational professionals and pupils. This is perceived as leading, at best, to the development of an instrumental attitude and, at worst, to anomie, deviance and violence among youngsters (Dubet, 1991). On the contrary, private schools are praised for the importance they give to the human factor, for the consensual interaction between educational professionals, parents and pupils and for their capacity to transmit self-confidence and a sense of well being to youngsters:

> In private schools, people are interested in you as a human being—that's the big difference. You feel like you are someone, and when you know you're someone, then you become someone... Its the whole affective aspect of things and then you have to find the means to create that affective part, and that's where the partnership comes in—something that doesn't necessarily exist in public schools. There needs to be a close partnership between parents, teachers, administrators, and pupils. To have that, there has to be a pedagogical project that everyone's behind. There's no real school project in public schools. That is, there's a big ministerial project, but no individual school project. (Mother teacher, father private-sector manager)

Some parents, especially professionals working in the public sector, are nevertheless critical of these schools, which are seen as over-protective and not helping children learn to be autonomous.

Nevertheless, there is on the whole a strong consensus among parents concerning private education qualities in the areas of instruction and care. This is not the case as concerns social integration where there are serious controversies among parents belonging to different middle-class fractions. Many parents emphasize the capacity of private schools to provide children with a sense of identification and community by developing a strong continuity between the values taught at home and in the school. Much more than public schools, private schools seem able to offer the type of class socialization desired by those parents, who are more likely to be managers and professionals working in the private sector:

> I think that the fact of going to a private school has to do with the parents' will. To begin with, parents have to make a major investment to send their children to a private school, so I think its above all the parents who are seeking values, values that will be continued with the teachers, you know what I mean, and because of this there are many more children who resemble my children, because that was what I wanted, in fact. The way they are raised at home should be continuous with, or should correspond to the education they receive at school. I mean little things, that seem insignificant but—being polite, to start with; you clean your plate—a whole bundle of little things like that, but they're important things; discipline of course, responsibility, responsibility toward others, respect for others, too, respect for teachers... (Father manager in the private sector, mother at home)

However, many others also emphasized the impact of social selection by private schools on segregation between schools and criticized the narrow type of socialization, the intolerance and the social hypocrisy to which pupils were exposed in private schools. If many parents make negative judgments on public schools because they do not have a coherent pedagogical and educational project, many others reprove private schools because they are not able to be agents of social integration.

MIDDLE CLASS PARENTS INDIVIDUAL AND COLLECTIVE ACTION AND THE REDEFINITION OF LOCAL EDUCATIONAL POLICY

Parental preferences exert an indirect but powerful influence on the prevalent educational rhetoric by remodeling and transforming the ideal of the public school. Parental individual and collective action exerts a direct and even more powerful influence on the redefinition of local educational policy. From an analytical point of view, it is possible to distinguish two different ways in which parental action influences policy. The first has to do with the aggregate effect of individual choices of public and private schools on the functioning of schools and school systems. The second concerns parental individual intervention in school affairs through discussion with staff and head teachers and participation at meetings and councils and through collective action in parents associations. In both cases however, it is possible to observe again important controversies concerning values, norms and practices by parents belonging to different middle-class fractions.

Middle-class parents educational strategies reflect parents' preferences and visions of schools, but also the material and symbolic resources of different local contexts. The diversity and accessibility of schools is an important material condition for choice, although the map of possible circuits of schooling varies according to parental social trajectories and positions (Ball et al., 1995; Broccholichi & van Zanten, 1997). Direct intervention in school affairs also varies according to the local configuration of relations in each school and in each local area. Others, that are neighbours, friends, members of the extended family or educational professionals, are important symbolic resources in the formation of judgement, in the construction of concrete plans and tactics and in the legitimation of final decisions. Educational strategies are socialized practices at an unconscious and a conscious level. They proceed, as other social practices from a deep-ingrained *habitus* informed by the social trajectory and by the social position of each family. However, given the increasingly problematic and critical dimension of educational decisions for middle-class parents they also proceed from conscious and more or less voluntary actions to penetrate, take profit or modify contexts and situations in interaction with others (Bourdieu, 1979; Bourdieu & Wacquant, 1992). Although the present economic and educational context is modifying the "taken-for-granted" attitude of bourgeois parents as well the lower class parents more fatalistic attitudes towards their children's educational futures, this strategic vision is still characteristic of middle-class parents (van Zanten, 1996).

PLAYING WITH THE RULES ON SCHOOL CHOICE

Quantitative studies have shown that middle-class parents are those who are more likely to make school choices in the public sector (Héran, 1996). This is done either officially by applying for specific options not offered in the local public school or by putting forward specific family problems or unofficially by giving a false address, or negotiating access with obliging head teachers. For instance in the area I studied parents could apply for a musical class option and for Russian as a language option which were both being offered by the most prestigious junior secondary school in the area studied. Using these strategies (very few of the parents were really interested in the content of the options) or illegal means to change to a public school with a better reputation supposes a great deal of anticipation and children's cooperation. For instance for children to be accepted in the musical option in secondary education, they had to have started very early musical lessons at the local academy of music, which would later certify the musical level of children, and be enrolled in the only primary school with a musical class. In addition to that, musical classes not only supposed a musical background but a lot of extra musical work at school and at home.

As options and reasons that are considered valid by local educational authorities to grant exemptions to enrollment in the local public school are not highly publicized, these strategies also suppose a lot of insider information which explains partly why teachers are the professional group most likely to use them (Ballion, 1990). The predominance of teachers also relates to the fact, however, that professionals from the public sector mostly use these strategies who do not want to choose the private sector for ideological reasons and who do not have enough economic capital to live near the most prestigious schools. It is important to note however that these possibilities for avoiding the local schools, especially those involving the choice of specific options, were frequently seen by parents as too complex and not necessarily beneficial for their children's career in the long run. English, for instance was considered a much more useful language than Russian in the present educational context. In addition to that, parents tended to see them as a form of fraud as they implied in most cases lying or pretending to obtain what they wanted. Despising the hypocrisy of the educational officials when dealing with exemptions was an important element of their critical view of local educational policy:

> I don't think it's right that they force a high school on us when the children are in middle school. We should have the right to send our children where we want; they should at least offer us a choice between several schools. If I hadn't chosen to use the private schools, I would only have had one possibility. Because if you ask for a special exemption to go to other public schools it is usually rejected. But some people do get exemptions, and personally that sort of thing drives me crazy. There're schemes, I know people who finagle their way, and really, that drives me crazy. Maybe you know, it works by whom you know, or else some people establish residency near the best middle school. (Father engineer, mother commercial manager)

In fact, most parents thought it much simpler—in the absence of financial or ability barriers—to send their children to nearby private schools. Almost one third of all families interviewed had sent at least one of their children to a private school or was seriously considering doing so. This decision supposed careful planning too as most private schools had waiting lists because of their good reputation, but also, in the case of less prestigious ones, because they did not have enough financial resources to expand. It also supposed additional personal and financial costs linked to distance and transportation. These costs were seen as too high by quite a large number of families who criticized the large periods of time children spent on private or public transport and school segregation by income. Some parents, however, especially some managers from the private sector, saw distance as strategic advantage as it would help children separate very early instrumental (school) and expressive (friends) dimensions of their existence. Choice of a private school was frequently influenced by informal conversations in and out of schools with other pupils, teachers, neighbors, friends and professional colleagues and, for some families, by the systematic interviewing of selected others. There were, however, important differences between families in the social meaning attributed to others' views on private schools. Middle-class managers from the private sector felt frequently that it was a social obligation in their social and local milieu to send children to private schools. On the contrary, many employees and professionals from the public sector thought that sending children to private schools was a betrayal of their political and social ideals and of the values of their social milieu and did not publicize their choices.

For many other families, however, the main decision, which had been taken or had to be taken, had to do with the link between residential strategies and educational strategies. This is both the consequence of the growing spatial mobility of the urban middle classes, especially of managers in the private sector, of the urban planning strategies of some communes and of the school policy of catchment areas. At least one other third of the families interviewed had taken into account school provision when moving and some were planning to move to be in the catchment area of a good school, especially when children were due to enter secondary school. This strategy supposed not only important financial resources and local contexts with an open and expanding real estate market, but also information on housing and on catchment areas. These factors introduced new forms of inequalities between families who have lived in the area or nearby for some time or who could use the social capital of family and friends living in the area to ask for advice and new comers with no connections. It is important to note that although the injustices linked to selection by mortgage was a main rationale for switching to a policy of school choice in many countries, French middle-class parents thought that moving was at least more honest than lying about their address (a practice not uncommon in some urban areas, especially in Paris where moving is a very costly strategy) or about motives for avoiding the local school. They also thought that by doing so they were being more sensitive to children's physical needs and to family well-being than families who chose to send their children to far away public or private schools.

The importance of proximity to school was also central to parents who, without choosing their place of residence in relation to school, presented the fact of sending their children to the local school as a conscious decision. These parents, frequently professionals or administrators in the public sector, tended to emphasize the social dimension more than physical needs or domestic well-being. This position, was not, however, entirely pure as it was frequently mixed with efforts to colonize schools to recreate acceptable learning and social environments (van Zanten, 2001). This implied three complementary strategies. The most important was trying to convince other middle-class parents to send their children to the local school through informal discussions and debates within the parents association:

> Several of the parents in my son's class, you know, the same level, have the same question (about which school to choose). So every once in awhile we get together and talk about it. If all of us, all the people at school C., decide to send their children to P., we can save P. But not many parents want to. There is a big core group at school C., a primary school where the quality is adequate. If all the children in all the sixth grade classes go to P., P. will become a better school than it is now. (Father engineer, mother housewife)

Another one was to put pressure on head teachers to have good, middle-class pupils insulated from others in ability classes. Another one still, that I explore in more detail further, was to use participation in schools to watch and monitor distribution of resources and teachers activity.

Although local education authorities do not officially recognize their influence, these parental strategies are having a profound impact on how schools function as schools adapt to parental supposed desires, but also to the strategies set up by other schools perceived as competitors. This impact varies according to the market position of each school, to its material and symbolic resources and to the degree of cooperation between the head teachers, the staff and parents (Gewirtz et al., 1995; Ball & van Zanten, 1998; Taylor, 2000). In the schools located in the most disadvantaged commune, two main changes were observed. The first one was an emphasis on discipline based mainly on constant surveillance, repression and effort to hide disruptive incidents when they took place. This reassured some middle-class parents but did not have any important long-term effect on causes and tended to divert teachers and head teachers from teaching concerns. The second one, already mentioned, was the setting of ability classes to retain the best middle-class pupils. Sometimes but not always successful in this respect, this response clearly reinforced segregation by ability, social class and ethnicity in the other classes (van Zanten, 2001).

In the schools located in the predominantly middle-class commune, which had more material and symbolic resources and were thus able to produce less reactive and localized responses, an interesting case of cooperation between schools emerged during the research. Five of the six secondary public schools elaborated a collective project to set up a European English option in each school in 2002 in order to counter-attack the attractive influence of similar sections in the two more prestigious private secondary schools. Although this would not have the same negative effect of ability classes in mixed schools, it is also another case of surface change encouraged by local competition and not by the desire to provide the best education for all children (Gewirtz et al., 1995). In fact, as in countries where choice is an official policy, parental strategies seem to be encouraging both socially and ethnically mixed schools and more homogeneous schools to recreate new forms of internal selection to be able to survive from public and private competition in an informal educational market.

INDIVIDUAL AND COLLECTIVE INTERVENTION IN PRIVATE AND PUBLIC SCHOOLS

School choice was not the only way in which parents influenced the functioning of schools. Almost all of the middle-class parents we interviewed declared themselves actively involved in schools through contact with teachers and head teachers and participation in school activities. Nevertheless, there were differences in the extent of participation allowed by schools and in the meaning given to participation by parents. In prestigious private schools, parents reported less attention given to parental wishes by head teachers and teachers and less demands for participation as these schools presented themselves as established, almost total institutions. Professional parents from the public sector indeed frequently suspected other parents, especially couples working in the private sector, to have chosen these private schools because they had no time to follow the children's schooling at home. They viewed choice of the private sector as a sort of parental abdication, not so different from that of lower-class families. In other private schools, parents reported a high degree of participation—sometimes perceived as excessive—asked from parents, including material and personal help to organize various academic and non-academic activities and a high degree of attention given to parental complaints and wishes. Head teachers reported on their side a high degree of tension between their Catholic mission and the need to keep their customers satisfied:

> In practice, we depend on a clientele—that's in quotes, of course; were not like a private company; we mustn't reason in terms of market share. Still, we

only exist because parents come here to enroll their children. That's because the product, in quotes, corresponds to their demand. I can't in good conscience do everything that the parents ask of me, because that would go against our mission; it would also be impossible to manage because parents ask for just about everything and its opposite. But neither can I become some kind of incorporeal guru on the pretext of our mission, and not be concerned in the least about the reactions of people and how the school works. (Principal, Sainte-Marie middle school)

Parental participation in public schools is also very variable. It is generally very important in attractive schools where there is a majority of middle-class parents. These parents think that their surveillance is necessary to maintain the quality of the school. These parents are particularly critical of the present internal organization of French secondary schools where teachers still enjoy an important individual autonomy from head teachers and parents. They are putting pressure on them to adopt managerial changes inspired from the functioning of the private sector. These should entail a stronger leadership from the head teacher, more cooperation between teachers and a better integration of parents as critical users. At the same time that these changes would allow parents to participate more strongly in the local regulation of education activities, many of them saw them as a way of preparing their children more effectively to their future work conditions in private firms:

Teachers want to be independent. I've got a fair number of teachers in my family, and I know their kind. They've always run their own classes, and the headmaster has no power over them! What business can work if the boss is not responsible for his employees? We're in a totally aberrant system. The inspector is the only one with real influence, but inspections are few and far between and the teachers are told beforehand. This is really ineffective. Inspections should take place without teachers being forewarned. The teachers feel like their secret garden is being invaded. And parents can't do much. We get the dates of parent-teacher meetings late—the headmaster does this deliberately. He shouldn't, because parents could contribute a lot. (Father computer technician, mother at home)

Parental surveillance is also oriented towards the monitoring of their children's career through changes on the instrumental, expressive and social goals of schooling. Their influence is growing in these areas despite strong teacher resistance. As concerns the instrumental dimension, one area in which this influence is clearly visible is that of evaluation. In our study, the number of written and oral tests and the amount of homework appeared considerably higher in prestigious private and public schools than in other schools. This was so both because parents put a lot of pressure on learning results and on accountability and because these schools were competing with each other to appear attractive to competitive parents and children. As concerns the expressive dimension, parents seemed to exert some influence on a more personalized, patterned (Laureau, 1989) treatment of their children in the schools as concerns homework or punishments. Finally, as concerns the social dimension of schooling, it is clear that many parents tried to build a relation of complicity with teachers, playing on the similarity of social status, in order to reinforce not only the special instrumental and expressive attention given to their children, but also the transmission of social-class values and manners.

This form of managed trust (Vincent, 2001) was also very important in some mixed schools where parents worried more about disruptive incidents, academic level and the need to keep a balance between teachers attention to children with learning problems and other special needs and teachers attention to their own children. This kind of parental intervention is from the point of view of middle-class parents' influence on policy, particularly interesting to analyze because its resists simplistic classification. On the one hand, these parents can be seen as displaying, individually, a consumerist attitude to protect and favour their own children. On the other hand, many of the collective actions in which they engage at the school and at the local level are conducted on behalf of all children or of pupils with special needs. Theirs is a good example of internal contradictions in middle-class approach to policy and the kind of goal confusion this may entail.

Many parents, especially those who occupy managerial and professional positions in private organizations view participation in parents associations in the same utilitarian terms that they view their individual intervention in schools. Although in public schools there is still a strong tradition of teacher and school insulation from parents, those who are perceived partly as insiders and who do services to school can benefit from information and special treatment:

> The best way to see how teachers react is from the inside. You say hello in the morning, you go to the meetings, you've got more contacts, you go on school outings—that way you're in good contact with people and you can see how the group does things, how it lives... It's partaking in the associative life of the school, but I won't deny that there are other things involved... When you're known and people have esteem for you, to move into first grade, if you've got three teachers and one is really popular, better—obviously I've never had to worry (laughter). You get to know the teachers, and it also enables you to get your children into the right class... That way I can see what the strong and weak points of certain teachers are. And I don't mind telling you it's for two reasons: get yourself known and to some degree looked up to, and get yourself into a position where you can talk easily with them. But you're giving so as to get. I know the principal will take good care

of my children. I'll do all I can, but I'm expecting something in return. (Father engineer, mother kindergarten classroom assistant)

For other parents, however, parents associations should be a place for the construction of the public good through discussions on important educational problems such as the causes of educational inequalities or of violence in schools and the solutions that the schools can provide to them. These parents, who are frequently parents who work in the public sector and send their children to public local schools, feel nevertheless frustrated in many cases because in these schools only a handful of middle-class parents—many of whom are teachers themselves—participate in these groupings. Because they are not representative of all parents neither in numbers, nor as concerns their social make-up, associations are not able to exert an important influence on schools.

These contrasted parental attitudes towards schooling are more or less reflected in the positions defended by the two main national associations of parents, the PEEP and the FCPE. The PEEP, whose membership is mostly middle-class with a predominance of parents working in the private sector, is in favor of school choice, school autonomy, and increased parental intervention in education. Parents who adopt a utilitarian vision see PEEP local associations as helpful sources of information and advice on schools, teachers and educational strategies. In predominantly middle-class communes and schools, head teachers see them as useful links between professionals and parents. And because their positions are on the same wavelength of present policy-in-practice they can exert an important influence on local policy-making and work closely with local educational authorities. On the contrary, the position of the other national association, the FCPE, whose membership is more socially mixed and comprises more middle-class parents working in the public sector, is more difficult. Officially, its members are against school choice and competition between schools; in practice many of them are active choosers. This contradiction between discourse and practice makes them less credible in the perception of head teachers and local educational authorities and diminishes the capacity of local FCPE associations for collective action.

In addition to these two national associations, there has been an increase in the last decade in the number of parents who support independent associations, especially in middle-class communes and schools. Because they do not depend on national and regional structures, these associations are able to react in a quick and flexible manner to various problems. Their model is that of the modern enterprise that defines objectives and methods, relies on individual initiatives and teamwork and gives a lot of importance to internal and external communication. Inside schools they support daily, direct, individual exchanges with head teachers. At the local level, they work hand in hand with municipalities and although they lack the legitimation of national institutions, they do exert a growing influence on local educational policy. In fact some aspects of the competition between local educational authorities and local political bodies has to do with their capacity to listen to parents, to respond to their demands but also to use them as spokespersons. On the other hand, parents associations in private Catholic schools, which are also part of a national association, the APEL, are not important actors at the school and the local level. Despite the general insistence on a "community" of parents and teachers linked by a set of common values, participation is considered mainly an individual affair. Parents associations, although playing an important financial role, are traditionally weakly organized and cannot counterbalance the important powers of the head teacher.

CONCLUSION

Middle-class parents' views and actions are thus contributing in not always visible but powerful ways to education restructuring at the local level. Although parents have no official decision powers on questions such as school provision, curriculum, pedagogy or evaluation, they are in fact influencing strongly the choices that teachers, head teachers and local educational authorities and local political bodies make everyday in these matters. At a more symbolic level, they are also contributing to a radical transformation of the image and the role of public and private schools. After a long period of exclusion from educational policy-making, are we witnessing a new wave of parentocracy in education (Brown, 1990)? In fact, it is difficult to separate parental influence from that of competition between schools and from that of the changing balance of power between the Central State and local educational centers (schools, local political bodies and local educational authorities). Present models of analysis are unable to capture these new and complex processes. What is needed to understand education restructuring, as well as restructuring in other social domains, at least in the French context, is a new model of public action. This model should take into account the blurring of distinctions between Central and local, between the State and civil society and between hierarchical, market and community modes of regulation of educational systems (Duran, 2001).

Sociological reflection on this topic should not stop, however, at the level of changes in organization. The value dimension also has to be integrated in the analysis and to point controversies as concerns principles and goals. As I have suggested at different points in this article, middle-class parental influence is reinforcing social, ethnic and academic segregation within schools and between schools, especially between public and private schools. This process maintains and reinforces educational inequality and exclusion. It can be seen, to a large extent, as a powerful reaction, both risky and conservative, to changes in the economy and in society, which have increased competition between social classes around educational assets. However, if this is so it is because the voices that are more influential are those of some fractions of the middle-classes, especially those of managers and professionals working in the private sector. These groups are particularly preoccupied with the degradation of their work conditions and those of their children and tend to view education, more and more, as a private good. On the contrary, administrators and professionals working in the public sector have a more complex Weltanschaung that tries to reconcile their private interests and the public good. Although their position is not exempt of criticism, it could support new practices and policies oriented toward equality and inclusion. However, this can only happen if policy-makers are able to listen to their voices and to build on them rather than to let education restructuring develop in an—perhaps only apparently—uncontrolled way at the local level.

NOTES

1. The analyses presented here are based on a research project on "Urban and school segregation in metropolitan contexts" which comprises interviews with 120 parents, mostly middle-class, conducted in two different communes, one predominantly middle-class and the other more socially mixed, of the Parisian periphery between 1999 and 2001.

REFERENCES

Adonis, A., & Pollard, S. (1997). *A class act: The myth of Britains classless society.* London: Hamilton.

Ball, S. J. (1994). *Education reform: A critical and post-structural approach.* Buckingham: Open University Press.

Ball, S. J. (2002). *Class strategies and the education market: The middle class and social advantages.* London: RoutledgeFalmer.

Ball, S. J., Bowe, R., & Gewirtz, S. (1995). Circuits of schooling: A sociological exploration of parental choice of school in social class contexts. *Sociological Review, 43*(1), 52–78.

Ball, S. J., & Vincent, C. (2001). New class relations in education: The strategies of the fearful middle classes. In J. Demaine (Ed.), *Sociology of Education Today.* London: Palgrave.

Ball, S., & van Zanten, A. (1998). Logiques de marché et éthiques contextualisées dans les systèmes scolaires français et britannique. *Éducation et sociétés, 1,* 47–71.

188   A. van ZANTEN

Ballion, R. (1982). *Les consommateurs décole.* Paris: Stock.

Ballion, R. (1990). *La bonne école: Évaluation et choix du collège et du lycée.* Paris: Hatier.

Barroso, J. (2000). Autonomie et modes de régulation locale dans le système éducatif. *Revue française de pédagogie, 130,* 57–71.

Beck, U. (2001). *La société du risque: Sur la voie dune autre modernité.* Paris: Alto-Aubier.

Bernstein, B. (1967). Open schools—open society? *New Society, 14,* 351–353.

Bidou, C. (1984). *Les aventuriers du quotidien: Essai sur les nouvelles classes moyennes.* Paris: Presses Universitaires de France.

Boltanski, L., & Chiapello, E. (1999). *Le nouvel esprit du capitalisme.* Paris: Gallimard.

Bourdieu, P. (1979). *La distinction: Critique sociale du jugement.* Paris: éditions de Minuit.

Bourdieu, P., & Passeron, J. C. (1970). *La Reproduction: Critique du système denseignement.* Paris: Seuil.

Bourdieu, P., & Wacquant, L. (1992). *Réponses: Pour une anthropologie reflexive.* Paris: éditions du Seuil.

Broccolichi, S., & van Zanten, A. (1997). Espaces de concurrence et circuits de scolarisation. Lévitement des collèges publics dun district de la banlieue parisienne. *Les annales de la recherche urbaine, 75,* 5–17.

Broccolichi, S., & van Zanten, A. (2000). School competition and pupil flight in the urban periphery. *Journal of Education Policy , 15*(1), 51–60.

Brown, P. (1990). The third wave: Education and the ideology of parentocracy. *British Journal of Sociology of Education, 11*(1), 65–85.

Cherkaoui, M. (1982). *Les changements du système éducatif en France, 1950–1980.* Paris: Presses Univeritaires de France.

Collins, R. (1979). *The credential society: A historical sociology of education.* New York: Academic Press.

Desrosières, A., & Thévenot, L. (1982). *Les Catégories socio-professionnelles.* Paris: La Découverte.

Dubet, F. (1991). *Les lycéens.* Paris: éditions du Seuil.

Duran, P. (2001). Action publique, action politique. In J.-P. Leresche (Ed.), *Gouvernance territoriale et citoyenneté urbaine: de la coordination à la légitimité.* Paris: Pédone.

Gewirtz, S., Ball, S. J., & Bowe, R. (1995). *Markets, choice, and equity in education.* Buckingham: Open University Press.

Héran, F. (1996). Ecole publique, école privée, qui peut choisir? *Économie et statistique, 293,* 17–39.

Kenway, J., Bigum, C., & Fitzclarence, L. (1993). Marketing education in the postmodern age. *Journal of Education Policy, 8*(2), 105–122.

Lareau, A. (1989). *Home advantage: Social class and parental intervention in elementary education.* London/New York: Falmer Press.

Lipovetsky, G. (1983). *Lère du vide: Essais sur lindividualisme contemporain.* Paris: Gallimard.

Murphy, R. (1988). *Social closure: The theory of monopolization and exclusion.* Oxford: Clarendon.

Pakulski, J., & Waters, M. (1996). *The death of class.* London, Sage.

Parkin, F. (Ed.) (1974). *The social class analysis of class structure.* London: Tavistock.

Peters, B. G. (1993). Managing the hollow state. In K. Eliassen & J. Kooman (Eds.), *Managing public organizations*. London: Sage Publications.

Popkewitz, T. S. (2000). Rethinking decentralization and the state/civil society distinctions. In T. S. Popkewitz (Ed.), *Educational knowledge: Changing relationships between the state, civil society, and the educational community*. Albany: State University of New York Press.

Prost, A. (1981). *Histoire générale de lenseignement et de léducation en France, tome IV, Lécole et la famille dans une société en mutation*. Paris: Nouvelle librairie de France.

Robson, G., & Butler, T. (2001). Coming to terms with London: middle-class communities in a global city. *International Journal of Urban and Regional Research, 25(1)*, 70–86.

Savage, M., Barlow, J., Dickens, P., Fielding, T. (1992). *Property, bureaucracy, and culture: Middle-class formation in contemporary Britain*. London: Routledge.

Taylor, C. (2000). Hierarchies and local markets: the geography of the lived market place in secondary school provision. *Journal of Education Policy, 16(1)*, 197–214.

Vincent, C. (2001). Social class and parental agency. *Journal of Education Policy, 16(4)*, 347–364.

Weiler, H. (1990). Decentralisation in educational governance: An exercise in contradiction. In M. Granheim, M. Kogan, & U. Lundgren (Eds.), *Evaluation as policymaking: Introducing evaluation into a national decentralised educational system*. London: Jessica Kingsley Publishers.

Westergaard, J. (1995). *Who gets what ? The hardening of class inequality in the late twentieth century*. Cambridge: Polity Press.

van Zanten, A. (1996). Stratégies utilitaristes et stratégies identitaires des parents vis-à-vis de lécole: Une relecture critique des analyses sociologiques. *Lien social et politiques, 35*, 125–135.

van Zanten, A. (2001). *Lécole de la périphérie. Scolarité et ségrégation en banlieue*. Paris: Presses Universitaires de France.

van Zanten, A. (2002a). Educational change and new cleavages between head teachers, teachers, and parents: Global and local perspectives on the French case. *Journal of Education Policy, 17(3)*, 289–304.

van Zanten, A. (2002b). Les classes moyennes et la mixité scolaire dans la banlieue parisienne. *Les Annales de la Recherche Urbaine, 93*.

van Zanten, A. (2002c). La mobilisation stratégique et politique des savoirs sur le social: Le cas des parents délèves des classes moyennes. *Education et Sociétés, 9*.

van Zanten, A., & Ball, S. J. (2000). Comparer pour comprendre: globalisation, réinterprétations nationales et recontextualisations locales. *Revue de lInstitut de Sociologie, 1(4)*, 113–131.

CHAPTER 9

CREATING A DISCOURSE FOR RESTRUCTURING IN DETROIT

Achievement, Race, and the Northern High School Walkout[1]

Barry M. Franklin
Utah State University

Not surprisingly, the efforts of educators, parents, policy makers, and others to address problems of low academic achievement, particularly as they occur among children of color in urban schools, not unlike other school reform initiatives, have their starts and stops, cycles, accomplishments, and downright mistakes. There is in fact a distinct lineage to these attempts involving ruptures and continuities among a number of competing lines of descent over time. Most of the elements of this lineage have to do with different classroom strategies for teaching low achieving children. They include the establishment of special classes and schools, the creation of remedial programs apart from special education but outside the regular classroom, the introduction of curriculum modifications within the regular classroom, the reduction in class size, and the development of compensatory and alternative educational programs (Franklin, 1998). More recently a sixth strategy has appeared on the scene that unlike these earlier

Educational Restructuring: International Perspectives on Traveling Policies, pages 191–217

approaches focuses not on what transpires in the classroom but in the governing of schools. Known as restructuring, it is developing its own lineage involving such patterns as decentralization, community control, recentralization, and various forms of parental choice. It is this last approach, that of restructuring, that I will focus my attention on in this essay.

EDUCATIONAL HISTORY AND THE PROBLEM
OF SCHOOL RESTRUCTURING

There is a large and conceptually rich research literature on urban school reform, the most recent of which devotes attention to problems of academic achievement and the role of restructuring in its remedy (see for example, Anyon, 1997; Bizar & Barr, 2001; Bryk, Sebring, Kerbow, Rollow, & Easton, 1998; Henig, Hula, Orr, & Pedescleaux, 1999; Hess, 1995; Hill, Campbell, & Harvey, 2000; Orr, 1999; Portz, Stein, & Jones, 1999; Ravitch & Vitgeritti, 1997, 2000).[2] A good portion of this research is historical and focuses on situating the issue of school reform in the politics, economics, and culture of American cities over time, exploring the policy debates surrounding reform initiatives, and examining the interplay between reform and issues of race and social class. The issues of academic achievement and restructuring appear in this literature in the context of considering the expansion of the school population as a result of the movement of European immigrants and Southern Blacks into the cities of the Midwest and Northeast, the conflict between urban school authorities and immigrant and black communities over the apparent inability or unwillingness of city schools to educate their children, and the development of an array of curricular, pedagogical, and governance reforms to address these problems (Cohen, 1990; Katznelson & Weir, 1985; Mirel, 1993; Peterson, 1985; Podair, 2002; Raftery, 1992; Ravitch, 1974; Rury & Cassell, 1993; Tyack, 1974).

Detroit represents a case in point. In 1971, the city implemented a school decentralization plan that would last ten years until 1981 (Berkowitz, 1973; Mirel, 1993). This was not the first nor last time that Detroit's school system was to be restructured. Between 1880 and 1916, the administration of the city's schools shifted from a ward-based board to a board that was elected at-large, back to a ward-based board, and finally back again to a board elected at large. And in 2000, the district underwent a reorganization that saw the city's elected board of education replaced by a board appointed by the mayor and the replacement of the superintendent by a more powerful board appointed chief executive officer (Franklin, 2003).

The interpretation that most scholars offer of the events in the twenty or so years preceding the 1971 decentralization is one that attributes the problems facing Detroit's schools to the long term effects of the demographic shifts and economic changes that occurred in large American cities in the two decades following World War II. This spatial reordering spurred forward the mutually reinforcing factors of residential and employment discrimination, suburbanization, deindustrialization, and a racialized politics that taken together led to a significant decrease in the city's white population coupled with a pattern of plant relocations, downsizing, job loss, and capital flight. The result was the destruction of the city's manufacturing infrastructure, the erosion of its tax base, persistent poverty, and economic dependency (Darden, Hill, Thomas, & Thomas, 1987; Fine, 1989; Mayer & Hoult, 1962; Sugrue, 1996). It was a transformation that accounted for any of a number of problems that the city's schools began to experience during the 1960s including racial segregation, the lack of adequate financial resources, a deteriorating physical plant, and a pattern of persistent low achievement on the part of its students.

Jeffrey Mirel's (1993) history of the Detroit Public schools offers a good picture of how within this explanatory framework educational historians typically look at events such as the city's schools attempts at restructuring. Mirel's account attributes the declining fortunes of the city's schools from their high point in the 1920s, where a consensus committed to the improvement of the school system reigned supreme, to the interplay between inadequate financial resources and increasing political conflicts. This lack of sufficient funds, which began to make its impact felt during the 1930s, set the stage for a prolonged struggle over several decades between the school board and the teachers union concerning salaries and necessitated a rationalization of capital construction and maintenance practices that favored schools in predominantly white areas in the outer fringes of the city at the expense of inner city black schools.

The 1930s also saw, according to Mirel, the beginnings of what would be a continuing weakening of the curriculum with the addition of a general track to the city's already differentiated high school program to provide a more practical course of study for students deemed incapable of mastering a traditional academic course of study. Over time, curriculum differentiation in Detroit would become a vehicle for watering down course content and lowering expectations for an array of diverse students, not only those who differed in ability and interest, but those who differed in class background and race. Mirel argues that taken together these financial problems and curriculum changes had the effect of convincing African American that the city offered their children an inadequate curriculum in schools that were physically deteriorating.

As Mirel tells his story, a coalition comprising liberal, labor, and black community and corporate leaders was able by the mid-1950s to secure sufficient influence over the city's board of education to begin to address the problems facing Detroit's schools. They offered the city, in his words, "a vision of the public schools broad enough to satisfy all concerned" (p. 404). Their agenda, according to Mirel, addressed the labor, financial, and curricular problems facing the schools, enlisted the support of conflicting groups, and promoted a common educational mission for the city's schools dedicated to academic excellence. Although successful in attaining many of its goals, the black-white racial conflict that emerged coupled with the continuing decline of the city's economy had by the end of the 1960s virtually destroyed this coalition and spurred forward the further decline of the city's schools that would set in motion the conflicts, bargaining, coalition building, and legislative action that would lead to the passage of the Michigan statute that would allow for decentralization.

CULTURAL HISTORY AND DETROIT'S DISCURSIVE REORDERING

My look at the restructuring in Detroit will take another path. Unlike Mirel and other historians of urban school reform, I will not be concerned with examining the competing and conflicting policies for addressing the problems facing the city's schools, particularly the pattern of low achievement affecting Detroit's black youth. My focus instead will be on another kind of spatial reordering that was occurring in Detroit in the two decades following World War II. This kind of shift, which we might think of as involving a reordering of conceptual or discursive space, did not involve changes in the physical world but in the linguistic arena and encompassed the terrain occupied by the concepts, categories, and classifications that were used as Detroiters thought, reasoned, and talked about all aspects of their social, economic, and political lives, including education. The arrangement of this conceptual space constituted a geography, albeit a conceptual one, whose ordering and reordering over time identified patterns of discursive conflict and disagreement as well as consensus and agreement surrounding matters of education (Lefebvre, 1991; Popkewitz, 1998; Popkewitz & Brennan, 1998; Soja, 1989, 1996).

In this essay, I will offer what might be called a cultural history of Detroit's 1971 restructuring of its school system. Such a history decenters the subject from the account and has instead as its focal point the language in which this restructuring initiative was framed (Popkewitz, Pereyra, & Franklin, 2001). This emphasis is important because of the critical linkage between discourse and the social practices that constitute schooling. Those practices, which include the classrooms, curricula, and pedagogy that mediate the distribution of knowledge, skills, and dispositions as well as the modes of governing the schools, do not simply arise de novo. Rather, these institutional forms are the products of certain kinds of reasoning and discussion about an array of matters involving teaching, learning, and the organization of schools that make the creation of certain kinds of policies and practices seem to be the sensible and compelling response to a particular set of educational dilemmas. In other words, the reasoning rules or discursive practices embedded in the language in which we think and talk about education serve to structure the kind of institutions that we actually establish in the conduct of schooling. From this vantage point, restructuring as a governing process appears differently than it does in more conventional accounts like that offered by Mirel. Its impetus is not to be located in the efforts of policy makers and politicians to frame legislation to recalibrate school governance. Rather, as I will argue in this essay, the momentum for restructuring comes from the cultural practices of ordinary and not so ordinary people mediated by the discourse in which they frame their experiences (Franklin, 1999).

THE NORTHERN HIGH SCHOOL WALKOUT

The starting point for this discussion will be a student boycott that occurred at Detroit's Northern High School in April of 1966. In singling out this walkout as the place for initiating a consideration of restructuring, I am not claiming this event as an originating moment in a linear historical account. In fact, I actually reject the idea of seeking the origins of things in that for any cultural practice such points are so numerous as to render such a search hopeless. Instead, what this walkout offers is one of many sites in which we can see the movement, interplay, and repositioning of discourses that entered into a linguistic reordering which in turn constructed the kind of linguistic terrain in which the restructuring of the city's schools became the reasonable course of action for the parties involved.

The Northern walkout began on the morning of April 7, 1966 when some 2,300 students at the all black high school responded to Superintendent Samuel Brownell's decision to close the school in anticipation of a student protest by walking out in mass and joining a group of parents who had congregated on the street in front of the school. What followed was a three-week boycott during which time its student leaders would press their demands for a host of changes at the school including the removal of the principal (Detroit Free Press, April 8, 1966; Fine, 1989; Gracie, 1967; Gregory, 1967; Mirel, 1993). The precipitating event behind the Northern boycott was the refusal of the head of the English Department, Thomas Scott, with the support of the principal, Arthur Carty, some two weeks before the walkout, to allow publication in the student newspaper of an editorial critical of the school and the education it offered Detroit's black youth. Written by a senior honors student, Charles Colding, and entitled "Educational

Camouflage," the article pointed to the failure of urban schools like Northern to provide a quality education. Colding decried such practices as social promotion, which he claimed was responsible for the low achievement of black students at Northern. He argued that the underachievement of Northern students when compared with the performance of students in such largely white Detroit schools as Redford High was unacceptable. Finally, he blamed conditions at Northern, which he asserted were not accidental, on segregation and on what he claimed was the widespread belief among Detroit educators that "Negroes aren't as capable of learning as whites" (National Commission on Professional Rights and Responsibilities, 1967, pp. 74–75).

The demands that Colding and other student leaders made as a condition for returning to school offer us something of a picture of how they constructed this protest. Their main demand was to have Carty removed as principal and that he not be replaced by Assistant Principal George Donaldson. The school administration, they felt, was paternalistic and authoritarian in their relations with students and the community, had ignored the inadequacies in Northern's curriculum and physical plant, and were responsible for its educational failings. Students further demanded that they be provided with information that would allow them to compare the academic standards existing at Northern with those of other Detroit schools. They wanted the board of education to furnish them with a plan detailing how the problems at the school would be corrected. They also demanded the creation of an elected student-faculty council to examine school problems and to make recommendations for their solution. The students asked for the appointment of a community agent to work with the parents of Northern students. They demanded the removal of the police officer who had patrolled the school prior to the walkout on the grounds that he treated students too harshly. And finally, the students wanted guarantees against reprisals for those participating in the walkout. By the end of April, the board agreed to these demands and the boycott came to an end (Gracie, 1967; *Detroit Free Press*, April 18, 1966; *Detroit News*, April 13, 1966, April 21, 1966).

THE BOYCOTT AS A DISCURSIVE CONFLICT

The Northern High School boycott represents one of numerous instances in Detroit during the decade preceding the decentralization of the city's schools that reveals the conflicting discursive practices or reasoning rules involved in the construction of two educational discourses, one black and the other white. From this vantage point, the boycott should be seen as a conflict over different constructions of the problem of black low achievement at Northern, particularly, and in Detroit schools generally. The language that black supporters of the boycott used to talk about the education of African American students in the city's schools embedded the issue of underachievement in a racial discourse. It was a discourse that enabled Black Detroiters to assert their need for a quality education while at the same time demanding that they be treated with self-respect and dignity. As one of the student leaders of the protest noted, "I am willing to give up everything to fight for an education. If we don't have an education, we don't have anything." She went on to say that when she thought about the boycott and other efforts of blacks to assert their rights, she felt "proud because the Negro stands proud" (*Detroit Free Press*, April 20, 1966).

Such discourses were a hallmark of black discussions of the walkout. Northern students attending the Freedom School that was established at St. Joseph's Church during the boycott wrote essays that attributed an array of inadequacies in both the school's facilities and in its curriculum to what they saw as the low expectations that white teachers and administrators held for black students. The assumption of the Northern staff, it was claimed, was that black students were "willing to accept anything, the leftovers, and this is what we are given." The prevailing belief about Northern teachers in these essays was that they "look and teach down to Negro students" and believe that "black boys and girls don't want to learn" (*Detroit Free Press*, April 27, 1966)

Parents of Northern students as well as many black community leaders framed their interpretations of the boycott in similar terms. Northern's principal and many of the school's teachers, in their comments and discussions, were viewed as being prejudiced toward blacks and consequently not holding high expectations for their academic performance ("Report of Community Hearings," 1966). The understanding of underachievement that African-American supporters of the boycott constructed was a racialized one that defined the condition as the result of prejudiced and discriminatory treatment of black students at the hands of white school officials. The concept of low achievement in their discourse had become a virtual code word for white racism.

Detroit's largely white educational establishment, most of whom opposed the walkout, also constructed the problem of underachievement using a racialized discourse. But the racialization was different. Their construction of low achievement was a psychologized one. Black students were seen by the white educators as being "indifferent to learning and to failure" (Gracie, 1967, p. 14). A typical high school curriculum, which was designed for students with aspirations for college and for middle class living, was not appropriate for them. What was called for were programs that recognized that "high school is terminal education for many people and each graduate should develop saleable skills" (Lewis, n.d.) Consequently for these educators, Northern was defined as a good school with a dedicated faculty that offered its students a sound education (*Detroit News,* April 18, 1966, April 19, 1966, April 25, 1966). Race in their discussion of low achievement was masked behind the veil of psychology. What appeared to be a neutral and scientific description of student learning problems was in fact a racial category.

DETROIT'S DISCOURSE ON DIFFERENTIATION AND RACE

To understand the Northern High School boycott, we need to situate the debate between the supporters and opponents of the walkout in an evolving discourse in Detroit on curriculum differentiation and race. Like other big city school systems, Detroit first began to address the problem of low achievement at the turn of the twentieth century as one phase of a larger educational reform movement to better link the school curriculum to a growing and increasingly diverse study body. Many educators of the day believed that a large portion of this new student body was less intellectually inclined and less capable than previous generations of students. They went on to argue, invoking the doctrine of social efficiency, that these students required a course of study that was less abstract than the existing curriculum, which emphasized the traditional disciplines of knowledge. In its place, these educators favored a curriculum tied more closely to practical needs and day-to-day concerns of youth. Consequently, they championed a differentiated curriculum that channeled students to an array of courses and programs, some preparatory and others terminal, that were thought to match their varying abilities, interests, and inclinations (Franklin, 1986; Kliebard, 1995). During the next half century, this principal of curriculum differentiation would provide the justification for the complement of special, remedial, and compensatory programs that public schools would launch in their efforts to provide for low-achieving students (Franklin, 1994, 2000). What the Northern protesters condemned as an inadequate curriculum and what Carty and his supporters touted as a good school program was in fact the product of such differentiation.

Two reports, the 1958 Citizens Advisory Committee on School Needs (CAC) and the 1962 Citizens Advisory Committee on Equal Educational Opportunity (EEO), provide examples of the kind of discussions of curriculum differentiation that were occurring in Detroit in the years immediately preceding the walkout. The understanding of curriculum differentiation held by the CAC, which was established as a vehicle for ensuring citizen participation in the making of school policy, is best reflected in remarks of the consultants who worked with the committee in their examination of curriculum issues. They argued that "wide differences in content and method may and probably should be evident between different classes of pupils of the same grade." This was the case, they went on to say, because "socio-economic and other factors operate in different regions of the city to make a uniform course of study unsatisfactory" (Detroit Board of Education, 1958b, p. 27). Differentiation, the CAC believed, offered a way for administrators to reconcile the competing demands facing the city's schools. It would signal their intent to provide all of the city's children with equal educational opportunity through a set of common goals. At the same time, however, the availability of diverse classes and curricular programs indicated their commitment to meeting the particular needs of individual students. For the high schools, this view legitimated the committee's continued support for a program comprising four courses, college preparatory, vocational, business, and general (Detroit Board of Education, 1958a). And for low-achieving children, the principle of differentiation supported the committee's recommendation for the establishment of separate remedial courses in reading and arithmetic (Detroit Board of Education, 1959).

The EEO Committee was created two years later in 1960 to study the factors that affected equal opportunity within the city's schools. The notion of such opportunity that this committee constructed did not require that all children should receive an "equal amount of schooling." Rather, it meant providing the child with "the kind and amount of schooling...that his capacities warrant" (Detroit Board of Education, 1962, p. 4). And having framed equal opportunity in that manner, curriculum differentiation was seen as the vehicle for its attainment. "It may seem something of a paradox," the report noted, "that equality can be achieved only by providing unequal education; but this paradox becomes clear when we realize that the students start school unequal in ability and experience, and that to offer them merely the same education in each case would be simply to continue the original inequality" (Ibid., p. 15).

Never far below the surface in discussions of low achievement and curriculum differentiation in Detroit was a racial discourse that pitted black parents and their children against white educators. The curriculum offered in those city schools with large black enrollments was typically seen by the city's African-American population as being "watered-down" and consequently harmful to any aspirations that black children might have for attending college (*Michigan Chronicle*, July 12, 1958; Hutchinson to Robinson, July 6, 1958). Beyond the curriculum itself, black discourse offered criticism of white teachers for not being interested in teaching African Americans. "By virtue of being colored, according to one viewpoint, "every Negro child is denied equal educational opportunity" (*Detroit Free Press*, July 21, 1960).

A good example of this discourse can be found in a March, 1958 conflict between members of the Parents Club at all black McMichael Junior High School and city school officials. The view of McMichael that Parents Club members framed in their comments was of a school that did not place many academic demands on its students. At the heart of this problem was a curriculum that was deemed to be inadequate. There were not, again according to the remarks of Parents Club members, sufficient science courses at the school for all of the entering ninth grade students, and those students who were able to take science did not have a regular textbook available to them but only a pamphlet. Students enrolled in English, it was also noted, were not encouraged, as were students at other city junior high schools, to buy the standard English textbook (*Michigan Chronicle*, March 22, 1958; Mirel, 1993).

A similar discursive construction of issues of learning and achievement at Detroit's Northwestern High School appeared four years later in a black community newspaper. The article depicted the school as an "attendance school," meaning that if a student simply attends long enough, "he will eventually be graduated from the school just as sausage is ground out of a machine" ("What's Wrong with our Schools," 1962). The cause for this situation was seen as the practice of social promotion. Teachers, it was asserted, often gave passing grades for student work that according to city-wide grading policies should have earned a failing grade. Two beliefs on the part of the city's white educators were seen as being at the root of this practice. One was the view that it was not possible to apply a single standard of performance to all of Detroit's students. The second held that any student who attends school on a regular basis and attempts to complete the work should be passed. From the perspective of black Detroiters such views were seen as being "favored by the people who believe that Negro children are inferior as students so there is no sense spending a lot of public money trying to educate them as white students are educated" ("Teacher Continues Northwestern Expose," 1962).

White discourse constructed the situation in decidedly opposite terms. The treatment given to black and white students was seen as similar. Yet, the opinion was offered that black children "do not seem to participate even though a definite effort has been made in their direction." The problem, according to this viewpoint, was "a lack of motivation" on the part of African American students. It was this construction of the situation that underlay the interpretation that school administrators offered concerning events at McMichael Junior High School. The curricular contrasts between McMichael and other junior high schools was justified by the fact that students entering the school were not seen as being prepared to undertake junior high school level work (*Detroit Free Press*, June 21, 1960). It was noted in that regard that of the five sections of students that made up the seventh grade, only one section was for "better students." The other four sections were composed of children who were described as "mediocre." The task of teachers in that setting, according to school administrators, was to "take the children along as fast as they will go" and toward that end "to adjust the work to meet a student's need." The use of different textbooks from those available at other schools was explained by the fact that it was often necessary to adjust course materials to the student's abilities (*Michigan Chronicle*, April 12, 1958).

Why Detroit's discourse on differentiation and race took the form it did with its support for curriculum differentiation on the part of the city's educational leadership and with a construction on the part of African Americans of the schooling offered their children as a form of racism is not all that difficult to explain. The support that the CAC, EEO, and many Detroit educators gave to curriculum differentiation did not exist in isolation. Nor did the construction of low achievement that appeared in the discourse of Black Detroiters. Rather, both appeared in the context of the longstanding intense dislike that much of Detroit's white, working class ethnics, who constituted the majority of the city's population, held toward blacks. The roots of this enmity stem back to the 1940s and are rooted in their fear that an increasing African American presence in the city posed for their economic security and cultural identity. Blacks, they believed, would take their jobs, lower their property values, and infest their neighborhoods with crime and vice. Limiting black employment opportunities in the city's automobile industry and maintaining residential and school segregation were the bulwarks of what they saw as their defense strategy. Whites who employed these tactics routinely sought to dissuade supporters of equal employment opportunity, housing integration, and school desegregation by admonition and intimidation. When those efforts did not work, and they often did not, some whites, particularly those who felt most threatened by blacks, turned to outright violence. At the same time, numerous white politicians in Detroit sought to advance their own careers by abetting this white resistance (Sugrue, 1996, 1995; Thompson, 2001a, 2001b).[3]

The result was a discourse among segments of the city's white population that constructed African-Americans as a decidedly negative influence on the life of the city. It was a discourse that allowed for the kind of racialized climate that would lead a largely white educational establishment to support curriculum differentiation despite the educational disadvantage it posed for the city's African-American students. And it was a discourse that would make the distrust that Detroit's blacks exhibited toward the city's schools seem reasonable and sensible.

A good picture of this discourse can be obtained from the correspondence received by the Detroit Board of Education President Remus Robinson during the early 1960s. Blacks, it was asserted in one such letter, "don't care to work." They would rather "just sit around and collect welfare checks." The construction of Detroit that was framed in this letter was of a "clean city until people from [the] South came." Now the city had become the "worst city in high crimes" with "colored prostitutes" all over and with "killings, robberies, assaults, and rapes on White women by colored men" (CFR to Robinson, n.d.). Another letter, this one from a University of Michigan student, criticized Robinson's support for integrating the school's student organizations. "Niggers and kikes in our sororities and fraternities indeed!" She urged Robinson, who himself was black, to "forget his stupid integration ideas!" The writer asserted support for segregation and warned the board president to keep his "punks in their place" (Anonymous student to Robinson, February 2, 1959). And still another letter reported the comments of a white teacher at Central High School to the effect that "negroes didnt like her and she didnt like negroes" (Butler to Robinson, December 14, 1960).

Blacks were, it seems, well aware of the antipathy that white Detroiters held out for them. The remarks of an African American teacher at Northwestern High School in 1962 characterizing the attitudes of the white principals who ran the city's secondary schools make the point. These administrators, he argues, had little interest in educating black children. Rather, their driving motive was to please their superiors at the board of education and in so doing to earn a promotion out of the city's black schools:

> A "good principal" will do whatever his bosses downtown ask him to do. The more a principal cooperates the sooner he will accumulate enough "gold stars" next to his name to move out of the depressed Negro school and into one of the lily-white schools (which will naturally be closer to his home as all of Detroit's high school principal are white). This means that he will keep cheating them every day in nearly every way. This means that he is guilty of criminal negligence, for a day lost in a kid's education is a day lost forever. ("Whats Wrong with Our Schools," 1962)

DETROIT'S CONTESTED DISCURSIVE TERRAIN

Neither the discourse on differentiation nor on race appeared simply as a black-white conflict. The positions that were taken on either issue were not that monolithic. There were among Detroiters generally different and conflicting discourses on the issue of curriculum differentiation. One viewpoint held that it was inefficient as well as damaging to students to create classrooms where the "dullard" had to compete with the "brilliant." Students who could not master the basic academic curriculum, it was argued, should be "sent to special schools to learn a trade." Underlying this position was the opinion that the central task of schooling in Detroit was to "accelerate the gifted ones." Yet, the conflicting position, namely that segregating children of different abilities was not desirable, was also voiced (Detroit Board of Education, 1957–58, pp. 2–3, 16).

A similar division existed within black discourse itself. One opinion that was voiced constructed the existence of individual differences as representing a desirable characteristic of a democratic society. The schools, according to this view, should attempt to maximize the potential of all students and aim toward the "equalization of competing skills." Heterogeneous grouping was seen as the best mechanism to achieve this end (Ibid., pp. 6–7). Also expressed within black discourse was the opinion that African Americans in inner city high schools often do not go to college but rather enter the labor force immediately after graduation. What was required was a differentiated curriculum that included remedial and vocational programs to provide for such students ("Statement of Charles Wells," 1964; "Minutes of Education Committee," 1965; "Vocational Education Subcommittee Report," 1965).

White and black discourse on race exhibited a similar pattern of conflict. On some issues, such as the existence of segregation, the opinions offered were divided along racial lines. Whites were more likely to doubt that their schools practiced racial segregation where blacks were convinced that this was the case (Citizens Advisory Committee on Equal Educational Opportunities, 1960). Yet, there were issues where the viewpoints within each group were divided. One such issue was the recommendation of the Citizens Advisory Committee on Equal Educational Opportunities that students throughout the city be allowed to transfer freely from school to school. There were blacks who voiced opinions in support of this recommendation on the grounds that residential segregation had virtually guaranteed that neighborhood schools would be segregated. And their were blacks who opposed this policy because they had reservations about sending their children to school outside of their neighborhoods and to place them in the hands of white teachers. The opinions of whites on this issue also differed. There were whites whose opinions were in line with the EEO Committee, and there were whites who were afraid that such a policy would threaten the existence of the neighborhood school as well as lead parents to attempt to have their children moved from school to school to avoid integration (*Detroit Free Press*, March 12, 1962).

The pattern of discourse surrounding the Northern High School walkout had similar features. At one level, it was clearly a black-white conflict. Black opinion constructed the city's schools as largely deficient institutions that were not providing their children with an adequate education. As one of the student boycott leaders commented to the *Detroit Free Press*, "right now the Negro needs an education, and he needs it bad" (*Detroit Free Press*,

April 20, 1966). The white viewpoint, on the other hand, challenged this assessment of Detroit's schools and believed that Northern was providing its students with an adequate education. As Arthur Carty noted about the Northerns curriculum, "we have all the courses they need here, if the kids want to take them." Whatever problems existed at Northern, he argued, had nothing to do with the school but were the result of the lack of student motivation coupled with poor parental involvement. "I have preached in churches and gone to block club after block club trying to persuade parents their children should work up to their full potential." Yet, very few parents took the time, he pointed out, to visit the school or to attend school meetings (*Detroit Free Press,* April 8, 1966, April 20, 1966, May 1, 1966).

Yet, black opinion exhibited divisions. Northern parents and community residents attending the public hearings following the walkout differed about the kind of curriculum that the school should offer. Some of those in attendance called for a more academically oriented school program noting that more French should be offered, that too many students were being placed in the general curriculum, that more homework should be given, and that a diploma from Northern should qualify a student for admission to college. Others thought that the emphasis should be on vocational training. One parent complained that her daughter had to take a business course after high school. "Shouldn't high school," she asked, "qualify a person for a decent job?" There were suggestions that more work in typing was needed, that the school should focus on preparing "productive citizens," and that Northern should work more closely with business and industry in preparing students for jobs. And still others thought that the curriculum should be more relevant to the lives of black children. Northern was criticized for teaching less "Negro history" than was taught in Southern schools and for offering a music curriculum that was "white" and out of date. One commentator suggested that students needed a history text that included more "Negro history" ("Report of Community Hearings," 1966)

This pattern of disagreement was not unique to Northern. Two years later, a committee of parents and teachers at Post Junior High School who were investigating community concerns following a walkout at the school reported a similar division to that existing at Northern over matters of curriculum. While some community members called for increases in remedial programs, others advocated an upgrading of vocational programs, and still others wanted an emphasis on African American history and culture. And while some community members called for more attention to the honors program, others felt that there should be a focus of attention on courses that addressed the "great social concerns of the day," especially racism, sex education, and drug dependence (Post Junior High School, 1968).

And similarly to the debate about curriculum differentiation and race, there were some divisions within the ranks of the contending parties to the

Northern walkout. The opinions voiced by the city two daily newspapers suggest, for example, that white opinion about the walkout was divided, at least initially. The *Free Press* was supportive of the student protesters and thought that Colding's editorial was correct in its assessment of both the school and of Arthur Carty (*Detroit Free Press*, April 9, 1966). The *News*, on the other hand, thought that Colding's complaints about the school as well as his solutions were "somewhat simplistic." (*Detroit News*, April 11, 1966). By the end of the boycott, however, the viewpoints offered by these two newspapers converged in defense of administrative authority and agreed that "submitting to student pressures" to remove Carty was a mistake" (*Detroit Free Press*, April 30, 1966; *Detroit News*, April 22, 1966).

The opinions of the city's teachers, two-thirds of whom were white, were also divided. There were teachers who voiced opinions in support of Carty and against the walkout, and there were teachers who framed their comments about the boycott in terms critical of Carty and the quality of education that was provided to students at Northern (*Detroit Free Press*, April 9, 1966, April 20, 1966, April 24, 1966; *Detroit News*, April 18, 1966, April 19, 1966, April 23, 1966, April 25, 1966). Yet, it appears that this conflict over the boycott had more to do with the pedagogical orientation, age, and organizational affiliation of teachers than it had to do with race. Those supporting the walkout tended to be pedagogically progressive, younger, and drawn from the ranks of the Detroit Federation of Teachers, the official bargaining agent for the city's teachers. Teachers who opposed the walkout were for the most part pedagogically conservative, older, and members of the rival Detroit Education Association (*Detroit Free Press*, April 9, 1966, April 20, 1966, May 1, 1966; *Detroit News*, April 20, 1966, April 23, 1966).

Yet, there was a critical difference between the discourse surrounding the walkout and the earlier talk concerning curriculum differentiation and race that we have considered. In the aftermath of the boycott, black discussions on curriculum differentiation and race had become more unified pointing to the hardening of the position that the city's African Americans were taking on these matters. In this discursive pattern, the problem of black low achievement was less likely to be seen as the result of deficient resources and low expectations than as the result of white control of the schools that served African American children. Blacks, according to this rationale, could never get a quality education "as long as our schools are being run by outsiders" (*Michigan Chronicle*, November 4, 1967). At the very least the schools in black communities had to be staffed by African American teachers and principals (*Michigan Chronicle*, November 11, 1967). Beyond organizational and structural changes, however, a new viewpoint had to be framed. It would be one that recognized that "black consciousness is a reality on our streets" and that "little black children are aware that they are black and that being black makes them a people separate and apart" (*Michigan Chronicle*, March 16, 1968).

The hardening of black discourse following the walkout was the result of the appearance on the linguistic scene of a black nationalist discourse. One of the oldest of an array of contending political ideologies that African Americans have advanced to describer their vision of freedom and equality, black nationalism rests on the a belief in race as the most important interpretive lens for examining American society (Dawson, 2001). Embedded in the discourse of black nationalists was the belief that whites could not be trusted to promote the cause of black equality. While they were not uniformly separatists in their outlook, black nationalists did not hold racial integration to be a high goal. They were much more interested in securing control of the institutions that existed within the black community. They challenged those moderate blacks who allied themselves with white liberals who favored racial integration, and who sought to attain access to existing political and economic institutions and to make them work for African Americans (Jennings, 1992; Georgakas & Surkin, 1975; Rich, 1989; Thompson, 2001b).

The discourse in which black nationalists framed their educational agenda was different than the way that other African Americans constructed their educational commentary. In his articles in the *Michigan Chronicle* in the four months following the walkout, Karl Gregory, Principal of the Freedom School, noted that black citizens could not trust their schools or rely on the honesty and integrity of the white educators who managed them. He claimed that the school system had not been providing black parents with the information that they required to recognize the failings of the city's schools. But he went further to claim that the difficulties of the city's schools were the result of the fact that blacks controlled neither their schools nor their community. "People needn't be shocked when residents of a community ask for changes in policies at their school. If students and parents are offended by police practices at a school and an apparent lack of effort on the part of the administration to promote quality education, they have not only the right but the responsibility to demand changes." In a democracy, he asserted, parents and students "must have a share in running their school" (*Michigan Chronicle*, May 26, 1966).

Rev. Albert Cleage, another leader of the black nationalist movement in Detroit, constructed the situation in very similar terms. At the heart of the deficiencies of the city's schools was that "not one Negro is in a policy-making position" (*Michigan Chronicle*, May 28, 1966). He believed that black children could not be educated in Detroit's schools as long as those schools were under white control. Student boycotts like the one that occurred at Northern, according to Cleage, did not mean that there was something wrong with black children. "All that it means is that they are sick and tired of going to schools where they are not learning anything. It means that they can't be expected to respect white teachers who have contempt and fear in their hearts for them. These explosions signify one thing—that there will be no education for black children until the black community controls its own schools" (*Michigan Chronicle*, October 28, 1967).

The discourse in which Cleage framed the issue spoke of the existence in Detroit's black community of a "Cultural Revolution" that was reconstructing the identity of the city's African Americans. They were increasingly becoming aware of their blackness and their separateness from white society. Blacks looked to the schools to provide their children with the knowledge of African history and the realization that black science religion, and philosophy had reached maturity when "the white man was a naked savage living in caves and eating raw meat." His construction placed a special responsibility on black teachers. If African American children "...go to school with a sense of black consciousness and black pride, hungrily seeking after understanding of self, and you tell them about George Washington, Abraham Lincoln and the plantation days, you are betraying the trust that black people have in you *(Michigan Chronicle*, March 16, 1968).

The introduction of a nationalist discourse into Detroit's ongoing black-white educational conflict constructed a new educational vision for the city's African American population. As the Inner City Parents Council framed it, the low academic achievement of black youth resulted from the "deliberate and systematic destruction of the Afro-American child's self-image and racial pride" on the part of the city's schools. The rejection of integration was from that perspective an assertion of "pride in their own history, culture, and power" (Inner City Parents Council, 1967, pp. 4, 12). The curriculum offered them a vehicle for attaining that separation. Black children required a "different educational orientation" than that provided to white children. The course of study had to offer black students "a knowledge of their history, their culture, and their destiny." The textbooks had to emphasize the worth and value of black people. Courses should be problem-centered and afford black children the opportunity to discuss the array of issues that faced their community (Ibid., 11). Black and white Detroiters, it seems, had come to speak two separate languages when it came to matters of schooling.[1]

RESTRUCTURING AND DETROIT'S DISCURSIVE REORDERING

The Northern High School walkout and subsequent boycott can be seen as a moment in time, albeit not the only one, that points to the set of cultural practices that made the restructuring of the city's schools seem to be a logical and reasonable response to the particular historical and social context of the moment. The boycott, in other words, offers us a picture of the linkage between the reordering of the city's discursive space for reasoning and talking about the education of African American youth and the introduction of a decentralized school system.

At the time of the walkout, Detroit's schools were organized into eight administrative regions, each comprised of several high schools and their feeder elementary and junior high schools and under the direction of a regional superintendent. Decision making authority, however, rested with the central administration and citywide board of education (Berkowitz, 1973). The five years following the walkout saw the passage of state legislation that eventually resulted in the establishment of a decentralized system comprised of eight regions, each with its own five person elected regional board and a regional superintendent selected from a list of eligible candidates submitted by the central board of education. While this legislation did allow these new regional boards some control over the employment of the regional superintendent, the employment and assignment of teachers, and the curriculum and testing program, most of the power was left in the hands of the central board. The legislation did, however, change the structure of the central board to include thirteen members comprised of the elected chairpersons of each of the eight regional boards and five at-large members elected citywide (Berkowitz, 1973; "Highlights of Public Act 48 of 1970," 1970).

There were an array of material conditions that provided an impetus for Detroit's decentralization. There was a continuing pattern of high school disturbances, albeit with an escalating rhetoric. A 1969 boycott at Northern High School offers a good example. Although the walkout only involved 125 students, it was couched by these students in the language of a "revolt." The demands voiced by these student protesters included the flying of the black nationalist's Unity Flag on the school's flag poll, the renaming of a reading room in the school in honor of Malcolm X, the introduction of a black studies curriculum, and the replacement of pictures of white luminaries throughout the school building with pictures of Malcolm X, Martin Luther King, Jr. H. Rap Brown, and Stokely Carmichael (*Detroit Free Press*, October 1, 1969; "Northern's Black Student Demands," n.d.). Second, blacks continued to protest the absence of black administrators and teachers in inner city Detroit schools. Third, incidents of violence including physical assaults on teachers and students were on the increase. And fourth, publication of citywide test scores lent credence to the claims of black Detroiters that the city's schools were failing African American youth (Mirel, 1993).

What seemed to shape or construct these empirical conditions into a call for decentralization was the belief voiced in the discourse of black

Detroiters that this restructuring would result in community control. As the Citizens for Community Control of Schools noted:

> We citizens of the Black community of Detroit, fully conscious of the fact that our children are not receiving a decent education, viewing the increasing deterioration in the educational situation in this city, and after innumerable presentations of our grievances and proposals to the Board of Education to no avail, have finally come to the conclusion that COMMUNITY CONTROL OF SCHOOLS is the only way to establish real accountability of the school system to the Black community. (*Foresight*, 1968)

Cleage made essentially the same point in the pages of the *Michigan Chronicle* in December of 1968 when he stated that "white people cannot do anything in a black ghetto unless black people are willing to accept it" (*Michigan Chronicle*, December 14, 1968).

The discursive shifts that were occurring among black Detroiters surrounding the Northern High School walkout that constructed the city's restructuring as a racial conflict were mediated by what Ian Hacking refers to as "elevator words," social constructs that are often defined circuitously with changing meanings (Hacking, 1999, pp. 22–23). In this instance, these words were decentralization on the one hand and community control on the other. The restructuring that Detroit's white educators had in mind was one that would decentralize the system by dividing it into smaller administrative units representing distinct geographical sectors of the city. Black Detroiters defined the restructuring process differently in terms of the notion of community control. The school system, as they saw it, should be divided into smaller units keyed to the city's geography. Those divisions, however, had to be such as to provide blacks control of the schools in those sections of the city where they constituted the majority of the population.

The debates over the Northern boycott, particularly the clash of African American students, parents and community leaders with the city's educational establishment, altered the ongoing discourse on curriculum differentiation and race then occurring in Detroit. The language in which the supporters of the walkout framed their criticisms of Northern with its emphasis on administrative incompetence, substandard facilities, uncaring teaching, and curriculum inadequacies racialized the concept of low achievement and constructed the education that Detroit was offering its black children as a decidedly inferior provision. At the same time the language in which many white Detroit educators framed their defense of Northern with its focus on the motivational and skill deficits of black youth also racialized the concept of low achievement but did so using a psychologized language that constructed the education that the city was offering black children as adequate and appropriate.

As a consequence, the diversity of opinion that existed among blacks and among whites began to give way to more uniform and rigid positions within each camp with the effect of further dividing blacks and whites. Differences about the efficacy of curriculum differentiation and the virtues of integration became lost in a discourse that constructed the education offered to their children in the city's schools as a form of racism and discrimination. Similarly, the different views that were to be found in the language of white Detroit school administrators about these same issues became submerged in a single discourse that constructed the problem of black low achievement as a problem of cultural disadvantage the cure for which lay in a differentiated, compensatory education. The Northern High School walkout serves as the marker for the emergence of this new linguistic terrain in Detroit.

CONCLUSIONS

In this essay, I used the lens that the Northern High School walkout offers to examine the interplay between race and education in the spatial reordering of Detroit. In the two decades following World War II, Detroit underwent a series of demographic and economic transformations that saw the movement of blacks and whites into separate physical terrain occupied by different neighborhoods, different schools, different work, and different lives. Accompanying this physical reorganization was another reordering that was not spatial in a geographical or physical sense but linguistically spatial in that it led blacks and whites to come to occupy separate discursive terrains comprising different constructs and categories.[5] One feature of this shift was the fact that black and white Detroiters came to think, reason, and talk about matters such as education in different and often conflicting ways, and as a consequence they settled on distinct curricular, pedagogical and governing practices as constituting the reasonable and sensible course of action for resolving particular educational dilemmas.

Looking at restructuring through the lens of a discursive reordering provides more than a strategy for historical interpretation. It also enhances our understanding of contemporary events. The 2000 mayoral takeover of the Detroit Public Schools offers a case in point. This effort at restructuring had a clearly different outcome than the introduction three decades earlier of decentralization. This time control of the schools passed from an elected board of education and became centralized in the hands of a chief executive officer and a board of education appointed by Detroit's mayor. The city and its schools had changed since the introduction of decentralization. In 1973, Detroit elected its first black mayor. Four years later, there was a black majority on both the city council and the board of education. And by 1980, the majority of the city's population was black (Henig, Hula, Orr, & Pedescleaux, 1999). Yet these political and demographic changes do not really explain why a black mayor and large numbers of black Detroiters would embrace the program of Michigan's Republican governor and its Republican-controlled and largely white legislature to remove authority for the schools from a popularly elected board of education

The discourse in which both proponents and opponents of this restructuring initiative framed their arguments does, however, offer an explanation. Support for the takeover came from a black and white coalition that included the governor, mayor, a few key black community leaders, the Republican majority in the state legislature, a handful of Democratic legislatures, the city's two major newspapers, Detroit's principal black newspaper, and about 40 percent of the city's black population. On the other side was a largely but not exclusively African American alliance comprising the vast majority of Detroit's Democratic legislative delegation, the Detroit City Council, several black community leaders, and about half the city's black population. The discourse of neither side, however, framed the issue in racial terms. What divided these two camps, however, was their assessment of the effectiveness of Detroit's schools in enhancing the social mobility of the city's children. Where the discourse of the proponents focused on the failure of the schools to provide black children with the knowledge and skills that they needed to get ahead, the opponent's discourse pointed to the improvements that Detroit's schools were making in providing black children with the competitive advantage that they needed to succeed in adult society. In effect, a discourse of social mobility had come to replace a racial discourse among black Detroiters, which had the effect of providing significant black support for this restructuring while curbing the likelihood that black opponents would frame the initiative as a racially motivated effort (Franklin, 2003).

The focus on discourse becomes particularly important when one looks at issues of governing schools in urban communities. Since the middle of the 1970s large US cities and their schools have, like Detroit, become for the most part black led. Where once African Americans were both a racial and political minority, in many cities they now constitute the majority of the population. This change requires that we embrace a different research strategy that looks beyond the conflict between a white dominated educational and political bureaucracy and a black citizenry to consider an array of players, both black and white, occupying different class positions with different degrees of power and influence, working in different economic and social sectors, and interacting in differing patterns of collaboration and conflict (Henig, Hula, Orr, & Pedescleaux). If we are to understand the interplay among these various players in this new terrain, we need to consider more than the public policies that are ultimately enacted in their name. We need to consider what lies behind those policies, namely the patterns of thinking and reasoning that they bring to debates over those policies and the similarities and differences in which they frame those policies.

More broadly, recent studies of school restructuring, which seem, at least in the US, to favor a retreat from decentralization in favor of efforts to increase the control of city and state governments over local school systems, seem to focus their attention on the institutional initiatives that are put in place to bring about this change in governing. The key players in this research seem to be the business sector, mayors, and state legislators with less attention being given to community groups and parents, particularly among minority populations (Kirst, & Bulkley, 2001). The problem with such an emphasis is that it ignores emerging patterns of governing as an outgrowth of globalization that are bringing the state and civil society more closely together by shifting the state from its traditional regulative role to that of an enabling institution that governs indirectly through the action of other agencies and groups (Rose, 2000; Wagner, 1998). What is occurring is best captured in Foucault notion of "governmentality" with its shift of attention away from state institutions and toward day to day cultural practices. According to Gordon:

> State theory attempts to deduce the modern activities of government from essential properties and propensities of the state, in particular its supposed propensity to growth and to swallow up or colonize everything outside itself Foucault holds that the state has no such inherent propensities; more generally the state has no essence. The nature of the institution of the state is, Foucault thinks, a function of changes in practices of government, rather than the converse. Political theory attends too much to institutions, and too little to practices. (1991, p. 4)

The growing tendency in the US, UK, and in other industrialized democracies to operate through public-private partnerships rather than through state agencies is a good example of this change (Franklin, Bloch, & Popkewitz, 2003). Capturing the governing processes within these new entities is not as simple as identifying their explicit programs and policies. Far more important are the common and differing patterns of thinking and reasoning among participants from different public and private sectors within these collaboratives as evidenced in the discourses in which they frame their goals, proposals, and actions. It is this focus on discursive practices that will move us along further in our understanding of this system of governing as it effects not only questions of school restructuring but other matters of educational and public policy.

NOTES

1.   The research reported in this essay was assisted by grants from the Spencer Foundation and the Horace H. Rackham School of Graduate Studies at the University of Michigan. The data presented, the statements made, and the views expressed are solely my responsibility. I am indebted to Lynn Franklin, Miguel Pereyra, Thomas Popkewitz, Kate Rousmaniere, William Reese, Charles Thomas, and Sapna Vyas for their critical reading of earlier drafts of this essay.

2.   For a review of some of this research in the contest of a discussion of the political economy of urban school reform, see Rury and Mirel (1997).

3.   For a broader and more national interpretation of this black-white working class hostility see Gestle, 1995, 2001).

4.   I have borrowed this description from the characterization that Jerald Podair (2002) uses to characterize black-white conflict over decentralization in New York City in 1968.

5.   I have drawn this line of argument from recent anthropological work on the role of discourse in the construction of racial identity in urban communities. See, for example, Gregory (1998).

REFERENCES

Anonymous Student to Robinson. (1959, February 2). Remus G. Robinson Papers, Box 5, Folder 9, *Archives of Labor History and Urban Affairs.* Walter P. Reuther Library: Wayne State University (hereafter RRP).

Anyon, J. (1997). *Ghetto schooling: A political economy of urban educational reform.* New York: Teachers College Press.

Berkowtiz, S. J. (1973). *An analysis of the relationship between the Detroit community control of schools and the 1971 decentralization of the Detroit Public Schools.* Unpublished doctoral dissertation, Wayne State University.

Bizar, M., & Barr, R. (Eds.). (2001). *School leadership in times of urban reform.* Mahwab: Lawrence Erlbaum Associates.

Bryk, A., Sebring, P.B., Kerbow, D., Rallow, S., & Easton, J.Q. (1998). *Charting Chicago school reform: Democratic localism as a lever for change.* Boulder: Westview Press.

Butler to Robinson (1960, December 14). *RRP.*

CFR to Robinson (n.d.). *RRP.*

Citizens Advisory Committee on Equal Educational Opportunity. (1960). *Minutes.* Detroit Public School Archives (hereafter DPSA).

Cohen, R. D. (1990). *Children of the mill: Schooling and society in Gary, Indiana, 1906–1960.* Bloomington: Indiana University Press.

Darden, J. T., Hill, R. C., Thomas, J., & Thomas, R. (1987). *Detroit: Race and uneven development.* Philadelphia: Temple University Press.

Dawson, M. C. (2001). *Black visions: The roots of contemporary African-American political ideologies.* Chicago: University of Chicago Press.

Detroit Board of Education. (1957–58). *Detroit citizens advisory committee on school needs.* Supplementary Materials (Part 1), DPSA.

Detroit Board of Education. (1958a). *Citizens advisory committee on school needs: Findings and recommendations* (abridged). DPSA.

Detroit Board of Education. (1958b). *Consultant's report to the school program (curriculum) sub-committee of the citizens advisory committee on school needs.* DPSA.

Detroit Board of Education. (1959). *One year after: A staff report on what has transpired since the Citizens Advisory Committee on School Needs made public its report and recommendations for the decade ahead.* DPSA.

Detroit Board of Education. (1962). *Findings and recommendations of the Citizens Advisory Committee on Equal Educational Opportunities* (abridged). DPSA.

Detroit Free Press. (1960–1969).

Detroit News. (1966).

Fine, S. (1979). *Violence in the model city: The Cavanagh administration, race relations, and the Detroit riot of 1967.* Ann Arbor: University of Michigan Press.

Foresight. (1968, January). Papers of New Detroit, Inc., Box 47, Folder 7, Archives of Labor History and Urban Affairs. Walter P. Reuther Library: Wayne State University (hereafter ND).

Franklin, B. M. (1986). *Building the American community: The school curriculum and the search for social control.* London: Falmer.

Franklin, B. M. (1994). *From "backwardness" to "at-risk": Childhood learning difficulties and the contradictions of school reform.* Albany: State University of New York Press.

Franklin, B. M. (1998). Low-achieving children and teacher heroism: A genealogical examination. In B. M. Franklin (Ed.), *When children don't learn: Student failure and the culture of teaching* (pp. 28–51). New York: Teachers College Press.

Franklin, B. M. (1999), Discourse, rationally, and educational research: A historical perspective of *RER. Review of Educational Research, 69,* 347–363.

Franklin, B. M. (2000). A historical perspective on teaching low achieving children: A first account. In B. M. Franklin (Ed.), *Curriculum and consequence: Herbert M. Kliebard and the promise of schooling* (pp. 128–152). New York: Teachers College Press.

Franklin, B. M. (2003). Race, restructuring, and educational reform: The mayoral takeover of the Detroit Public Schools. In L.F. Miron & E.P. St. John (Eds.), *Reinterpreting urban school reform* (pp. 95–125). Albany: State University of New York.

Franklin, B. M., Bloch, M., & Popkewitz, T. S. (2003). Educational partnerships: An introductory framework. In B.M. Franklin, M. Bloch, & T.S. Popkewitz (Eds.), *Educational partnerships: Democracy, citizenship, and salvation in a globalized world* (pp. 1–23). New York: Palgrave Macmillan.

Georgakas, D., & Surkin, M. (1975). *Detroit: I do mind dying. A study in urban revolution.* New York: St. Martins Press.

Gestle, G. (1995). Race and the myth of the liberal consensus. *Journal of American History, 82,* 579–586.

Gestle, G. (2001). *American crucible: Race and nation in the twentieth century.* Princeton: Princeton University Press.

Gordon, C. (1991). Governmental rationality: An introduction. In G. Burchell, C. Gordon, & P. Miller (Eds.), *The Foucault effect: Studies in governmentality* (pp. 1–51). Chicago: University of Chicago Press.

Gracie, D. (1967). The walkout at Northern High. *New University Thought, 5,* 13–28.

Gregory, K.D. (1967). The walkout: Symptom of dying inner city schools. *New University Thought, 5,* 29–54.

Gregory, S. (1999). *Black Corona: Race and the politics of place in an urban community.* Princeton: Princeton University Press.

Hacking, I. (1999). *The social control of what?* Cambridge: Harvard University Press.

Hartigan, J., Jr. (1999). *Racial situations: Class predicaments of whiteness in Detroit.* Princeton: Princeton University Press.

Henig, J. R., Hula, R. C., Orr, M., & Pedescleaux, D. S. (1999). *The color of school reform: Race, politics, and the challenge of urban education.* Princeton: Princeton University Press.

Hess, A. G. (1995). *Restructuring urban schools: A Chicago perspective.* New York: Teachers College Press.

Hill, P. T., Campbell, C., & Harvey J. (2000). *It takes a city: Getting serious about urban school reform.* Washington, D.C.: Brookings Institution Press.

Highlights of Public Act 48 of 1970 (1970), ND.

Hooks, B. (1990). *Yearning: Race, gender, and cultural politics.* Boston: South End Press.

Hutchinson to Robinson. (1958, July 6). Box 7, Folder 14, *RRP.*

Inner City Parents Council. (1967). *Programs for quality education in inner city schools.* National Association for the Advancement of Colored People-Detroit Branch Papers, Part II, Box 29, Folder 2, Archives of Labor History and Urban Affairs. Walter P. Reuther Library: Wayne State University (hereafter NAACP-II).

Jennings, J. (1992). *The politics of black empowerment: The transformation of black activism in America.* Detroit: Wayne State University Press.

Katznelson, I., & Weir, M. (1985). *Schooling for all: Class, race, and the decline of the democratic ideal.* New York: Basic Books.

Kirst, M. W., & Bulkley, K. E. (2001, April). *Mayoral influence and takeover: The different directions taken in different cities.* Paper presented at the annual meeting of the American Educational Research Association, Seattle, WA.

Kliebard, H. M. (1995). *The struggle for the American curriculum, 1893–1958* (2nd ed.). New York: Routledge.

Lefebvre, H. (1991). *The production of space* (D. Nicholson-Smith, Trans.). Oxford: Blackwell.

Lewis, C. S. (n.d.). *What makes Sammy fail.* Box 6, Folder 27, RRP.

Mayer, A. J., & Hoult, T. F. (1962). *Race and residence in Detroit.* Detroit: Institute for Urban Studies, Wayne State University.

Michigan Chronicle. (1958–1968).

Minutes of Education Committee. (1965, July 27). Detroit National Association for the Advancement of Colored People Collection, Part I, Box 14, Education Committee Folder, Archives of Labor History and Urban Affairs. Walter P. Reuther Library: Wayne State University (hereafter NAACP-I).

Mirel, J. (1993). *The rise and fall of an urban school system: Detroit, 1907–1981.* Ann Arbor: University of Michigan Press.

National Commission on Professional Rights and Responsibilities. (1967). *Detroit, Michigan: A study of barriers to equal educational opportunity in a large city.* Washington, D.C.: National Education Association.

Northern's Black Student Demands. (n.d.). Detroit Commission on Community Relations Collection, Human Rights Department, Part III, Box 46, Folder 6,

Archives of Labor History and Urban Affairs. Walter P. Reuther Library: Wayne State University (hereafter DCCR).

Orr, M. (1999). *Black social capital: The politics of school reform in Baltimore, 1986–1998.* Lawrence: University Press of Kansas.

Peterson, P. E. (1985). *The politics of school reform, 1870–1940.* Chicago: University of Chicago Press.

Podair, J. E. (2002). *The strike that changed New York: Blacks, whites, and the Ocean Hill-Brownsville crisis.* New Haven: Yale University Press.

Popkewitz, T. S. (1998). *Struggling for the soul: The politics of school and the construction of the teacher.* New York: Teachers College Press.

Popkewitz, T. S., & Brennan, M. (1998). Restructuring of social and political theory in education: Foucault and the social epistemology of school practices. In T.S. Popkewitz & M. Brennan (Eds.), *Foucault's challenge: Discourse, knowledge, and power in education* (pp. 3–35). New York: Teachers College Press.

Popkewitz, T. S., Pereyra, M. A., & Franklin, B. M. (2001). History, the problem of knowledge, and the new cultural history of schooling: An introduction. In T. S. Popkewitz, B. M. Franklin, & M. A. Pereyra (Eds.), *Cultural history and education: Critical essays on knowledge and schooling* (pp. 3–42). New York: Routledge.

Portz, J., Stein, L., & Jones, R. R. (1999). *City schools and city politics: Institutions and leadership in Pittsburgh, Boston, and St. Louis.* Lawrence: University Press of Kansas.

Post Junior High School. (1968, May 1). Subcommittee investigating the concerns of the community and recommendations made to the school and the board of education previous to the walkout, Box 45, Folder 35, DCCR.

Rafftery, J. R. (1992). *Land of fair promise: Politics and reform in Los Angeles schools, 1885–1941.* Stanford: Stanford University Press.

Ravitch, D. (1974). *The great school wars: New York City, 1805–1973: A history of the public schools as battlefield for social change.* New York: Basic Books.

Ravitch, D., & Viteritti, J. (Eds.). (1997). *New schools for a new century: The redesign of urban education.* New Haven: Yale University Press.

Ravitch, D., & Viteritti, J. (Eds.). (2000). *City schools: Lessons from New York.* Baltimore: The Johns Hopkins University Press.

Report of community hearings. (1966). Box 12, Folder 17, NAACP-II.

Rich, W. (1989). *Coleman Young and Detroit politics: From social activist to power broker.* Detroit: Wayne State University Press.

Rose, N. (1999). *Powers of freedom: Reframing political thought.* Cambridge: Cambridge University Press.

Rury, J. L., & Cassell, F. (Eds.). (1993). *Seeds of crisis: Public schooling in Milwaukee since 1920.* Madison: University of Wisconsin Press.

Rury, J. L., & Mirel, J. (1997). The political economy of urban education. In M.W. Apple (Ed.), *Review of research in education* (vol. 22) (pp. 49–110). Washington, D.C.: American Educational Research Association.

Soja, E. W. (1989). *Postmodern geographies: The reassertion of space in critical social theory.* London: Verso.

Soja, E. W. (1996). *Thirdspace: Journeys to Los Angeles and other real and imagined places.* Oxford: Blackwell.

Statement of Charles L. Wells, Chairman, Education Committee. (1964, April 24). Box 14, Education Committee Folder, NAACP-1.

Sugrue, T. J. (1995). Crabgrass-roots politics: Race, rights, and the reaction against liberalism in the urban north, 1940–1964. *Journal of American History, 82,* 551–578.

Sugrue, T. J. (1996). *The origin of the urban crisis: Race and inequality in Detroit.* Princeton: Princeton University Press.

Teacher continues Northwestern expose. (1962, February 19). *The Illustrated News.* Box 7, Folder 55, RRP.

Thompson, H.A. (2001a). Rethinking the collapse of postwar liberalism: The rise of Mayor Coleman Young and the politics of race in Detroit. In D. R. Colburn & J. S. Adler (Eds.), *African American mayors: Race, politics, and the American city* (pp. 223–248). Urbana: University of Illinois Press.

Thompson, H.A. (2001b). *Whose Detroit? Politics, labor, and race in a modern American city.* Ithaca: Cornell University Press.

Tyack, D. (1974). *The one best system: A history of American urban education.* Cambridge: Harvard University Press.

Vocational Education Sub-Committee Report. (1965, October 7). Box 14, Education Committee Folder, NAACP-I.

Wagner, P. (1994). *A sociology of modernity: Liberty and discipline.* London: Routledge.

What's Wrong With Our Schools. (1962, February 12). *The Illustrated News.* Box 7, Folder 55, RRP.

ABOUT THE CONTRIBUTORS

Yang-tien Chen, Assistant Professor at Taipei Municipal Teachers College, Taiwan. His interests focus on educational reform in Taiwan and the historical fabrications of national imaginaries that have been embodied through the reforms.

Sally Power, Professor of Education and head of the School of Educational Foundations and Policy Studies, Institute of Education, University of London. Her research interests include policy sociology in general, including the changing relationship between public and private provision and education and the middle class.

Marny Dickson, Kings College, London University. Her research interests related to policy studies.

Ines Dussel, FLACSO/Argentina. Her research is related to educational theory and policy, and the history of education in Latin America.

Barry M. Franklin, Utah State University. His research interests are in the areas of curriculum policy, urban school reform, and history of education.

Sharon Gewirtz, Kings College, London University. Her research interests are in the sociology of education and policy studies.

Sverker Lindblad, Gothenburg University and Uppsala University, Sweden. He is at present doing education policy analyses and comparing classroom interaction in different cultural contexts.

Educational Restructuring: International Perspectives on Traveling Policies, pages 219–220
Copyright © 2004 by Information Age Publishing

Meg Maguire, Kings College, London University. Her research interests are in the sociology of education and policy studies.

Johan Muller, the University of Cape Town, South Africa. He research is related to the sociology of curriculum theory and policy.

Thomas S. Popkewitz, the University of Wisconsin-Madison, USA. His research is concern with the systems of reason that govern pedagogy and research.

Fazil Rizvi, the University of Illinois, Champaign-Urbana, USA. He is currently working on globalization and educational policy related to student mobility and the internationalization of higher education.

Agnès van Zanten, Observatoire Sociologique du Changement, the Centre National de la Recherche Scientifique and to the Fondation Nationale des Sciences Politiques. She has conducted sociological and comparative research on the relationship between schools and local communities, on parents' educational strategies on local educational practices.

Printed in the United States
24385LVS00001B/225-262

9 781593 111809